ALSO BY TERRY GOLWAY

So Others Might Live

The Irish in America

For the Cause of Liberty

Irish Rebel

Full of Grace

WASHINGTON'S GENERAL

WASHINGTON'S GENERAL

Nathanael Greene and the Triumph of the American Revolution

Terry Golway

A John Macrae / Holt Paperback

Henry Holt and Company | New York

Holt Paperbacks
Henry Holt and Company, LLC
Publishers since 1866
175 Fifth Avenue
New York, New York 10010
www.henryholt.com

A Holt Paperback® and ® are registered trademarks of
Henry Holt and Company, LLC.

Distributed in Canada by H. B. Fenn and Company Ltd.

Library of Congress Cataloging-in-Publication Data
   Golway, Terry, 1955–
      Washington's general : Nathanael Greene and the triumph of the
   American Revolution / Terry Golway.—1st ed.
         p.   cm.
      Includes bibliographical references and index.
      ISBN-13: 978-0-8050-8005-6
      ISBN-10: 0-8050-8005-8
      1. Greene, Nathanael, 1742–1786.   2. Generals—United States—Biography.
   3. United States. Continental Army—Biography.   4. United States—History—Revolution,
   1775–1783—Campaigns.   I. Title.
   E207.G9G65 2005
   973.3'3'092—dc22
   [B]   2004052259

Henry Holt books are available for special promotions and
premiums. For details contact: Director, Special Markets.

Originally published in hardcover in 2005 by John Macrae Books/Henry Holt and Company

First Holt Paperbacks Edition 2006

Designed by Paula Russell Szafranski

Map art © 2004 David Cain

Frontispiece: *Nathanael Greene,* by Charles Willson Peale, from life, 1783, courtesy of
Independence National Historical Park

Printed in the United States of America
10   9   8   7   6   5   4

For John Wright and Rita Kerrigan

CONTENTS

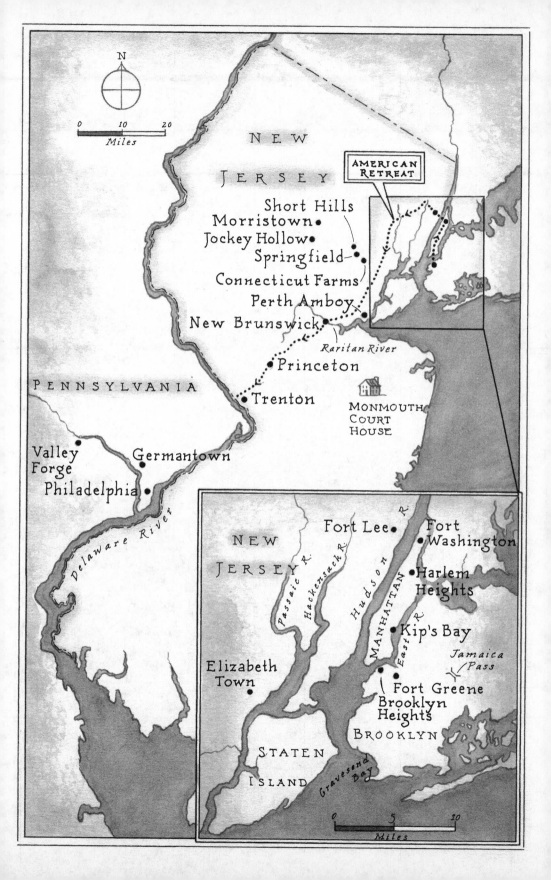

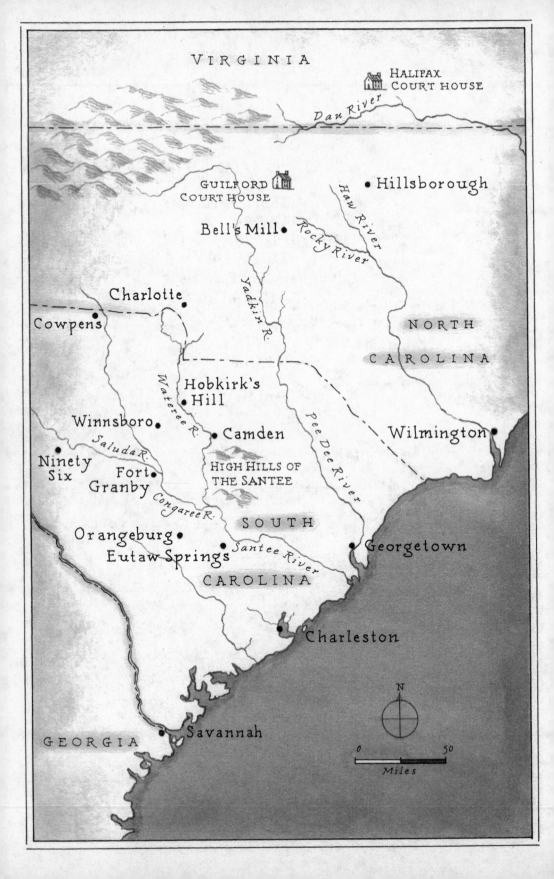

1 | The Quaker General

Even in an army filled with inexperienced officers and citizen soldiers, Nathanael Greene was an unlikely warrior. He walked with a slight limp, possibly the result of a childhood accident. He was reared in Rhode Island as a Quaker, the son of a devout family that loathed war. His formal education ended once he learned to read and write. His first taste of war came during the siege of Boston in 1775—and he already was a general.

How and why Nathanael Greene, merchant, ironmaster, and only lately a fervent patriot, came to command Rhode Island's little army in 1775 remains one of the great mysteries of the American Revolution. Many others in that rebellious colony had more experience and training, including some friends of his. Until he donned the epaulets of a general officer, he was a private in a local militia called the Kentish Guards. His presence in the ranks was notable, but not for any evident leadership skills. Rather, he stood out because of his limp. His comrades and friends were mortified as Greene spoiled the splendid, uniform look of their parades on the village green of East Greenwich, near his home in Coventry.

It's possible that Greene's overnight promotion from private to general was a tribute to his family's political connections, which were considerable. Or perhaps the Rhode Island legislators who commissioned him were impressed with the force of his personality, which was formidable. Whatever the case, Nathanael Greene became general of the Rhode Island Army of Observation in May 1775 before he ever heard the roar of a cannonade, experienced the shock of an enemy assault, or tried to pierce the fog of war.

The appointment had consequences for the army and for the nation that Rhode Island's lawmakers could not have imagined. Had he not been given command of his home colony's troops, he very likely would not have become the Continental army's youngest brigadier general. And if he were not a brigadier, he would not have come to George Washington's attention so early in the war, if ever.

Perhaps. But then again, Nathanael Greene was a young man determined to make a name for himself. He had not left behind a successful business and a charming bride to become just another officer in a ragtag army. Greene was a fervent patriot, but he was an ambitious man, too. Insecure and sensitive to criticism, and yet not a modest man, he longed for fame and yearned for fortune. The war offered a chance at both, and he seized the opportunity. By July 1776, this thirty-three-year-old military neophyte was one of George Washington's most important advisers. Barely a year removed from civilian life, Greene was given the task of defending New York City during the summer of 1776 as a huge British task force prepared to invade Long Island and crush the Revolution in its infancy. That appointment, at so critical a time for the fledgling nation and its army, was a testament to Greene's leadership abilities and his self-taught grasp of military tactics and strategy. It also was a reflection of Washington's trust in this young man he barely knew. And his place in the army's leadership demonstrated that the years he spent schooling himself in the art of war, furtively reading military classics by Julius Caesar and Frederick the Great in violation of his family's pacifism, were well spent.

In becoming one of the Continental army's greatest soldiers, Nathanael Greene personified the power and potential of the new American idea—especially its rejection of the Old World's aristocratic governments and equally aristocratic military commanders, and its embrace of merit and virtue as society's ultimate arbiters. While the Greenes of Rhode Island were not without political influence, Nathanael Greene was hardly the sort of man who might hold an impressive title in the British army, as did his future antagonist, the well-educated, wellborn Lord Charles Cornwallis. Indeed, during Greene's long service from the war's beginning to its triumphant and unlikely end, this self-taught amateur fought many bitter battles against two symbols of the Old World: Cornwallis, a professional soldier, and Baron Wilhelm von Knyphausen, a commander of mercenaries who knew no loyalty other than to war. These opponents, who fought Greene in New York, New Jersey, Pennsylvania, and the Carolinas, represented all that the American Revolution opposed: inherited power, unearned titles, and imperial militarism. Nathanael Greene spoke for the New World notions of a citizen soldiery and a merit-based society.

While his appointment as Rhode Island's general remains a puzzle, his rise in the Continental army is not. His grasp of military strategy, his competence, his organizational skills, and his persistence in defeat led Congress to promote him quickly from brigadier to major general. Washington's appreciation for Greene's talents was such that on at least two occasions, fellow officers and politicians described Greene as the commander in chief's favorite officer, as the man Washington had designated to succeed him if he were killed or captured. There is no documentary evidence to suggest that Washington had such a succession in mind, but he did hear the gossip about his relationship with Greene, and he never denied it.

Greene was at Washington's side from the liberation of Boston to the long retreat through New Jersey in 1776; from the disappointments of

Germantown and Brandywine to the terrible months at Valley Forge; from the unexpected victory under a merciless sun at Monmouth to the snowdrifts of Morristown. For more than half this time, not only did Nathanael Greene command troops in the field and offer Washington important strategic advice, but he also served in the unglorious and unappreciated role of quartermaster general—the purchaser and transporter of the army's supplies. It was work he loathed; it was a duty he fulfilled. He complained about it. But he did it.

His service to his nation and to his commander in chief was distinguished by its remarkable competence and admirable for its sacrifice, for like every other American rebel, Nathanael Greene was a volunteer who left behind family and private interests when his country called. Until late 1780, however, Greene seemed destined to be remembered, if at all, merely as one of several competent major generals who served on Washington's staff. He never had the chance at independent command and never emerged from Washington's considerable shadow. He told Washington, in a phrase filled with self-pity, that history does not remember quartermaster generals.

And he wished, desperately, to be remembered. He wished for the glories he imagined when, as a young adult, he put aside Quaker texts in favor of Caesar's *The Civil War*. But circumstances seemed to dictate that such fame would not be his. With undisguised envy, he bitterly complained of the undeserved laurels heaped upon Horatio Gates, a man he despised, after the Battle of Saratoga. They would never be his, these tributes and orations, not as long as he dutifully served in Washington's shadow.

In the summer and fall of 1780, however, as the army edged closer to the abyss of defeat and failure, Nathanael Greene saw an opporunity to gain what had been denied him. The hated Gates had suffered a catastrophic defeat outside Camden, South Carolina. It was the second time in four months that the Southern Army of the United States had been shattered. With Gates's defeat, organized resistance in the South ended. The British under Lord Cornwallis began the process of reannexing Georgia and the Carolinas, while casting covetous eyes on Virginia, the home of George Washington, Patrick Henry, and Thomas Jefferson.

For the Continental army and the nation itself, there had been many crushing moments since 1775, and Greene had been an eyewitness to all of them. But in 1780, the blows to American arms and morale were ceaseless. Blizzards in January turned winter quarters in Morristown, New Jersey, into a frozen horror, far worse than Valley Forge. The Continental dollar became nearly worthless by spring, and so Americans declined to sell their goods to the army that was fighting in their name. The southern army, then under Benjamin Lincoln, surrendered en masse in Charleston in May. In August, Lincoln's successor, Gates, was annihilated. Prospects for victory never seemed dimmer. Equally disturbing for Greene, his infant son and vivacious young wife were ill back home in Rhode Island, and his own health was precarious—asthma left him gasping for breath most nights.

Then, after defeat, came treachery. In late September, Greene's friend Benedict Arnold nearly succeeded in handing over West Point, the key American stronghold on the Hudson River, to the British. Greene, who was temporarily in command of the main American army while Washington conferred with the French in Connecticut, did not shield his troops from the gravity of the moment. Had Arnold succeeded, he told them, the cause surely would have been lost. Even before Arnold's treachery, Washington had warned Congress that the army might be forced to disband for want of money and supplies.

In the fall of 1780, the American cause was as close to collapse as it had ever been, even during the fateful closing weeks of 1776. Rumors now spread through the American army: Horatio Gates, it was said, would be sacked for his loss at Camden. A new commander would be sent south to take his place, with nothing less than the fate of the cause, of the country, of the army, weighing on his shoulders. Who would it be? Congress reserved for itself the right to make such promotions, suspicious as it was of the motives of even so great a man as George Washington. But Congress had sent Benjamin Lincoln to the South, and Congress had sent Horatio Gates to the South, and both had been soundly beaten. Would a chastened Congress abide by Washington's wishes in choosing the southern army's third commander in six months? Washington's capable young aide Alexander Hamilton earnestly hoped so. He told a friend in Congress that if it was intent on removing Gates, "for God's sake . . . send Greene."

There was little question that Nathanael Greene wanted Horatio Gates's job, doomed though it seemed to be. He wanted it even though the possibility horrified his wife, Caty, who was a favorite of Washington's. Back home with the Greene family in Rhode Island, Nathanael's brother Jacob wrote that Caty was "much alarmed" by rumors that her husband might be sent south, and Jacob himself warned Nathanael against pursuing the post. "Nothing but Disgrace and Disappointment has Attended Every Commander in that Station," he wrote, accurately. Greene knew that Caty, the mother of four children born since the Revolution began, was at her wit's end with anxiety and fear. "Poor Girl," Greene wrote, "I am afraid it will prove almost fatal to her, as she is very fond of domestic life, and has a most horrid Idea of the war to the southward." *Horrid* would hardly do justice to the American plight in the South and would not begin to describe the bloody civil war between American patriots and American loyalists in the backcountry of Georgia and the Carolinas.

Nevertheless, on October 3, 1780, Greene wrote to a friend in Congress, where Gates's fate would be decided. If, he told John Mathews of South Carolina, "you find it necessary to appoint another officer to [the southern command], and think I can be useful in that quarter, my best endeavors will not be wanting to protect the people and serve my Country."

When he heard that Gates might not be sacked after all, Greene wrote to General Washington to ask for Benedict Arnold's old job as commandant of West Point. Even with its limited prospects for glory, West Point was a vital post, and its next commander would have the chance to rebuild its defenses and revive the garrison's morale. Not glorious work, but necessary work all the same. And while Nathanael Greene was not adverse to self-pity and complaint, he had never shirked the call to duty, however unpleasant or unglorious. Washington granted his request, writing to him on October 6: "I commit this important Post to your care in full confidence in your prudence, vigilance, activity and good conduct." But the commander in chief added a caveat: everything could change, including Greene's assignment, because of the army's "uncertainties."

Greene invited Caty to join him at the garrison for the coming winter. He knew she would be relieved to hear that he was not going to the South after all. "I shall be happy to receive you to my arms, as soon as you can render it convenient to come," he wrote. Caty and Nathanael had been together through every winter of the war, and they had the children to prove it. They were very much in love, for all their difference in age (she was twenty when they married in 1774; he was thirty-two) and in demeanor. He was solid and dependable. She was lighthearted and vivacious. He was a voracious reader determined to prove to his social betters that he was just as smart as they were. She relied on her charm and stunning appearance, which were more than enough to win attention from not only her husband but his friends, too. Nathanael rarely seemed to mind her preference for the company of men, and she bore with patience his exhortations to improve herself. War and separation surely had taken a toll on their marriage; he once conceded to her, "Our felicity is not perfect." Greene, insensitive to his wife's loneliness and anxiety, regularly wrote home with tidbits about the pretty young women he met while staying in the homes of fellow patriots in New Jersey and Pennsylvania. When she called him on it, though, Nathanael beat a hasty retreat, in phrases husbands have used before and since. "I declare upon my sacred honor," he wrote, ". . . as much as I respect them as friends, I should never be happy with them in a more intimate connection. . . . I will venture to say there is no mortal more happy in a wife than myself."

And he was, in fact, happy to be married to Caty and often told her so. "O, sweet angel how I wish—how I long to return to your soft embrace," Nathanael once wrote to her from camp.

As Nathanael settled into his new assignment, Caty prepared for her annual trek to winter quarters. The prospect of months away from the extended Greene family, and even her own children, thrilled her. She was not a typical officer's wife, content with her place in life as a companion and mother. She longed for the company of friends like Martha Washington, for the attention of young officers like the Frenchman Lafayette, whose language she spoke. Even in Valley Forge and Morristown, where winter was cruel and deadly, there were parties and balls and dancing once the snows melted. And nobody enjoyed them more than Caty Greene. Winter camp, even with its burdens and deprivations, was her refuge from dreary domestic life.

While she sometimes left her children with relatives in Rhode Island for months at a time, this year she would not travel alone. Four-year-old George Washington Greene, born during the siege of Boston, would travel with her, no doubt to the delight of the father young George barely knew.

Nathanael Greene was at West Point less than a week when a letter arrived from his friend, the roly-poly artillery specialist Henry Knox. He told Greene that Gates was about to be fired after all, and that Congress had decided to let Washington name a new commander in the South. "Who will that person be?" Knox wondered. "You may ask me the same question, but I protest I know not."

Neither did Greene, although he was certain it would not be him. He had badly miscalculated, angling for and receiving the West Point command because he believed Congress would not dare recall Gates. But now Congress had done the unexpected, and where was he? Stuck at West Point. How long he had dreamed of a chance to win battlefield glory, and how often it had been snatched from him! And now the fortunes of war had conspired against him once again. On October 15, from his desk at West Point, he wrote a letter to a longtime friend and business partner, Jeremiah Wadsworth. Noting that Gates had been relieved of his command, he speculated on several candidates for the post, none of whom was named Nathanael Greene. "Perhaps I should have gone, had I not come to this place; but being fixed here it will be difficult for the General to call me away immediately without giving umbrage to some of the rest of the General officers." Greene was not angry, and his concern about what the other general officers might be thinking was typical of a man who spent a great deal of time and energy monitoring what was being said (or not being said) about him. He seemed resigned to his fate, so much so that he told Wadsworth that he didn't really want the southern command after all.

It was too late. A few hours after he wrote to Wadsworth, Greene received a message from General Washington. Congress, Washington wrote, had given him the power to appoint a new commander for the southern army. "It is my wish," he wrote, "to appoint you." He asked Greene to leave for the South immediately.

Nathanael Greene, the self-taught soldier from Rhode Island, had been offered the most important command of the war, short of becoming commander in chief. The enemy's finest general, Lord Cornwallis, was marching through the South, returning Georgia and South Carolina to the king's rule and preparing to do the same in North Carolina. He already had annihilated two American armies and ruined the reputation of two generals, Lincoln and Gates. There was little reason to believe the Americans could stop him from marching north to Virginia and cutting the fledgling Republic in half.

Greene accepted the impossible assignment, as Washington knew he would. Greene had been at Washington's side since Boston in 1775, and he had yet to disappoint his commander in chief. But he did have one request: he asked Washington if he could put off his journey to the South for a short time. He wanted to return home to Rhode Island for a few days to attend to his "domestic concerns." His youngest child, eight-month-old Nathanael Ray, was recovering from a serious illness that almost killed him. He knew that Caty would be distressed, to put it lightly, to learn that he would not be spending the winter at West Point. And through the long years of war, he had yet to see all four of his children together in the same room.

And he knew this opportunity might never come again.

He handed his letter to a waiting messenger and then reflected on the stunning turn of events. Before long, he had second thoughts about his self-indulgent request. Who was he, after all, to ask for family time at such a critical moment in the nation's history? Who was he to ask George

Washington, of all people, to grant him such an indulgence? Hadn't Washington himself sacrificed everything, without complaint? Greene quickly sent his commander a letter withdrawing his request for a short leave. It didn't matter; Washington denied Greene's original request. The war hinged on the battles to come in the South. There was no time for "domestic concerns."

Greene would have to break the news to Caty that there would be no winter camp this year, no socializing, no parties with some of the New Jersey patriots they had come to know so well after three winters in that pivotal state. He composed a "my dear Angel" letter to his wife, breaking the news in language that suggested he, too, was heartbroken: "What I have been dreading has come to pass. His Excellency General Washington . . . has appointed me to the command of the Southern Army. . . . This is so foreign from my wishes that I am distressed exceedingly." This is an odd sentiment from a man who had lobbied for the post, but Greene had just received a heartrending letter from Caty in which she poured out her "suffering in such a feeling manner as melt[ed his] soul into the deepest distress."

Perhaps after receiving Caty's letter, Nathanael Greene yet again had second thoughts about his new assignment. But it was too late. The fate of the nation now rested primarily on his shoulders. He made plans to send his baggage to North Carolina, dispatched a flurry of letters to colleagues and family, and paused for a few moments to read a letter from an old friend, Thomas Paine. Greene and Paine had marched side by side through New Jersey in the dreadful fall of 1776. Now, Paine wrote from Philadelphia: "Though I do not write much I pray often, if fervency of hoping and wishing can be called prayer, and these will constantly attend you on your expedition."

As he prepared to leave, Greene realized that Caty might well have left Rhode Island as soon as she heard that he was to be commandant of West Point. If she had, she wouldn't know of the change in plans. So he crossed to the east bank of the Hudson in hopes of finding his wife on the road to West Point. She never showed; in fact, as it turned out, she hadn't left Rhode Island at all. But he could delay his mission no longer. He could not wait to hold her once more, to spend another night with her.

"Could I leave you happy I should go with a heart as light as a feather," Greene wrote in one of three farewell letters he sent to Caty, "but the thought of leaving you in distress renders me exceeding wretched."

After stopping for a conference with Washington, this wretched man began his journey to the South in late October 1780 to take charge of a shattered army.

If he failed, all was lost.

2 | A Downright Democracy

Nathanael Greene was born into the raucous, iconoclastic colony of Rhode Island on July 27, 1742. His father and namesake lived with his second wife, Mary Motte, and their expanding family in a two-story house overlooking Potowomut Creek near East Greenwich on the western shore of Narragansett Bay. The sounds and sights of Yankee enterprise and industry surrounded them, from the mills, from the forge, from the well-tended orchards, from the furrowed fields.

The Greenes came to America from Britain because of religion, or more precisely, because of disputes over religion. The future general's great-great-grandfather, John Greene, was a surgeon who left his hometown of Salisbury to cross the Atlantic with his wife and five children in the mid-1600s. At the time of his departure, he was a disciple of the charismatic preacher Roger Williams, who had just left England in hopes of founding a purer church in the virgin forests of New England. This was the age of sectarian splits in the once formidable monolith of Western Christendom, the residue of Martin Luther's dramatic challenge to the papacy in the early sixteenth century. Dissent inspired more dissent, and even dissent within the dissenters themselves. In England, men like Williams questioned the sanctity of the established Church, itself the product of Protestant rebellion against Roman Catholicism. The religious unity of Europe was shattered, with nations defining themselves as much by their denomination as by their language and culture, and willing to go to war with heretical neighbors. Independent clerics were emboldened to preach their individual versions of holy truths and gathered around them communities of fellow believers.

When the Puritans despaired of reforming the Church of England, they looked westward to a new promised land in America. John Winthrop abandoned England for the Massachusetts Bay Colony, setting sail in 1630. Williams followed in early 1631, and the pious Dr. Greene and his family arrived shortly afterward.

The New World, however, quickly proved to be no refuge from the divisions and dissents of the Old. Williams shocked the citizens of Boston when he asserted that political authorities should not have the power to enforce religious dogma. More disputes followed as Williams preached the importance of individual conscience, insisting that the phrase "so help me God" should be removed from the colony's oath of allegience. It was, he said, offensive to those who didn't believe in God.

Those who didn't believe in God? This was too much for the Bay Colony's fathers, and no doubt its mothers as well. Williams was banished from the colony, and so in early 1736, he and his band of followers, including Dr. Greene, slogged through the snow and ice of a New England winter to found a new refuge, which they called Providence.

The new colony, which eventually was called Rhode Island and Providence Plantations (still the state's official name), became a sanctuary for all manner of dissenters from the Bay Colony. Included among them was a man named Samuel Gorton, a fiery and uncompromising preacher who taught that men and women were equal. This odd notion and other radical ideas landed him in prison in Providence—his dissents were too much even for Roger Williams—and eventually to exile. Gorton made few friends in Providence, but he did win over Dr. John Greene. When

Gorton left Providence to found his own town, Warwick, John Greene packed his bags for the third and last time.

It was not, however, the end of the Greene family's spiritual journey. By the time Nathanael Greene was born, the family had converted from Gorton's sect to Quakerism. The plain-living, devout, and pacifist Quakers established a strong presence in Rhode Island in the late seventeeth century, and while they were an insular group that believed in only the most rudimentary education for their children, they quickly achieved economic and political power in the colony. Nathanael Greene Sr. was a prosperous entrepreneur who, together with his brothers, owned a business that included a farm, an iron forge, and a sawmill.

The Greenes built an extensive trading network with far-off towns in other colonies. But whatever else those merchant vessels brought to the wharves of Rhode Island, they carried nothing to sway Nathanael Greene Sr. from the unadorned purity of his faith. He became the spiritual leader of the Quaker congregation of East Greenwich, which met two miles from the Greene home. Every Sunday the Greene family, clad in black homespun, tramped the primitive road from their house to the Quaker meetinghouse, where the children sat in silence in rough-hewn pews as the congregation waited for God to inspire Nathanael with his weekly dose of wisdom. The Greene family patriarch was a devout and earnest man determined to pass Quaker dogma to his children. But it was less his preaching than his honorable way of life that made a strong impression on the son who bore his name. "My Father," Nathanael Greene Jr. once wrote, "was a man [of] great Piety, had an excellent understanding; and was govern'd in his conduct by Humanity and kind Benevolence."

Nathanael Greene Jr. was his father's second child by his second wife. Four more boys would follow the eldest, Jacob, and Nathanael Jr., adding to the two boys Nathanael Sr. had with his deceased first wife, Phoebe Greene. The Greenes led a comfortable existence in their fine old house, built in 1684 by Nathanael Sr.'s father. Woods and fields surrounded the home, and a stream babbled its way through the property. The Greenes were not frontier settlers living in rural isolation and ever wary of natives with hostile intentions. They were prosperous merchants in a thriving settlement, and their fortunes continued to improve as Nathanael Sr. bought out his brothers and became the sole proprietor of Nathanael Greene & Co. around the time of Nathanael Jr.'s birth.

The family was not only prosperous but numerous and well-connected, too. Blood relations held an assortment of prominent places in the colony's government and business life, and they were aligned by interest and eventually by marriage with one of the colony's two political factions, the Ward family. The Wards and their supporters were bitter opponents of Governor Stephen Hopkins and his supporters, the most prominent being the famous Brown family.

Affluence and influence, however, did not assure the Greene brothers a carefree, luxurious childhood. Quite the opposite. Quaker tradition, not to mention the necessities of running a family business in the New World, demanded an appreciation for labor and industry even among children. So the Greene boys were reared to value hard work for its own sake. They spent their days working in the mills or in the fields, learning the trades they would need when they inherited the business.

Formal education, though, was another matter entirely. Nathanael Greene Sr. shared the Quaker belief that book learning was a worldly luxury that could only lead to temptation, heresy, and other sins. A tutor instructed the Greene boys in their letters, so that they could read the Scriptures and several Quaker-approved books, and in their numbers, so they could work their business ledgers. All else, they were told, was vanity, or worse. "My Father was a man of Industry and brought up his children to business," Greene wrote years later. "Early, very early, when I should have been in pursuit of Knowledge, I was digging into the Bowels of the Earth after Wealth."

Although Nathanael Greene Jr. admired his father's benevolence and piety, he resented the narrow confines of Quaker childhood, and his father's strict regimen and rejection of books and ideas. The younger Greene wrote that his father "was over shadow'd with prejudices against Literary Accomplishments." In most Quaker households, those prejudices constituted an unquestioned way of life. But as Nathanael Greene

Jr. grew to adolescence—a husky, big-shouldered young man of five feet, ten inches with blue eyes and a thirst for knowledge—he questioned the authority that forbade reading, inquiry, and education. It was, he would later write, a tradition that "has prove'd to be a fine nursery of Ignorance." On his own, with no mentors to encourage him, he was forming ideas that were very much at odds with his father's.

He didn't realize it, but he was beginning to act very much like a Rhode Islander.

The chief justice of New York was astonished by what he found during a visit to Rhode Island in 1773, when affairs between the colonies and Britain were falling apart. He wrote to the earl of Dartmouth in London that Rhode Island's "government (if it deserves that name) is a downright democracy." The chief justice, a man named Daniel Horsmanden, did not use the phrase as a compliment. Indeed, he found little about Rhode Island worthy of praise. In most of the other American colonies, including New York, the king appointed the governor. In Rhode Island, however, the governor was elected, and therefore, Horsmanden sneered, he was "entirely controlled by the populace." Similarly, "all other magistrates and officers" were elected, he complained.

To twenty-first-century eyes, Rhode Island in the eighteenth century would hardly qualify as a democracy, downright or otherwise. The vote was confined to white, adult male property owners, and not all of them at that. Representation in the colonial Assembly was skewed in favor of certain towns, at the expense of others.

To a colonial servant of the Crown in the early 1770s, however, Rhode Island seemed very much like a radical experiment in self-government. Though the colony followed the custom of linking voting rights to property ownership, it was not so difficult for a white, Protestant male in Rhode Island to gain the right to vote. In fact, in a survey of five Rhode Island towns, the historian David S. Lovejoy estimated that in 1757 between 75 and 84 percent of adult males were eligible to vote, a remarkably high figure. Political conflict between the colony's two dominant factions often was uproarious and chaotic, a harbinger of modern partisan politics. Election of delegates to the colony's General Assembly took place twice a year, while candidates for positions ranging from governor to justice of the peace were elected every spring. Campaigns were never-ending and often highly personal.

Even more astonishing was the degree to which Rhode Island seemed independent of the king and Parliament. The colony's charter, granted in 1663 during the reign of King Charles II, gave Rhode Island residents the same rights "as if they . . . were borne within the realme of England." The General Assembly passed whatever laws it wished, as long as they were consistent with the laws of England. In reality, England interfered very little in the Assembly's proceedings, leading Governor Stephen Hopkins to say in the 1750s that "the King and Parliament had no more right . . . to govern us than the Mohawks." Long before Americans considered the possibility of independence, Rhode Islanders conducted themselves as if they were, if not independent of Britain, then at least a self-governing province under the Crown.

But it was more than just Rhode Island's sense of independence and its feisty democracy that made the colony so distinct. The legacy of Roger Williams still was very much evident in its tolerance for dissenters, nonconformists, and other outsiders. The colony's charter promised that no person would be "molested [or] punished . . . for any differences of opinione in matters of religion." If they were "behaving themselves" and not using their liberty to promote "lycentiousness and profaneness," members of all faiths were granted freedom of religion. And so French Huguenots, Congregationalists, Quakers, and even Jews streamed into the colony. Though Jews, like Catholics, were barred from voting, the colony's General Assembly declared in 1684 that they could "expect . . . good protection" in Rhode Island.

In a sense, Rhode Island had no choice but to tolerate the presence of so many people of so many faiths, because only through toleration could Rhode Island develop as a single colony. Its four main towns— Providence, Portsmouth, Warwick, and Newport—risked being divided up piecemeal among its larger neighbors if Rhode Island's leaders let religious differences get in the way of forming a colonywide government.

The colony's disregard for convention was played out in business as well as in government. The colony's economy, in fact, was based on a surly defiance of Britain's attempts to regulate colonial trade. Rhode Island was a small place without resources or cash crops, without much of anything except Yankee ingenuity and seaports. So it became a prototype for what economists hundreds of years later would call a service economy. Trade, not cotton, not grain, was the core of its economy, and trade was based on molasses. The colony's seaports became a point of entry for molasses from the West Indies, providing Rhode Island with a commodity it could use to trade for other goods and produce from larger colonies. The molasses trade led to the development of distilleries throughout Rhode Island, which provided rum to the colonies and provided barter for slave traders working Africa's west coast.

The molasses trade developed and prospered because merchants, government officials, and ordinary citizens had simply ignored an act of Parliament. In 1733, Parliament ordered a tax of six pence on every gallon of molasses imported from foreign countries, including parts of the West Indies not under British rule. The Sugar Act of 1733 was a protectionist measure designed to assist the British-controlled molasses industry, but it soon became clear that collection of these taxes would have made molasses too expensive. So the taxes were ignored, or at very least were collected only sporadically; by one estimate, customs officials were content to collect about 10 percent of the taxes due. Rhode Islanders liked the arrangement, and the Crown's appointees quickly learned to ask no questions. Three thousand miles away from London, blessed with a charter that offered them a reasonable facsimile of self-government, proud of their tradition of tolerating dissenters, Rhode Islanders took great delight in thumbing their collective nose at dictates of the English government.

Much of what we know about young Nathanael Greene is based not on records but on stories and legends handed down to his grandson

George Washington Greene who met some of Nathanael's brothers and contemporaries. In writing of his grandfather's earliest years, George Washington Greene described a childhood that was by turns idyllic and laborious. Fields and forest were their most intimate neighbors, with the nearest large town, East Greenwich, two miles away. In the summers, the boys swam in nearby streams after a long day in the fields or the forge. Then it was off to a friend's home, often a journey of several miles, for an evening's entertainment. Strict Quaker custom regulated even these pastimes, and the Greene boys, like their peers, were forbidden to dance.

Of course, as parents through the centuries have learned to their dismay, there is nothing so alluring to a young person as a forbidden pleasure. Somehow, in the darkened countryside of Kent County, Rhode Island, far from the disapproving gaze of his preacher father, Nathanael Greene learned to dance. Perhaps around a discreet bonfire in a lonely field, perhaps on the earthen floor of a deserted forge, this inquisitive Quaker boy tapped his feet to fiddle music and met the children of other pious households. He was limping even then, but the young ladies of Kent County were a good deal more tolerant of this disability than his future militia comrades—most of the time. One partner, however, couldn't help but blurt out what others noticed without comment. "You dance stiffly," the young lady said, her eyes perhaps drifting to the future general's slightly lame right leg.

Greene had a quick answer. "Very true," he conceded. "But you see that I dance strong."

Young Nathanael was a fugitive at these dances and socials, as were many of his friends. Only through elaborate playacting and the active cooperation of his brothers could he make his way from house to fields undetected. Greene family legend has it that on dance nights, Nathanael went off to bed like a good boy, only to sneak out a window when the coast was clear. (It has been suggested that his limp may have been the result of an injury suffered during one of these perilous escapes.) He climbed down from his second-story room and dashed off into the darkness, sneaking back into his room hours later with nobody the wiser—except for his coconspiring brothers. This plan of campaign required intense preparation, shrewd planning, and, on at least one occasion, no shortage of courage. Sometimes, even parents figure out that their children are up to no good, and Nathanael Sr. made such a discovery one chilly night. Young Nathanael came waltzing home to find his father not only awake but on lookout duty outside the house. Ominously, Nathanael Sr. had a bullwhip in his hands. A careful survey of the landscape convinced young Nathanael that he had made a terrible strategic error—he had left himself no line of retreat. So, legend says, he crept over to a pile of shingles near the house, placed a few under his coat to defend the most likely area of attack, and then walked toward his father to meet his fate. His screams of agony, family members later said, were very convincing.

The overpowering figure of pious, strict, and occasionally well-armed Nathanael Greene Sr. dominated his sons into their young adulthood. His influence became even more profound when the only female in the Greene household, young Nathanael's mother, Mary, died when Nathanael was eleven years old. The effect of the Greenes' loss can only be guessed at, for later in life, Nathanael wrote little about his mother. The continued influence of his father and his rigid ways, however, was ever present in Nathanael's letters. "I lament the want of a liberal Education; I feel the mist [of] Ignorance to surround me," Greene wrote. "For my own part I was Educated a Quaker, and amongst the most Supersticious sort, and that of itself is a sufficient Obstacle to cramp the best of Geniuses, much more mine."

As he made the journey from child to adolescent after his mother's death, young Nathanael devoured the few books he was permitted to read. His intense studies of the Bible, the essential text for children of all pious colonial families, gave young Nathanael a moral and literary framework that would serve him well into adulthood. To complement the Scriptures, Greene and his siblings read from approved Quaker texts, including a book cowritten by the sect's founder, George Fox. With the lumbering title *Instructions for Right Spelling and Plain Directions for*

Reading and Writing True English, this workbook was written specifically for Quaker households, its exercises designed not only to teach grammar and spelling but to reinforce Quaker theology. Greene no doubt spent a great deal of time with Fox's work, and although he developed into a clear writer of "True English," he was not much of one for "Right Spelling."

Among the other approved books Greene read, and reread, were *The Journal*, another text by George Fox, and a Quaker classic titled *An Apology for the True Christian Divinity* by Robert Barclay. Though the books sought to reinforce Quaker principles and demonstrate the fallacy of other denominations, the authors' skepticism of tradition and authority and their emphasis on individual conscience prompted Greene to ask more questions and to demand more answers.

Somehow—perhaps he solemnly promised that he'd never dance again!—he persuaded his father to hire a tutor named Adam Maxwell, a local schoolmaster and immigrant from Scotland. Tradition has it that Maxwell instructed Nathanael in mathematics and Latin, but Greene's grandson suggested that the Latin lessons were short-lived, if they existed at all. Clearly, though, somebody inspired Greene to study classic Roman authors, for later in life he demonstrated an easy familiarity with Seneca, Horace, and Euclid, and an intimate knowledge of the writings of a Roman general named Julius Caesar. Their works were not on the Quakers' list of necessary reading.

Late in their lives, Greene's brothers would recall seeing Nathanael climb upstairs, book in hand, to read by himself by candlelight in his bedroom. He read between chores, during his journeys to Newport, across Narragansett Bay, and he read at the forge and the mill. Decades after Nathanael's death, his brothers proudly displayed a well-worn seat by the family forge. There, Nathanael tried to manage the irons in the fire while reading whatever book caught his fancy that day. According to George Washington Greene, "he would often forget himself in his book long after the last kernel had been shaken from the hopper."

His brothers did not share Nathanael's eagerness to learn and to read.

So his was a lonely pursuit, and he rarely met inquisitive peers or possible mentors as he carried out his chores in and around the family home. But when he visited Newport, New England's second-busiest seaport (Boston was the busiest), he encountered men of education and knowledge, men who traded in ideas as well as goods, men with libraries and college degrees. Though extremely self-conscious about his own lack of formal education, Greene sought out men from whom he believed he might learn something, a trait that would serve him well on the battlefield. It must have taken no small amount of courage and self-confidence for this young Quaker to strike up conversations with men of letters in Newport. But he did, and for his efforts he formed friendships with such well-educated men as Ezra Stiles, a minister and future president of Yale University.

Greene's grandson tells a possibly apochryphal story about Nathanael's first encounter with the learned and influential Stiles. Greene was in a bookstore, perhaps for the first time, in Newport, and he announced to the proprietor that he wished to buy a book. "Which one?" the proprietor asked. Flustered, the country boy from the forges of Potowomut was stuck for an answer. His embarrassment won the sympathy of a fellow patron, Stiles, who struck up a conversation with Greene about books and writers. The two men, one a learned clergyman, the other an earnest student, became friendly, and Greene often visited the older man when he was in Newport.

Whether or not the story of Greene's encounter at the bookstore is true, it's not hard to imagine that the young man felt a little unsure of himself as he ventured ever so cautiously into the wide world beyond the forge. He persisted nevertheless and became friendly with a young college student known only as Giles, who inspired Nathanael to further bury himself in books. Soon, Nathanael Greene was a walking incongruity: a self-taught child of the Enlightenment, dressed in the unadorned black garb of a Quaker. On his business trips to Newport, he sold miniature anchors he made at the family forge, and with the proceeds he began buying books. Through the influence of his new friend Stiles, he read John Locke's influential treatise *Essay on Human Under-*

standing, which celebrated inquiry and intellectual independence. He read the classic English work on the law, Sir William Blackstone's *Commentaries.* And he devoured *The Drapier's Letters,* a series of articles written in the 1720s by the Irish satirist and rabble-rouser Jonathan Swift. Writing under the guise of a shopkeeper named M. B. Drapier, Swift argued vehemently against British economic policies in Ireland and helped inspire a campaign that thwarted Parliament's attempt to introduce inferior currency in Ireland. But Swift went beyond just the issue of the moment. He wrote, "All government without the consent of the governed is the very definition of slavery." And, addressing his fellow Irish, he said, "You are and ought to be as free a people as your brethren in England." Jonathan Swift quickly became Nathanael Greene's favorite author.

Yet there is no evidence that young Nathanael Greene sought to apply the rhetoric of Jonathan Swift to Rhode Island or to America. Still in his twenties, single with no immediate prospects for a family, he was very much a work in progress, still unsure of where life would take him, and without a guide to help him on the journey. Through his contacts in Newport and the friendship of Ezra Stiles, he knew of a larger world beyond the forge, the farm, and the mill. As yet, though, he simply wasn't sure how he might fit into that world. And that world was beginning to change.

Strapped for cash and stuck with bills from the French and Indian War, Parliament turned its eyes westward in the 1760s, toward the colonies in North America. The military power of Britain offered the colonists security; the economic might of the empire made their prosperity possible. It was time, then, to extract some measure of revenue from those subjects of the Crown scattered in the towns and forests of America.

Of all the measures Parliament might have considered, of all the taxes it might have levied, none would have been worse for Rhode Island than the Sugar Act. It was not a new tax; the Sugar Act had been passed in 1733 and was promptly disregarded. Beginning in May 1763, however, it became a real tax. Parliament ordered that the duty of six pence per gallon on non-British molasses from the West Indies was no longer to be ignored or evaded or bribed away. Colonial governors and customs officials were put on notice that they could no longer act as if they knew nothing about uncollected molasses duties. To illustrate the point, Royal Navy warships took up positions in American ports. Parliament ordered them to "seize and proceed to condemnation of all such Ships and Vessels as you shall find offending" against the newly muscular Sugar Act. In December 1763, HMS *Squirrel* set up operations in Newport. For reasons best known to the Royal Navy's commanders, the ship bore a name not likely to inspire much in the way of fear or respect from notably irrascible Rhode Islanders. The *Squirrel*'s twenty guns, however, got the point across.

The crackdown was meant for all of His Majesty's colonies, but Rhode Island had the most to lose. By the 1760s, the colony's prosperity and development were linked inextricably to the molasses trade, and that trade was based on the informal agreement among merchants, politicians, and customs officials to act as though the Sugar Act didn't exist. The six-pence tax would have made the cost of importing molasses from non-British sources prohibitive, and there was only a limited amount of molasses from British possessions, not nearly enough to satisfy demand. Enforcement of the tax on foreign molasses, then, threatened Rhode Island's financial health and prosperity. A Rhode Island merchant soon reported that "all business seems to wear a gloom not before seen in America."

Inspired by their merchant colleagues in Boston, who were prepared to resist enforcement of the molasses tax, Rhode Island's politicians and businessmen drew up a written protest and dispatched it to London. The document emphasized the importance of molasses to Rhode Island's economy: rum, the Rhode Islanders said, was "the main hinge upon which the trade of the colony turns, and many hundreds of persons depend immediately upon it for a subsistence." The merchants painted a picture of desperation: "Two-thirds of our vessels will become useless. . . . Our mechanics and those who depend upon the merchant for employment must seek for subsistence elsewhere. . . . An end will be put to our commerce." The Rhode Islanders and other American protesters knew that the Sugar Act was due for renewal (or expiration) in early 1764, and they hoped their arguments would carry some weight with Parliament. New legislation in 1764 lowered the tax to three pence per gallon, but it was hardly a victory for colonial merchants. Parliament made the molasses tax permanent, and it increased taxes on sugar from foreign colonies as well as adding taxes on other, non-British goods.

What made the Sugar Act of 1764 historic, and even more threatening, was Parliament's assertion that it had a right to levy taxes to raise revenues, especially to pay for the thousands of British soldiers in America. Previously, taxes were considered a means by which Parliament regulated trade. The government of George Grenville warned that colonists could expect further taxes in the future, including the possibility of "certain Stamp Duties."

A few months after the *Squirrel* arrived to remind Rhode Island of its new obligations, sailors aboard another Royal Navy vessel, the *St. John,* were accused of stealing goods from Newport's merchants. As an indication of just how tense affairs had become in Newport by the spring of 1764, residents gained access to a fort and opened fire on the *St. John,* but dispersed before the *Squirrel*'s guns could be brought to bear. When the *Squirrel*'s commander, Captain Richard Smith, discovered that the man who had fired the first shots actually acted on orders from local officials, he condemned Rhode Island as a "licentious republic" in need of drastic change. Smith demanded apologies; local officials were equally angry. They wanted to know why the gunners hadn't sunk the *St. John*.

The following spring, angry Newporters again took action against the Royal Navy when the captain and crew of the *Maidstone* virtually shut down the port by seizing merchant sailors and fishermen coming in and out of the port and putting them to work on His Majesty's ships. This practice, known as impressment, was common on the seas (and would become one of the flashpoints in the War of 1812) and in seaports, but the *Maidstone*'s captain was particularly ruthless. Newport struck back in early June 1765. A group of about five hundred citizens made off with one of the *Maidstone*'s boats and burned it, to the delight of all.

This was a shocking act of defiance, but only one manifestation of Rhode Island's anger. In late 1764, Governor Hopkins published a treatise titled *The Rights of the Colonies Examined,* which argued vehemently against the Sugar Act. He also complained against the latest outrage: the Stamp Act. Parliament, he argued, had no right to collect taxes without the consent of the colonists themselves. Furthermore, he wrote, the American colonies were "entitled to equal liberty and freedom with their fellow subjects in Europe."

Hopkins's arguments helped move the roiling debate in America toward issues larger than any single tax or law. The issue, as Hopkins and others were making clear, was liberty.

After limited debate in Parliament, the Stamp Act passed the House of Commons on February 27, 1765, and the House of Lords on March 8. Unlike past taxes, the Stamp Act did not concern itself with trade regulation. It was designed to raise revenue, specifically, to help pay for British troops stationed in America that cost the treasury three hundred and fifty thousand pounds a year. Military tribunals called Admiralty Courts were given jurisdiction over those accused of violating the new law.

Reaction throughout the colonies was swift and certain. In Rhode Island, the public's outrage inspired a small insurrection in Newport in late August. The colony's legislators asserted publicly that Parliament had no right to impose such a tax on the colonies.

Despite the protests and violence, the Stamp Act remained on schedule, due to take effect on November 1. A load of stamped paper arrived in Newport Harbor a few weeks before the deadline, inspiring a new round of denunciations. A special supplement to the *Newport Mercury* of October 28 reported the imminent death of "North American Liberty." A few of Liberty's friends "went a few Days ago to wait upon the poor old Gentleman, and found him indeed gasping his last, and now find him reduced to a Skelton," wrote the newspaper's correspondent, identified only as "A Mourner." The Mourner invited the people of Newport to a public funeral and burial for old man Liberty on the morning of November 1.

The ceremony took place at the appointed hour, with none of the violence of previous demonstrations. A standoff followed: the stamped paper remained on board a British ship in the harbor; the stamp master, Augustus Johnston, remained in his office but incapable of action; and all eyes turned to Samuel Ward, who had succeeded Hopkins as the colony's governor. He ordered that Rhode Island set aside Thursday, November 28, as a day of Thanksgiving. This seemingly innocuous gesture was, in fact, a work of political genius. Ward played the role of dutiful royal subject in asking "Almighty God" to bless and protect King George III's "most precious life," which was nice enough. But Ward added a few more requests for the Almighty. He prayed that "our invaluable Rights, Liberties and Privileges, civil and religious, may be precious" in God's sight, and that "He will be pleased to frustrate every Attempt to deprive us of them."

Ward's language did not go unnoticed. Other colonial radicals cheered his sly maneuver, noting that no other governor had yet asked for God's intercession on behalf of American liberty.

In late December, Stamp Master Johnston resigned. Governor Ward informed London of Johnston's resignation and further asserted that the tax was "inconsistent with" Rhode Island's "natural and just rights and privileges." As for the act itself, Ward reported that he couldn't enforce it because, after all, he had no stamped paper.

It was sitting in the cargo hold of a British ship in Newport Harbor, and nobody dared unload it.

The hated Stamp Act was repealed in 1766, but tensions between the colonies and Parliament continued, and Rhode Islanders in particular kept a wary eye out for further limitations on their liberty and their commerce. There was no shortage of them: the Townshend Acts imposed taxes on glass, lead, imported paper, and, most famously, tea, while the Declaratory Act asserted Parliament's right to legislate for and tax the colonies. The Townshend taxes inspired throughout the colonies an agreement to stop importing British-made goods, but for some of Rhode Island's merchants, love of commerce trumped love of liberty. They continued their trade with Britain, just as other Rhode Islanders traded with the French during the French and Indian War. Merchants in Boston and Philadelphia sent messages to Newport suggesting that the Rhode Islanders reconsider their position, lest they find themselves with no markets within the colonies. The British were not alone in bemoaning Rhode Island's iconoclasm and sense of independence.

Nathanael Greene spent the turbulent 1760s in Potowomut, continuing his work in the family business and trying to find some balance between the Quaker tradition of his family and his own intellectual curiosity. He took a small step into the colony's civic affairs when he joined three other men, including his tutor, Adam Maxwell, in petitioning the Rhode Island Assembly to relocate Rhode Island College from the town of Warren to East Greenwich, not far from the family homestead. Greene very likely wrote the petition, which described East Greenwich as "abounding with Every necessary supply to render the Scholars Comfortable." Included among the town's amenities, Greene wrote with impressive earnestness, was "a post office."

The petition failed, and the college was moved to Providence and eventually renamed Brown University. Greene's involvement in the campaign, however, further illustrated how far he was straying from the parochial, insular traditions of his faith and family. The distance became a good deal greater in November 1770, when Nathanael's father died in Potowomut at the age of sixty-three. The surviving sons inherited the family business, but Nathanael continued to shake loose other parts of his father's legacy. It is in letters written after his father's death that Nathanael begins to complain about his lack of education and about his father's hostility toward literature and the world of ideas.

There are few indications of any radical political activity on his part during his twenties, but he continued to visit Newport on business and he could hardly have missed the new spirit of the times in that city, where rioters had taken to the street to protest the Stamp Act and other British policies. And as an avid reader, he surely must have devoured the flowery denunciations of Parliament regularly available in the *Newport Mercury,* which briefly sported a front-page slogan reading, "Undaunted by TYRANTS—We'll DIE or be FREE."

Greene's regimen of self-improvement continued, too, and he found himself attracted to military histories, beginning with Caesar's. While the Roman's book had a narrative flow and battlefield descriptions designed to capture the reader's imagination, Greene's further reading showed that he had moved beyond mere narrative and was looking for actual instruction in the art and science of war. In his letters, Greene mentioned that he read *Instructions to His Generals* by the Prussian militarist Frederick the Great, and *Mes Reveries,* by Maurice de Saxe, the famed French marshal. Greene's unlikely interest in warfare, along with his general thirst for secular knowledge, nurtured his private rebellion against religious traditions he regarded as unreasonable and arbitrary. Tales of great battles and triumphant generals offered him an exciting glimpse of glory beyond the Quaker meetinghouse and the gristmill. And these books did not simply stir his imagination; they also offered him instruction in battlefield tactics and strategy. As he would demonstrate in later years, Greene learned these lessons well, however irrelevant they might have seemed at the time.

For the moment, however, Greene's only personal knowledge of combat was restricted to that fought on legal battlefields. He and his brothers were frequent visitors to the Court of Common Pleas in East Greenwich, usually in pursuit of an unpaid debt. Court documents from the era show numerous legal actions, some involving family squabbling, related to foundry and forge. Nathanael Greene began his studies of Blackstone's *Commentaries* because of the number of lawsuits involving the family business.

Through his twenties, Greene's health began to show signs of afflictions he would later suffer on the battlefield. He complained of asthma attacks that kept him awake at night, and his right eye was slightly scarred after he was innoculated against smallpox during a visit to New York.

The scar, which occasionally became infected, was nothing compared to the disease itself, one of the most prolific killers of the era. Greene's willingness to risk innoculation further demonstrated his free-thinking, independent spirit, for even in progressive Rhode Island in the early 1770s, smallpox innoculation was illegal.

Just before his father's death in 1770, Nathanael had moved from the Greene homestead to Coventry, about ten miles to the west, where Nathanael Greene & Company opened a new foundry. The twenty-eight-year-old bachelor built himself a new house, which he called Spell Hall, and made sure that it included a splendid library and study. And while he enjoyed the company of his growing collection of books, he was hoping for more animated companionship, too. He had fallen in love with Anna Ward, a daughter of Samuel Ward, the colony's occasional governor and leader of one of Rhode Island's political factions. But Anna, known as Nancy to her family, apparently wasn't attracted to the young Quaker gentleman. Nathanael was crushed when it became apparent that Miss Ward had no intention of returning his affections. The humiliation became all the more intense when one of Nathanael's younger brothers, Christopher, married another one of Samuel Ward's daughters, Catherine, in 1774, formally linking the Greene family to the politically powerful Wards.

The aborted relationship between Nathanael and Nancy was not in vain, at least not for posterity's sake. Nathanael became friendly with her young brother, Samuel Ward Jr., who was precisely half Nathanael's age and, at age fourteen in 1770, already was a student at Rhode Island College. Nathanael and the lad he called Sammy corresponded through the early 1770s, and Nathanael's letters have survived. They are filled with spelling mistakes and earnest pronouncements about the world, like this offering from 1771: "To pursue Virtue where theres no Opposition is the Merit of a common Man, But to Practice it in spight of all Opposition is the Carrector of a truly great and Noble Soul."

What's striking about Greene's early letters to Sammy is the absence of any discussion of Rhode Island politics or the raging controversies of the day. He used the opportunity to lament his formal education, while offering Sammy advice about life and learning. "Study to be wise and learn to be prudent," he told Sammy. "Learning is not Virtue but the means to bring us an aquaintance with it. Integrity without knowledge is weak and useless, and Knowledge without integrity is dangerous and Dreadful. Let these be your motives to action through Life, the relief of the distressed, the detection of frauds, the defeat of oppression, and diffusion of happiness."

At the age of thirty, Nathanael Greene was absorbed in introspection, self-improvement, and the misery of unrequited love. But great events would soon offer him the opportunity to put his words of wisdom to the test.

3 | The Making of a Rebel

Lieutenant William Dudingston, commander of the British navy schooner *Gaspee,* was a man who took his job very seriously. He and his ship were part of the navy's crackdown on the colonial smuggling racket, and he had a reputation as a particularly aggressive enforcer of His Majesty's revenue laws. Several years earlier, in 1769, he had assaulted fishermen in Pennsylvania for no apparent reason. Not surprisingly, then, customs officials in Boston decided he was just the man to send to Rhode Island, the colony that had turned smuggling and evasion into an art form.

Rhode Islanders, of course, had some experience in dealing with customs and revenue officials who had no appreciation for their local traditions. And, like Dudingston, they were not shy about expressing their feelings. In the summer of 1769, the warship *Liberty* had sailed to Newport to enforce laws against smuggling and evasion of duty. After several confrontations with vessels suspected of carrying contraband, the *Lib-*

erty opened fire on a particularly quarrelsome captain and his crew. The next day, the *Liberty*'s captain was introduced to the ways and means of angry Rhode Islanders. As he set foot on a wharf in Newport, the captain was surrounded and was told to order his crew off the ship. He had little choice but to comply. A select committee of Newport citizens boarded the vessel, cut it loose, and scuttled it. A few days later, the *Liberty* made for a fine bonfire. Nobody was ever prosecuted for this daring display of dissent. Rhode Island authorities later described the suspects merely as "Persons unknown."

Lieutenant Dudingston would put an end to this kind of insolence.

Dudingston and the *Gaspee* arrived in Narragansett Bay in early 1772, and Rhode Island's merchants quickly discovered that he was a man who meant business. He disdained the tradition of presenting his commission to Rhode Island's governor. He demanded that all ships lower their colors in tribute as they passed the *Gaspee*. Vessels of all sizes were subject to search, and Dudingston's well-armed crew made sure that their searches were thorough.

Dudingston had nothing but contempt for the colony and its merchants. He complained that Rhode Islanders acted as if "they have every right to carry on" their illicit trade "without interuption." He was not wrong. But he was determined to change the way this irrascible colony conducted its business affairs. On February 17, 1772, he seized an opportunity to make his point.

The merchant vessel *Fortune* was anchored in Narragansett Bay, its hold filled with fourteen hundred gallons of rum, a hogshead of brown sugar, and forty gallons of "Jamaican spirits." At the vessel's helm was Rufus Greene, a young cousin of Nathanael Greene and his brothers. The firm of Nathanael Greene & Company owned the *Fortune*.

An officer from the *Gaspee* set out from the mother ship and boarded the *Fortune*, instructing Rufus Greene to retreat into the cabin while the vessel was searched. Greene asked the officer under whose authority he was acting. "If you do not go into the cabin, I'll let you know," the officer replied. The officer's drawn sword indicated the source of his authority, and Rufus Greene was hustled off toward the cabin, where he was roughed up and thrown against a chest of drawers. The *Gaspee* towed Greene's ship into Newport Harbor.

Dudingston decided to send the *Fortune* and its cargo to Boston, where an Admiralty Court—and not a local jury—could decide its fate. By law, however, the case should have been tried in Newport, but Dudingston decided that this was one evasion of the law that the Crown would support.

Word of the *Fortune*'s seizure and of the rough treatment cousin Rufus suffered quickly made its way to Coventry. Nathanael Greene was furious. He put aside his pining for Nancy Ward and his endless exercises in self-improvement to win some measure of justice and compensation for what he regarded as an act of officially sanctioned piracy. In a letter to his friend Sammy Ward, Greene wrote that he was in pursuit of a "Searover," or pirate, who had taken "a quantity of Our Rum and carried it round to Boston (contrary to the Express words of the Statute)." The "illegality of [the] measure," he went on, "created such a Spirit of Resentment That I have devoted almost the whole of my Time in devising and carrying into execution measures for the recovery of my Property and punishing the offender."

Those measures would include a lawsuit against Lieutenant Dudingston himself, demanding that he compensate the Greenes for their losses. The case of *Greene v. Dudingston* became a legal sensation in Rhode Island, a notable act of defiance, and indicated that Nathanael Greene was emerging from his forge and his library to take an active role in his times. The suit forced Dudingston to spend months evading Rhode Island officials, who were authorized to arrest him as part of the Greene family's complaint.

Even as Nathanael Greene prepared his case, the *Gaspee* became the terror of Narragansett Bay through the spring and summer of 1772. Dudingston and his crew not only harassed all manner of vessels but regularly raided farms and businesses. Dependent on seaborne trade, Rhode Island's economy suffered as Dudingston's aggressive searches and willingness to open fire on uncooperative vessels made the very act of entering Narragansett Bay a dangerous proposition. One prominent Rhode Islander and a future member of the Continental Congress, Henry Marchant, described Dudingston as a "very dirty low fellow" who ordered his crew "to commit many Outrages upon the Possessions and Property of the Inhabitants on Shore."

Rhode Island's governor, Joseph Wanton, dispatched a letter of protest to Dudingston's immediate superior, Admiral John Montagu, who was based in Boston. The admiral defended Dudingston and then issued a blunt warning to Wanton: "I am . . . informed the people of Newport talk of fitting out an armed vessel to rescue any vessel the King's schooner may take carrying on an illicit trade," Montagu wrote. "Let them be cautious [about] what they [do] for as sure as they attempt it and any of them are taken I will hang them as pirates."

Wanton's written reply was simple and utterly in keeping with Rhode Island tradition: "I do not receive instructions for the administration of my government from the King's Admiral stationed in America."

Lieutenant Dudingston's aggression continued into late spring. On June 9, 1772, the *Gaspee* fired a shot across the bow of the merchant ship *Hannah* in Narragansett Bay. The *Hannah*'s captain, Benjamin Lindsay, chose defiance rather than surly compliance. He decided to try to outrun the *Gaspee*. Dudingston immediately gave chase, but this time his zeal betrayed him. Lindsay moved into shallow waters off Namquit Point, and the *Gaspee* ran aground. Lindsay and the *Hannah* got away and sailed for Providence. When the *Hannah* arrived in port, Lindsay spread the news: the hated Dudingston and his despised ship were stuck and vulnerable in shallow water about six miles away.

The city's leading citizens and merchants convened that night in a tavern to plan Rhode Island's revenge on the *Gaspee*. They dispatched a man with a drum to parade up and down the town's streets to spread word of the *Gaspee*'s misfortune and recruit volunteers for an attack. Sixty-four citizens turned out at the wharf and set out in longboats before midnight, headed toward the stricken warship. They were spotted as they approached the *Gaspee*, and soon Lieutenant Dudingston appeared on deck, armed with a pistol. He asked the intruders in the longboats to identify themselves.

A voice replied: "I am the sheriff of the county of Kent, God damn you! I have got a warrant to apprehend you, God damn you!" The sheriff, Abraham Whipple, had been trying to serve Dudingston with papers since Nathanael Greene and his brothers filed their lawsuit, naming the lieutenant as a defendant.

The sheriff demanded that Dudingston surrender. Dudingston declined. A shot rang out, hitting Dudingston in the groin. The Providence men quickly boarded the *Gaspee* and overpowered its crew. One of the raiders asked the wounded Dudingston if he planned to "make amends" for the rum he had seized from the *Fortune*. A medical student in the boarding party dressed the lieutenant's wound, and Dudingston and his crew were herded into small boats and taken to shore. Humiliated, they could only watch as the Providence raiders put their warship to the torch. By morning, the *Gaspee* was a smoking hulk.

Once again, Rhode Islanders had committed an outrage against the Crown, and British officials and even the king himself were furious. The secretary of state in charge of American affairs, Lord Hillsborough, resigned, and Lord Dartmouth replaced him. His Majesty ordered a royal commission to investigate the crime and bring those responsible to justice. Some British officials, including Massachusetts governor Thomas Hutchinson, believed that a few hangings would remind Rhode Island of the price of insubordination.

Samuel Adams, the Boston rabble-rouser who was closely monitoring events in Rhode Island, regarded the *Gaspee* insurrection as a glimpse of what was to come. "I have long feared this unhappy contest between Great Britain and America would end in rivers of blood," he wrote to Rhode Island's deputy governor, Darius Sessions. "Should that be the case, America, I think, may wash her hands in innocence." In the meantime, Governor Wanton had little choice but to issue a proclamation on June 12 offering a reward of one hundred pounds "to any Person or Persons who shall discover the Perpetrators of the . . . Villainy." King

George personally raised the amount of the reward to five hundred pounds two months later.

As was the custom in Rhode Island, the Perpetrators remained at large. The reward went unclaimed. But Rhode Island authorities did catch up with at least one criminal suspect. Three days after the attack on the *Gaspee,* the Kent County sheriff arrested Lieutenant Dudingston as he lay in a hospital bed. The arrest allowed the case of *Greene v. Dudingston* to proceed in court.

The *Gaspee* affair was a milestone in Nathanael Greene's life. His letters, which had been apolitical until now—the correspondence contains no reference to the Boston Massacre in 1770 or its aftermath—soon were filled with condemnations of Britain's rule in America. He continued to press his case against Dudingston, eventually winning a judgment of about three hundred pounds sterling. It's not certain whether Greene actually received the money from Dudingston, but there's no question that the family business could have used it. In August 1772, the Greenes' forge in Coventry burned to the ground. It was a financial and personal disaster. One bright morning just after the fire, Nathanael sat amid the ruins and read a letter from his friend Sammy Ward. He replied quickly, describing the scene around him: "I was surrounded with Gloomy Faces, piles of Timber still in Flames, Heaps of Bricks dasht to pieces, Baskets of Coal reduced to ashes. Everything seemed to appear in Ruins and Confusion." The calamity, coming even as *Greene v. Dudingston* was being argued in Kent County courts, had a terrible effect on Nathanael. He suffered through an asthma attack that kept him nearly sleepless for four nights, leading to an inflammation in one of his eyes. He even despaired of his surroundings. "If Coventry ever was tolerable, it has now become insupportable," he wrote. And once again, his thoughts turned to Sammy's sister, who remained beyond his reach. He told her he would stop writing if that was what she wished, but he desperately wanted to continue their correspondence. Their letters offered Nathanael hope, however dim, of a future with Nancy.

His morbid self-absorption gave way to engagement and fury when Greene heard rumors that he had been identified as one of the leaders of the *Gaspee* raiding party. The royal commission hearing evidence in the case interviewed one of the *Gaspee* crew members, who said that he recognized a man "named Greene" among the raiders. If there was, in fact, a man named Greene among the *Gaspee* boarding party, most likely it was Rufus, the captain of the ill-fated *Fortune*. But beyond the question of his innocence, Nathanael Greene had good reason to fear being named as a suspect in the affair. He had heard further rumors claiming that *Gaspee* suspects would be transported to London for trial.

Of his accuser, Greene said, "I should be tempted to let the Sunshine through him if I could come at Him." Again, as with the seizure of the *Fortune,* Greene transformed his personal travail into a political epiphany. Questions of freedom and liberty no longer were distant or merely academic. They now were unavoidable; they affected him, and, he realized, they affected all other Americans as well.

He told Sammy Ward that the *Gaspee* commission was "Justly Alarming to every Virtuous Mind and Lover of Liberty in America." If the commission succeeded in tempting witnesses "to Perjury," he wrote, "this Court and mode of Trial . . . will naturally Affect all the other Colonies." He went on to condemn the colony's General Assembly, which had not vigorously protested the commission's work, as a "Pusillanimous Crew and betrayers of the Peoples Liberties."

Although he now feared for the liberties of his fellow colonists and had reason to resent the power and prerogatives of the Crown, Nathanael Greene—like most Americans—was not prepared for radical solutions to their complaints. The king remained a popular figure in America, and Britain's tax and revenue policies were blamed on Parliament and the king's ministers. Greene himself still honored Rhode Island's connection to the mother country. His favorite horse, a stallion, was named Britain.

His connection to his faith was undergoing a similar transition. He was becoming ever more impatient with what he regarded as the irrational and anti-intellectual cant of his late father's brand of Quakerism, and yet he had not broken completely with the traditions of his childhood. But Nathanael's occasional appearances at the Quaker meetinghouse in

East Greenwich, near the family homestead in Potowomut, did nothing to persuade him that he was making a mistake as he drifted away from his father's faith.

One such meeting featured a particularly pompous and long-winded minister whose sermon inspired only cynicism from Nathanael as he sat in the congregation, wishing he were somewhere else. The minister's talk, Greene wrote, was "so light that it evaporated like Smoke and left us neither the fuller nor better pleased." Indeed, the experience, and perhaps his never-ending search for a bride and companion, left him "in the dumps . . . brooding over mischief and hatching Evils."

Greene's impatience with conventional religious practice was not confined to criticism of Quakerism. He lashed out when the colony's clergymen protested the performance of a play called *The Unhappy Orphan*. Stage performances were prohibited under Rhode Island law, and a holy ruckus followed the play's debut. "Priests and Levites of every Order [cry] out against it as a subversion of Morallity and dangerous to the Church," Greene wrote. But he took the side of the actors, one of whom he knew.

It was not entirely surprising that Nathanael Greene eventually found himself suspended from the Quaker meetings for an infraction of their code of behavior. The suspension was ordered in July 1773, and for years, historians stated that it was a punishment for Greene's having attended a military exercise of some sort. Such activity, it was assumed, constituted a breach of Quaker pacifism. More recently, however, Greene scholars have argued persuasively that the suspension was related to Nathanael's appearance at a public house or some other disreputable place. The official record states that Greene and one of his cousins, Griffin Greene, were punished for having been seen at "a Place in Coneticut of Publick Resort where they had No Proper Business." Historians for decades assumed that the "Publick Resort" was a military parade, but the editors of Greene's published papers note that the phrase was used at the time to describe alehouses and the like. Given Greene's convivial personality (at around this time, he attended a friend's wedding and wound up celebrating the occasion for several days), not to mention his clear disregard of Quaker tenets, it is not hard to picture him enjoying himself in an alehouse.

But even if he was drinking and not drilling in Connecticut, Greene's heretical interest in military matters was undeniable. He continued to study Caesar and Frederick the Great and cited famous campaigns from the past, like Hannibal's in northern Italy, in his letters. His correspondence with Sammy Ward offers a tantilizing but mysterious clue about his interests at the time. In two letters in the early 1770s, well before the colonies and Britain marched to war, Greene referred to himself as "the colonel." Nobody is quite sure why. But if his self-styled title betrayed a secret ambition, Greene set his sights far too low.

The organized boycott of British goods began to sputter out in late 1770, after the government withdrew duties on most items except tea. In Boston, however, agitators continued their boycott, even though one of the city's leading citizens, John Hancock, made a fortune importing tea from Britain.

The East India Company, the tea-trading firm that had become one of Britain's largest institutions, was perilously close to bankruptcy in the early 1770s. Parliament tried to bail out the company in May 1773 by eliminating colonial middlemen from the tea trade. The East India Company was given permission to ship and sell directly to designated American agents, drastically lowering the cost of its tea. Stouthearted patriots would be sorely tempted to reconsider their principles, American merchants would be cut out of the action, and only the company's agents would make money on the deal.

Ships carrying the tea sailed into Boston Harbor in late November and early December 1773. And on the night of December 17, the city's most radical agitators disguised themselves as Mohawk Indians, sailed into the harbor, boarded the merchant ships, and dumped the offending tea into the sea. The Boston Tea Party electrified America's radical leaders and enraged Britain's politicians. In March 1774, Lord North introduced legislation in Parliament called the Boston Port Act. It was

Britain's reply to the Tea Party: the port of Boston was ordered closed, and its government and administative functions were transferred out of the city. General Thomas Gage was dispatched to Massachusetts to become the colony's military governor, and he would have command of four thousand troops who would enforce the Crown's laws.

In addition to the Boston Port Act, Parliament passed a series of laws that became known in the colonies as the Intolerable Acts. Royal officials accused of crimes would be tried not in the colony in which the crimes took place but in Britain or in another colony. The Quartering Act ordered that colonial authorities provide British troops with housing and supplies. And the Massachusetts charter was rewritten to give the new military governor extensive powers over the town meetings that had helped give birth to the colony's agitation.

Other colonies rallied around stricken Boston, even as rumors circulated that more oppressive measures were under consideration. John Sherwood, Rhode Island's agent in London, wrote to Governor Wanton, warning him: The prime minister may be considering a bill to "Vacate Your Charter, and to add part of Your Colony to the Province of Massachusetts Bay, and part to the Colony of Connecticut." Sherwood added that he found the report hard to believe. Nevertheless, with the great port of Boston closed and their neighbors in Massachusetts under martial law, Rhode Islanders had reason to believe that anything was possible, given their own record of defiance. Wanton set aside June 30 as a day of fasting and prayer. In keeping with custom, Rhode Islanders were asked to pray for the king, and while they were at it, for the "relief . . . of the town of Boston." A correspondent identified only as "the Preacher" wrote in the *Newport Mercury* that it was "now high time for the Colonies to have a grand Congress to complete the system for the American Independent Commonwealth, as it is so evident that no other plan will secure the rights of this people from rapacious and plotting tyrants." Such a congress did, in fact, convene in 1774—the First Continental Congress. But the Preacher's goal was more radical than most of the delegates, who sought a more peaceful resolution to the growing conflict.

Nathanael Greene followed events in Boston closely, and he often visited the city, sixty miles from his home in Coventry, during the crisis in 1774. At some point during his journeys to Boston, he met a portly young bookseller named Henry Knox, who shared not only Greene's love of literature but also his growing interest in military science.

The Boston Port Act and the Intolerable Acts solidifed Greene's evolution into a fledgling revolutionary. His letters now were filled with language that Samuel Adams would have enjoyed. Britain's political leaders, he wrote, seemed "determined to embrace their cursed hands in American Blood, and that once Wise and Virtuous Parliament, but now Wicked and weak Assembly, lends an assisting hand to accomplish their hellish schemes." He condemned the soldiers in Boston as "insolent above measure." And, like Adams, he saw events speeding toward a violent end. "Soon very soon expect to hear the thirsty Earth drinking in the warm Blood of American sons. O how my eyes [flash] with indignation and my bosom burns with holy resentment."

It was not only resentment that so agitated Greene's bosom. Quite the opposite. He had fallen in love, again, this time to a nineteen-year-old beauty he had known since she was a little girl. Her name was Catherine Littlefield, and she was a cousin of Sammy Ward's. Catherine's mother died when she was ten, so she left her home on Block Island and moved to the home of her mother's sister, who was married to William Greene, a distant relation of Nathanael's and a prominent political leader in the colony. Nathanael Greene was an occasional visitor to William Greene's house, so he watched the couple's niece, known to her friends as Caty, blossom into a charming and flirtatious young woman who enjoyed the company of men. One observer described her as a "small brunette with high color, a vivacious expression, and a snapping pair of dark eyes." Other descriptions insist, with equal enthusiasm, that those dark eyes actually were violet.

Her aunt, Catherine Ray Greene, was just as charming and lovely as Caty Littlefield. When Catherine Ray was younger and single, she fell in love with the married but frequently obliging Benjamin Franklin. Franklin and young Catherine Ray carried on a memorable correspondence indicating that they were on the verge of intimacy, but never actually got there. However, they remained friendly once Catherine Ray married into the expansive Greene family.

Catherine Ray Greene was a strong influence on her niece, seeing to it that she took French lessons and developed an interest in the world outside their home. That latter assignment was relatively easy, because the outside world was very much a part of the Greene household. William Greene was building a political career that would lead to his election as governor of Rhode Island during the Revolution, and so his home became a meeting place for colonial patriots and other ambitious men. Young Caty Littlefield prospered in this highly masculine world, and not just because of her beauty. Though not especially well-educated, she was smart and charming, and men gravitated toward her.

After an apparently short courtship, the wedding between Nathanael Greene and Catherine Littlefield took place on July 20, 1774, in East Greenwich. The ceremony was small, restricted, in Nathanael's words, to "only a few Choice spirits." Among those choice spirits were several well-connected friends of Greene, including not only Sammy Ward but a lawyer named James Varnum and a future member of the Rhode Island Supreme Court named Thomas Arnold. They were typical of the kind of company Nathanael Greene cultivated. Both men were younger than Greene, were college educated, and were involved in the colony's civic affairs. Though Greene still remained self-conscious about his incomplete education, he surrounded himself with young friends who had the schooling he wished for himself. He knew he still had much to learn, and he was comfortable in the company of those who could teach him something.

He brought his bride back to his home in Coventry, a three-story house that no longer seemed such a lonely place. Relatively late in life, at a time when his friends despaired of him ever finding a bride, thirty-two-year-old Nathanael Greene began his new life as a married man with all its attendant responsibilities.

It quickly became obvious, however, that he was hardly settling down.

Just a few weeks after his wedding, Greene joined his friend James

Varnum and other leading citizens from and near East Greenwich in raising money for the suffering citizens of Boston. Greene's was among eighty
signatures on a public subscription that deplored the "Late, Cruel, malig-
nant and more than savage Acts of the British Parliament." Greene contributed two pounds, eight shillings to the fund, the second-highest single
donation. The money was used to buy food and livestock for Boston.

As America's emerging political leaders convened in Philadelphia for
the First Continental Congress, Nathanael Greene was moving beyond
rhetoric and subscription lists. The avid student of battles past took his
first step toward a military career of his own by joining a private military
company based in East Greenwich. It was one of many militia units
forming throughout the colonies as tensions over Boston worsened. The
new militia met several times a week to drill, train, and study under the
supervision of two former officers in the British army. Tradition has it
that Nathanael Greene was responsible for recruiting one of the officers
after they met during one of Greene's visits to Boston. Greene also
brought back a musket from Boston, hiding it in a farmer's load of hay
until they were safely beyond the watchful eyes of British soldiers.

In October 1774, after a few weeks of training, the amateur soldiers
of East Greenwich asked the Rhode Island Assembly to incorporate
them as a recognized state militia for Kent County. Approval was quick in
coming, and so Nathanael Greene became a private in the new Kentish
Guards. With their red coats with green trim, white waistcoat and pan-
taloons, and hats with a black cockade, they were a frequent sight in East
Greenwich.

Few of these citizen soldiers were more enthusiastic than the newly
married Nathanael Greene, who expected to become one of the company's leaders. It is hard to imagine, then, the wound he suffered in late
October, when the troops overlooked Greene in electing their officers.
Several militiamen took Greene aside and told him he was an embarrassment to the company. It was, they said, his limp; slight though it was, it
took away from the company's manly, martial appearance. It simply
wouldn't do, the men told Greene, to have an officer with a limp. Who
would take such a company seriously?

Greene was crushed. He immediately wrote a heartrending letter to the unit's new captain, James Varnum, confiding that it was a "stroke of morification" to be told that he was "a blemish to those with whom [he] associated." He went on to say, "I confess it is my misfortune to limp a little but I did not conceive it to be so great." After such an embarrassment, so completely unexpected, he was prepared to leave the company. "My heart is too sus[c]eptible of pride, and my sentiments too delicate, to wish a connexion where I am considered in an inferior point of light," he wrote.

He sent the letter to Varnum and then reconsidered. He did not resign from the Kentish Guards. But the episode showed a side of Greene that would become familiar to his colleagues in the years and conflicts to come. He was extremely sensitive to criticism, whether explicit or perceived, and it didn't take much for him to take a plunge into waves of self-pity.

The guards continued to drill and parade, with great effect. Greene and his fellow militiamen, like all American patriots, followed events in Boston with increasing anxiety as General Gage tightened his grip over the city. On the night of April 19, 1775, an express rider galloped into East Greenwich with news that a British column had opened fire on patriots in Lexington and Concord. Greene heard the news in Coventry. He said his farewells to his bride of less than a year, mounted his horse—but not his beloved Britain, for the stallion had been stolen some time ago—and rode to East Greenwich. With Varnum in command, the Kentish Guards set out for Massachusetts at daybreak on April 20 to provide whatever assistance their embattled countrymen might require.

Was this war or another terrible incident, like the Boston Massacre? Was this little outfit of part-time, unpaid militiamen prepared to face some of the best-trained soldiers in the world?

The men from East Greenwich soon learned that there would be no answers to such questions, at least not at the moment. When they reached Pawtucket, they learned that Governor Wanton had ordered them to halt their march to Massachusetts. Though Wanton had delivered some fine, defiant words to Crown authorities in the past, he was not prepared for the next step in Anglo-American relations. He was not quite a Tory, but he was more sympathetic to British authorities than the Kentish Guards were.

Most of the militiamen obeyed Wanton's order and returned to East Greenwich. Not Nathanael Greene. He and several other guards continued on the road to Massachusetts, no doubt stewing over the lack of ardor and patriotism among their friends. Finally, however, a messenger arrived with news that the British had retreated from the countryside and were back in Boston. Greene and his party reluctantly turned back for home.

The bloodshed in Lexington and Concord led lawmakers in Providence to propose that Rhode Island form an "Army of Observation" that would "repel any insult or violence that may be offered to the inhabitants" of the colony. Governor Wanton and his chief deputy opposed this dangerous escalation and were soon deposed. (The lawmakers refused to administer the governor's oath of office to Wanton, who had recently been reelected.) Lawmakers then went ahead with plans to authorize the raising of an army of fifteen hundred soldiers.

And, on May 8, 1775, the Assembly offered command of this army to a thirty-two-year-old private in the Kentish Guards, Nathanael Greene.

Given his personal and family connections to Rhode Island's political leaders, Nathanael Greene clearly was not an unknown quantity. His influential friends and relations surely knew of his intense interest in military affairs and his patriotism. Perhaps his performance in the Kentish Guards also recommended him. Whatever the case, just six months after he was considered a "blemish" on the good appearance of the Kentish Guards, Nathanael Greene was given an army and the title of general.

Greene's commission ordered him to "resist, expel, kill and destroy" any enemies who might invade or assault America, "in Order to preserve the interest of His Majesty and His good subjects." Even at this late date, America's enemies did not include King George III, at least not in the eyes of all but the most advanced radicals. Men acting in the king's name, men like Gage and the government's ministers, were the enemy—but not the king himself.

Greene spent the next few weeks organizing his army, arranging for supplies, and conferring with his officers. By late May, he was on his way toward Roxbury, near Boston, to choose a campsite for his army. The Rhode Islanders were preparing to join other patriots in laying siege to General Gage's hated troops now trapped inside Boston.

He left Caty behind in Coventry, telling her to rely on his brothers and their families for support. Caty was just beginning to feel the effects of her first pregnancy, and now her husband was off to war.

4 | An Uncommon Degree of Zeal

From the forests, farms, and towns of New England marched men bearing muskets, rifles, axes, and a grievance, heading for the outskirts of Boston to join a fledgling army poised to challenge the finest soldiers in the world. They gathered in a semicircle around the port city, cutting off the British from communications and supplies by land. These New Englanders were acting on their own accord, for there had been no national call to arms, no formal declaration of hostilities. They heard only an appeal from the Massachusetts Committee of Safety, which issued a cry for help in defending "our wives and children from the butchering hands of an inhuman soldiery."

General Gage knew it would be a mistake to underestimate these hostile Americans. He suspected, however, that his superiors in London might make that very mistake. After news of the skirmishes in Lexington and Concord reached Britain, the Irish-born politician and writer Edmund Burke spoke for many in Parliament when he complained that

Crown troops had conducted a "most vigorous retreat" in the face of "feeble Americans."

Feeble was not the word Gage used in describing his opponents. True, the Americans were poorly equipped, and their leaders were middling militia commanders at best. Still, the British commander understood that the men gathered on the hills outside Boston were motivated, brave, and dangerous. "The rebels are not the despicable rabble too many have supposed them to be," he wrote. In fact, he said, they possessed an "uncommon degree of zeal and enthusiasm." Knowing that many skeptics in Britain would cite the unimpressive American performance during the French and Indian War, Gage warned that this war would be different. The Americans "never showed so much conduct, attention and perseverance as they do now."

Presiding over the siege was a heavyset merchant and militia commander named Artemas Ward, a veteran of the French and Indian War. Ward, no relation to the powerful Ward family of Rhode Island, was not the most inspiring or charismatic of figures, not the kind of leader who could turn a collection of militiamen, adventurers, and smooth-faced teenagers into an army. Still, he was the best available officer, in the judgment of the political radicals of Massachusetts.

Nathanael Greene reported to Ward's headquarters on May 23, 1775, and immediately offered to serve under the senior general's command. On the face of it, Greene's gesture might not seem so extraordinary. Ward, after all, held the seemingly explicit title of commander in chief. But his authority formally extended only to troops from Massachusetts. The Rhode Island troops technically were an independent army, accountable only to Greene and to the colony's political leaders. As militia from other New England colonies dug in outside Boston, there was no attempt to coordinate a common supply system or command structure, no sense that the troops were part of a unified army. Each colony jealously guarded the independence of its militia.

In one of his first acts as a professional soldier, however, Nathanael Greene rose above the petty, parochial pride that would often be the bane of this fledgling army. Greene realized, far earlier than most of the Revolution's political leaders, that this would be a national struggle, requiring strong, centralized leadership. In placing his troops under the command of an officer from Massachusetts, Greene in an instant swept aside local and regional distinctions for the good of a common cause and foreshadowed his arguments on behalf of strong national government and a standing army of professional soldiers. To his bitter frustration, however, the young nation's political leaders were skeptical of both.

After his consultations with Ward, Greene and his troops were assigned to the right wing of the besieging army in Roxbury, under the immediate command of Major General John Thomas of the Massachusetts militia. Greene scoured the area near Jamaica Plains to locate a suitable camp for his army and found one in the former estate of a onetime governor of Massachusetts, Francis Bernard. Its sixty acres of fields and hills lay behind a large pond, a perfect defensive location. Greene told Thomas that the pond would protect his troops from a surprise frontal assault, and that a hill to the rear of his position would allow "a most excellent post for observation." Greene had yet to fight his first battle, but it was already clear that his self-education in military science had not been in vain.

Soon after establishing camp, Greene appointed the Reverend John Murray as the Rhode Island army's chaplain. Chaplains were common among the intensely religious New England units—their fiery sermons would soon become the object of some curiosity when troops from other regions joined the siege—but the likes of Reverend Murray were not. He was the American founder of Universalism, a creed that shocked the rock-ribbed congregationalists of Massachusetts. Greene had met Murray in 1772 at James Varnum's home after the minister delivered a sermon in Newport. Greene's onetime tutor, Adam Maxwell, also was acquainted with the clergyman. Neither Greene nor his friends seemed offended by Murray's heretical beliefs, including his insistence that there would be no eternal punishment in the hereafter, and that salvation was available to all people.

It is hardly surprising that Rhode Island in general and Nathanael

Greene in particular would find a place for such an unconventional clergyman in the colony's army. Murray's clerical colleagues were less welcoming, however, and the reverend's presence in camp became something of a minor scandal as the siege wore on. But Greene's support for Murray never wavered; in fact, two years later, he came to Murray's defense when critics questioned not only the clergyman's theology but his political allegiance as well. Murray was accused of spying for the British, a charge that prompted Greene to write a public letter describing the reverend as an "honest man and a good Christian." The latter assessment was a good deal more controversial than the former.

Greene himself often sounded like a New England moralist as he attempted to turn his Rhode Islanders into a disciplined fighting unit. The behavior of his troops, most of them backwoodsmen and farmers—not the pious Quakers or eager college students of his youth—shocked him. They certainly exhibited no working knowledge of the Ten Commandments, particulary the proscription against taking the Lord's name in vain. This virginal general, his military record as yet devoid of combat, his experience of command limited to the employees of Nathanael Greene & Company, had read of the glories of military conquest but knew precious little about the raucous life of a common soldier in the field. In his orders on June 4, 1775, Greene told his officers to "Supress as much as [possible] all Debauchery and Vulgar Language Inconsistent with the Character of Soldiers." Vulgar language? Inconsistent with the character of soldiers? The troops must have had a good laugh.

Greene, however, saw his soldiers as the living symbols of American liberty. Their fellow citizens were likely to judge the righteousness of the cause by the righteousness of the troops, and Greene was determined to be righteous, indeed. But he had his hands full: the Rhode Island troops already had earned a reputation as first-class swearers. A soldier from Connecticut camped near the Rhode Island contingent in Roxbury wrote that his ears were "filled with the most shocking oaths . . . the tremendous name of the great God is taken at the most trifling occasions."

Some of the Rhode Islanders were equally enthusiastic drinkers. One of them, a soldier named Peter Young, was hauled before a court-martial after getting drunk. His superiors testified that Young behaved "in a very indecent and contemptuous manner, damning the man that confined him [and] throwing his hat about the guard-house."

All of this horrified Greene. He believed that the fledgling rebellion would succeed only if the American civilian population supported the soldiers fighting in their name. Debauchery and vulgar language were more than breaches of military discipline; potentially, they were public relations disasters. As the siege dragged on, Greene continued to keep a tight watch over the behavior of his troops.

Meanwhile, as a sign of just how serious the standoff had become, three of Britain's top generals, Henry Clinton, William Howe, and John Burgoyne, landed in Boston in late May. Impatient with General Gage's conservative approach, they were determined to break the siege as quickly as possible. The very idea of American amateurs holding some eight thousand of His Majesty's crack soldiers hostage was unthinkable! Burgoyne could hardly believe it. "Let us in," he said of himself, Clinton, and Howe, "and we'll soon make elbow room!"

Late May and early June found Nathanael Greene shuttling between military drills in Roxbury and political consultations in Rhode Island. The colony's Committee of Safety, which included Greene's older brother Jacob, retained civilian control over the army and was given ambiguous authority over supplies. Appropriating money for gunpowder and blankets was one thing; getting them to the troops was quite another task, and an exasperated Greene complained that the legislature had devised "no mode of supply."

On June 2, as he prepared to leave Providence for Roxbury, Greene composed a note to Caty. He would have been happy, he wrote, if he "could have lived a private life in peace and plenty." But, he said, "the injury done my Country . . . calls me [forth] to defend our common rights, and repel the bold invaders of the Sons of freedom. The cause is the cause of God and man." Furthermore, he wrote, "[I am] determined to defend my rights and maintain my freedom or sell my life in the attempt."

What Caty thought of her husband's fervent patriotism is anybody's guess, since her letters have not been preserved. But Nathanael's pledge to "sell" his life for the good of his country surely frightened her. The peaceful little world of her aunt and uncle's homestead and the splendid isolation of her childhood home on Block Island had left her unprepared for war and the prospect of becoming a general's widow at the age of twenty. She was singularly untaught in the domestic skills expected of most colonial housewives. Her formidable aunt and surrogate mother, Catherine Ray Greene, had made sure that young Caty learned French but was less concerned that she learned how to prepare meals or mend a pair of trousers. Aunt Catherine's legacy had made Caty a more interesting character, but her in-laws came to regard her as useless in the practical business of running a household. Nathanael's brother Jacob and his wife, Peggy, moved in with Caty and took over the house. Caty was not pleased, but there was little she could do about it.

When Greene returned to camp on June 3, he discovered that the Rhode Island troops had taken advantage of their commander's brief absence. Discipline had broken down; so had the supply system. Some of the troops had disabled their muskets and were preparing to march home. The men in charge of the commissary had been attacked, and they, too, were about to desert. Morale was abysmal. Greene quickly restored order and cracked down on rowdy behavior—he persuaded the Massachusetts legislature to ban the sale of alcohol inside the camp—as well as lax soldiering. He found that many captains and other junior officers were reluctant to impose discipline on their troops, "some through Fear of offending their Soldiers, some through Laziness and some through Obstinancy." This simply would not do. "I have warned them of their Negligence many times," he wrote. And, he promised, he would "break them."

The orders flew off his desk. Soldiers considered physically unfit were forced to undergo an extra hour of daily exercise, from ten to eleven o'clock in the morning. Regiments paraded regularly, soldiers received crash courses in weapons training, and officers were told to keep a strict account of their unit's ammunition. For the sake of martial appearance and good morale, no soldier without shoes was allowed on the parade grounds, and officers were expected to keep their uniforms neat and clean. Greene led by example, rising early, inspecting his troops, attending to the dozens of prosaic details that come with command, and working in his tent long into the night. "My task is hard and my fatigue great," he wrote to brother Jacob. "The numerous Applications you cannot conceive of unless you were present to behold the Round of Business." Such leadership was not lost on his men. Despite the discipline, tedium, and grunt work, Greene soon reported, "[My] officers and Soldiers generally are well Satisfied, nay I have not heard one complaint."

Within weeks, Greene was beginning to see further progress. While the Rhode Islanders remained, in his words, "raw" and "irregular," he concluded that they were better disciplined and better organized than most militia units. Other observers shared that opinion. Samuel Ward Sr., the onetime governor of Rhode Island and a delegate to Congress, heard nothing but praise for Greene's troops. A clergyman named William Emerson, the grandfather of Ralph Waldo Emerson, was similarly impressed when he came upon the Rhode Island camp during a tour of the patriot fortifications. While most of the troops resided in "slapdash housing made of stone and turf," Emerson told his wife, one group lived in "proper tents . . . and looked like the regular camp of the enemy." These, he wrote, were the Rhode Islanders.

The newfound discipline and smart appearance of the Rhode Island troops reflected well on their commander. Other American generals began soliciting Greene's opinion and according him "the greatest Respect"—"much more than my Station or Consequence entitle me," he wrote. In a letter to Jacob, Greene tried hard to sound modest about his rise in reputation, but there was no hiding his pride.

> Were I to estimate my Value from the attention paid to my
> Sentiments and opinions, I should have great Reason to think
> myself some considerable Personage. But fatal Experience

teaches me every day that Mankind are apt to pay the
Deference due to the Station and not the Merit of the Person.
Therefore when I find myself surrounded by their flattering
Address, I consider them as due my office and not to Me.

The endless business of supplies and logistics required Greene to re-turn to Providence in mid-June for yet another conference with the colony's Committee of Safety. Befitting an army that came together spontaneously, with little thought given to support staff and supply lines, the soldiers were short of everything from blankets to tents to weapons. Greene was particularly concerned about his army's shortage of gun-powder and hoped to persuade the committee and Governor Nicholas Cooke, who had replaced Wanton as the colony's chief executive, to find and buy more.

He also found time to steal away to Coventry to visit Caty, but their re-union was destined to be brief. On June 18, two days after Nathanael showed up on the doorstep of Spell Hall in Coventry, a frantic messenger arrived with frightening news. The British, he told the Greenes, were as-saulting the American position on Breed's Hill and Bunker Hill in Charlestown, outside Boston.

Greene left immediately, rode all night from Coventry to Roxbury, and arrived to find the battle over and Charlestown a smoking ruin. The American position on the hills had been overrun, and so the day be-longed to the British. But victory had come at such a cost it was hard to imagine Generals Howe, Clinton, and Burgoyne toasting their good for-tune and laughing at Gage's timid ways. About twenty-three hundred troops stormed the American position, and more than a thousand were killed or wounded. Even more appalling was the toll taken of officers. The British estimated that they lost twenty-seven dead and sixty-three wounded. A shocked Howe wrote, "When I look to the consequences of [the battle], in the loss of so many brave Officers, I do it with horror— The Success is too dearly bought."

Once at Roxbury, Greene immediately prepared his troops for a pos-sible new attack on the American right wing. He dispatched an urgent message to members of the Rhode Island Committee of Safety: "[Send] about two Tons of Powder and as much ball as you can conveniently spare." His instincts were as sound as his experience was limited: The British briefly considered an assault on Dorchester Heights, to the right of Greene's position in Jamaica Plains, but decided against it. The troops were too dazed and too bloodied to mount another attack.

Though Greene missed the battle near Bunker Hill, he absorbed its lessons and would carry them with him for the rest of the war. Bunker Hill showed Greene and the Americans that they could redefine the very idea of victory in this war. To his brother Jacob, Greene wrote, "I wish [we] could Sell them another Hill at the same Price we did Bunkers Hill." In the coming years, Greene would have many opportunities to make such a transaction.

In Philadelphia, members of the Continental Congress realized that the hodgepodge collection of militia outside Boston was fighting not a local battle but a war for American liberties and so should have the support of all the colonies. On June 14, 1775, at the urging of John Adams and others, Congress officially adopted the troops in Boston, creating the Continental army. The new army required a new commander: George Washington, of Virginia. And a new commander required staff, so Congress appointed an adjutant general, paymaster general, quartermaster general, commissary general, four major generals, and eight brigadier generals. The last and most junior brigadier was Nathanael Greene, who became the new Continental army's youngest general. Eight months earlier, in October 1774, men in the Kentish Guards had told Private Nathanael Greene that he was unfit and unworthy for militia duty, that his limp was a blemish on the company. Now he was a brigadier general in the Continental army. Although not religious in the conventional sense, Greene in later years often spoke of his belief that the Almighty had a special interest in the American cause. Given his astonishing and perhaps inexplicable rise from militia outcast to brigadier general, it's hardly a wonder that even Greene was tempted to look heavenward for answers.

With his new title came a salary: one hundred and twenty-five dollars a month. Like his brother generals and members of Congress, Greene supplemented that meager income with profits from his private businesses, which he continued to manage from afar. He would need the extra income, once Caty gave birth to their first child.

The new commander in chief of the Continental army arrived in Cambridge on July 3, 1775. With him were several officers who were strangers to Greene, but with whom he would soon become familiar. Perhaps the most memorable member of Washington's party was an eccentric Englishman named Charles Lee, a major general who would become renowned for his sloppy dress, his affection for dogs (as opposed to human beings), and his undoubted ability as a career military man. The other newcomers included another former English officer, Horatio Gates, now Washington's adjutant general, and another wayward Quaker, Thomas Mifflin, who was Washington's aide-de-camp and soon to become the army's quartermaster general. Greene was destined to work closely with, and sometimes against, all of these men in the struggle to come.

On July 4, Greene sent a detachment of two hundred Rhode Island troops, armed with a letter of welcome, to the new commander's headquarters. Washington accepted the gesture and reciprocated by inviting Greene to headquarters for a personal meeting. And so the tall, remote Virginian met the broad-shouldered, hearty Quaker from Rhode Island, beginning a relationship and a friendship that profoundly affected the course of the war. At first, they seemed to have as much in common as Virginia did with Rhode Island; in other words, not much. Washington came from a family of proper Anglicans—people likely to look askance at Quakers, Puritans, and other noncomformists—and grew to adulthood in a colony that was as orderly as Rhode Island was chaotic, as aristocratic as Rhode Island was democratic. Washington himself was as distant as Greene was eager to please. But they shared far more than they realized at that first ceremonial meeting. Washington's bearing and confidence—but not his writing—hid the fact that his formal education was hardly any better than Greene's. His unlettered mother, widowed when George was eleven, had no money to send him to Europe for a ruling-class education. Just as Nathanael Greene spent his formative years toiling at the family forge, the teenage Washington worked his mother's farm, far from the libraries and schoolhouses of Virginia's wellborn sons. And like Greene, he was unwilling to settle for the fate that destiny and circumstances had in mind for him. So he read, and read some more. Like his new subordinate from Rhode Island, George Washington was a son of the New World of opportunity through self-improvement.

Perhaps Washington recognized in Greene something of himself—a less polished, less refined version for sure, but a decent reflection all the same, a competent man, a patriot, and a man, like himself, willing to sacrifice his fortune for an idea. And perhaps Greene saw in Washington the mentor he wished Nathanael Greene Sr. had been. From the very beginning of their association, Greene looked up to Washington as a surrogate father, a man he would defend against enemies and whose patience he would test repeatedly.

Washington decided to give Nathanael Greene the chance his peers in Kent County denied him because he walked with a limp.

Neither man left an extended written record of their first meeting, but their actions as the siege wore on spoke to the immediate respect they developed for each other. In a letter to Samuel Ward, Greene described Washington in glowing terms.

> I hope we shall be taught to copy his example and to prefer
> the Love of Liberty in this time of publick danger to all the
> soft pleasures of domestic Life and support ourselves with
> manly fortitude amidst all the danger and hardships that
> attend a state of war. And I doubt not under the Generals
> wise direction we shall establish such excellent order and
> stricktness of [discipline] as to invite Victory.

Greene and many other officers in camp began referring to Washington as "His Excellency," a gaudy, Old World honorific that seemed decidedly out of place among the flinty egalitarians gathered in the camps outside Boston. Rank meant little among the rugged New England individuals who made up the new American army. Officers were known to stand in line for their food along with the men under their command. There even were reports of officers trained as barbers who shaved their soldiers. The New England troops were proud of their anti-aristocratic, anti-elitist army, but some officers, including Greene, were horrified. Such familiarity would not help in administering the discipline the raw Americans needed. Washington, whose bearing and background practically defined the notion of Virginian aristocracy, quickly made it clear that the old ways were over. In a letter to Congress, he condemned "Familiarity between the Officers and men, which is incompatible with Subordination and Discipline."

Inadequate supplies continued to bedevil the army. On July 4, the day after Washington took command, Greene condemned a shipment of moldy bread from Providence. A few days earlier, enraged Rhode Island troops had discovered that a welcome supply of beef actually was horse meat. A disgusted Greene told Governor Cooke, "[I am] willing to spend and be spent in so Righteous a Cause, but unless I am supported by the helping hand of Government, my indeavors will be defeated and your expectations blasted." If well-fed, well-supplied troops are derelict in their duties, he wrote, they can and ought to be punished "with great justice." But if they are suffering from hunger and want, "they excuse all their misconduct." And there was no shortage of misconduct: Washington's general orders through the summer of 1775 frequently made reference to the general's approval of whippings meted out to insubordinate or otherwise misbehaving soldiers.

Turning these farmers and tradesmen into something resembling an army was an enormous challenge. But Washington and his generals also had to achieve another kind of transformation, one that even the lash could not help bring about: they had to turn these farmers and tradesmen into Americans.

The new Continental army was, in fact, a New England army commanded by a Virginian. Not until thirteen companies from Pennsylvania, Virginia, and Maryland arrived in midsummer did the army begin to resemble the vast and diverse enterprise that Congress envisioned. But these men were strangers to one another and regarded one another with suspicion, skepticism, and even fear—not unlike their political leaders in Philadelphia. Washington himself was not immune to parochial sectionalism. In a far too candid letter to his cousin, Lund Washington, he referred to New England troops as "dirty and nasty." He also complained to a fellow Virginian about the "unaccountable kind of stupidity in the lower class of these people which . . . prevails but too generally among the officers of the Massachusetts part of the Army." The New Englanders, for their part, were repulsed by the crude frontiersmen from the southern states. These troops were accomplished riflemen, rightly known for their marksmanship—they picked off three British officers in two days not long after arriving—and their toughness, but their insolence made them few friends among the New England regiments. The southerners were themselves puzzled by their northern brethren: "Such Sermons, such Negroes, such Colonels, such Boys [and] such Great, Great-Grandfathers," one southern soldier wrote. To the astonishment of the southerners, blacks were serving alongside whites in some of the New England units, and within a few years blacks would make up about 15 percent of the Continental army. Among those who advocated for black recruitment was Nathanael Greene's cousin Christopher, who would go on to command a small unit of blacks from Rhode Island.

Nathanael Greene intuitively understood that success of the cause depended on men willing to put aside their sectional prejudice and pride, if not their racial prejudices. When New Englanders complained that Washington seemed to favor his fellow southerners, Greene was quick to compose a masterfully diplomatic defense of a man he admired almost to the point of hero worship. In a letter to Samuel Ward Sr., Greene explained carefully that Washington "had not had time to make himself thoroughly Acquainted with the Genius" of the New England troops. "His Excellency has been taught to believe the People here a superior Race of Mortals, and finding them of the same temper, disposition, passion and prejudices, Virtues and Vices of the common People of other Governments, they Sink in his Esteem."

To help break down the sectionalism that even he was guilty of, Washington reorganized the army into three integrated divisions, eliminating the notion of separate provincial armies. He also tried to break up regiments based on geography, but officers and troops alike objected and Washington backed down. "His Excellency," Greene told Ward, "has a great desire to Bannish every Idea of Local Attachments." That task, Greene admitted, would continue to cause problems, because it "is next to impossible to unhinge the prejudices that People have for places and things they have had a long Connexion with." But Greene himself was a budding American nationalist who cared little for the regional prejudices that obsessed the war's soldiers and politicians alike. "For my own part I feel the cause and not the place," he wrote. "I would as soon go to Virginia as stay here."

He soon was on the move all right, not to Virginia but to a Virginian. Washington gave Greene command of a brigade of seven regiments—his three from Rhode Island plus four from Massachusetts—and redeployed him from Roxbury to Prospect Hill, north of Cambridge. And he was placed under the direct command of Major General Charles Lee of Virginia.

Greene took a liking to Lee, which spoke well of the Rhode Islander's open mind, for Lee was not easy to like. He was not much of one for personal hygiene, even by the standards of an army camp in 1775. His crude manner was more suited to backwoods Virginia than to the affluent circles he had frequented in his native England. Educated in Switzerland and literate enough to quote from the classics, he nevertheless repelled many members of his social class and station with his profanity and rude references.

He dubbed his headquarters "Hobglobin Hall" and once shocked Abigail Adams, who was visiting Lee, by insisting that she shake the paw of one of his dogs. Abigail's husband, John Adams, preferred to overlook Lee's personality tics because the general was, beyond doubt, a walking, swearing, publicity coup: an English general converted to the American cause. He also was the most experienced officer in the American army, having fought in the French and Indian War and as a soldier of

fortune in the Polish army. True, Adams wrote, Lee was "a queer creature," but it was important to "forgive a thousand whims for the sake of
the soldier and the scholar."

Greene certainly would have agreed with Adams. The Rhode Island
brigadier had yet to witness his first battle, whereas Charles Lee had
fought many battles, as he was more than happy to point out. Greene had
always sought out the company of men better educated than he, eager to
learn from them what he had not learned as a young adult working the
family forge. Lee was his latest mentor, and although Greene left little
record of their consultations together, it's easy to imagine him listening
attentively as the loquacious Lee expounded on his martial conquests,
some of which may actually have been true.

Certainly, Lee's stories were more exciting than the reality of camp
life as the siege continued through summer. Lee's tales were full of danger and glory, real and imagined; the siege of Boston was about boredom
and court-martials and worse. Greene reported to Governor Cooke in
early August: "Our troops are now very sickly with the Dysentery. There
was about a Week of exceeding hot Weather, [which] brought on this
distemper, but they are now getting better, and from the change of aid
and the healthy situation we [are] posted in, I hope we shall recover a
perfect state of health very soon."

In what may have been a related development, Greene found that his
men had become less than diligent about digging proper latrines, so that
soldiers had little choice but to "Void [their] Exerment about the fields."
Camp was foul enough already, with its acrid haze and dubious food and
lack of clean clothing. Dictating an order to an aide who, like many others on both sides of the conflict, spelled phonetically, Greene noted that
the health "of the Camps is greatly Dangred by these Neglects" and so
"it is Recomended to the ofisers of the Several Ridgments to put do attention" to the digging and maintaining of proper latrines. Greene had
yet to prove himself on the battlefield, but there was little doubt that he
grasped the importance of war's less glamorous essentials: supply, logistics, discipline, and the health and morale of the rank and file.

While the Americans suffered through the fetid summer in the high ground around Boston, conditions in the British-occupied city were a good deal worse. The civilian population decreased from seventeen thousand to fewer than seven thousand, and Greene was receiving reports from deserters and exiles about the deplorable state of affairs, including an outbreak of smallpox, for soldiers and the public alike. Greene summarized his intelligence from Boston in a letter to Governor Cooke: "Provisions bad, and [fuel] scarce, and . . . no harmony among the Troops. . . . Many of the People that [come] out are real Objects of pity, their suffering has been exceeding severe, especially among the poorer sort. Great Violence is done to the cause of humanity in that Town."

Violence, though not particularly great, was no stranger in the American camps. As the patriot lines moved closer to British forward positions, the long summer days often were punctuated with sniper fire—the two lines were within shooting distance of each other at some points—and periodic shelling. These exchanges did little damage and actually broke up the monotony of the siege. The green American troops took to chasing unexploded cannonballs as they rolled through the lines. But not all such skirmishes were without effect. In late August, Augustus Mumford, a member of the Kentish Guards who had joined Greene when he marched to Boston, was decapitated by a cannonball while digging entrenchments. Greene was devastated. In more than three months of siege and gunfire, he had lost no friends, indeed, no Rhode Island soldier had died, until now. He and Caty knew poor Mumford, and the loss was so powerful that Greene dispatched his friend Colonel Varnum to Rhode Island to break the news personally to Mumford's widow. Greene also sent a letter to Caty, who was four months into her pregnancy, to offer her some measure of comfort and reassurance. Addressing his wife as "My Sweet Angel," Greene wrote:

> The fears and apprehensions for my safety, under your
> present debillitated state, must be a weight too great for you
> to support. We are all in the hands of the great Jehovah, to
> him let us look for protection. I trust that our controversy is a

Righteous one, and altho many of our friends and rellatives
may suffer an untimely fate, yet we must consider the evil
Justified by the Righteousness of the dispute. Let us then put
our confidence in God and recommend our souls to his care.
Stifle you own grief my sweet creature and offer a small
tribute of consolation to the afflicted widow.

In late September, Greene's former tutor, Adam Maxwell, arrived in
camp with an urgent message from Henry Ward, the secretary of Rhode
Island and brother of Samuel Ward Sr. Henry Ward had come upon a
letter written in code and intended for British officials in Boston. Sus-
pecting treachery, he sent the letter to Greene via Maxwell, urging the
general to bring it to Washington's attention. Similarly alarmed, the
American general tracked down a Boston woman who had tried to deliver the letter to the British. After interrogation, the woman revealed the
letter's author: her lover, Dr. Benjamin Church, a onetime member of
the Massachusetts Provincial Congress and the colony's Committee of
Correspondence, a noted patriot orator, and the chief physician in the
American camp. He also was a British spy. The Americans brought in
two cryptologists, who broke Church's code and discovered that the letter contained information about American positions and troop strength.

Greene wrote back to Ward to thank him for his alert actions: "The
Author is found. You cannot guess who it is. It is no less a man that the
famous Doctor Church." The famous doctor got off with a relatively
easy sentence. He was driven from the colony, jailed for two years, and
then sent into exile in the West Indies.

The siege went on. Some twenty thousand men were now gathered
outside Boston. They drilled, they dug, they fired into the British lines,
and then they drilled and dug and fired some more. From the perspective of headquarters in Cambridge, the endless siege was an administrative nightmare. This large army required a constant and consistent
supply of food, clothing, fuel, and munitions. Its disruptive and sometimes disorderly presence tested the patience of neighboring citizens.
The troops had been living outdoors for months, which was not so harsh

when the weather was warm, but now the New England winter was approaching. Washington was well aware of the warnings written on his calendar. In a letter to Congress on September 21, he noted that the troops were ill-prepared for a winter siege: "So far as regards the Preservation of the Army from cold, they may be deemed in a state of nakedness. Many of the men have been without Blankets the whole campaign and those which have been in use during the Summer are so worn as to be of little Service." Not only were conditions bound to deteriorate as the year drew to a close, but the army itself would fall apart, too. Enlistments would begin to expire on December 1, and by the end of the year, virtually the entire American force would be free to return home.

Washington was growing weary of the stalemate. Impatient to show Congress and the American people that his army was doing more than simply playing a waiting game, he dispatched Benedict Arnold and a thousand men, including Greene's old friend Sammy Ward, north to reinforce an invasion of Canada under Generals Philip Schuyler and Richard Montgomery. The campaign was well under way by October.

In Boston, however, all remained as it was when Washington arrived in July. Reports of disease and low morale among the British troops in Boston gave the false impression that time was on America's side. In fact, with American enlistments about to run out, the opposite was true. Washington concluded that he ought to attack Boston while he still had an army. The twenty thousand Americans were more than double the British force of eight thousand, and they were in better health. The British commander, Gage, had been ordered back to London to explain himself, leaving William Howe in charge of the ravaged garrison. Washington called a council of war in Cambridge on October 18. The topic: an attack on Boston, which Washington had first raised with them some four weeks before.

Greene was one of eight generals who gathered in Washington's headquarters to discuss the plan. It was a heady experience for the Rhode Islander. Surrounding him were professional soldiers (the Englishmen Charles Lee and Horatio Gates), veterans of the French and Indian War (Artemas Ward, John Thomas, Israel Putnam, and William

Heath), and an experienced militia officer (John Sullivan, a major in the New Hampshire militia who had led a raid on Fort William and Mary in New Hampshire in 1775). These were the best and most experienced military men fighting on the rebel side, and there was Greene, yet to see his first battle, seated among them. He was, comparatively speaking, a boy among adults. Voicing an opinion among such company must have seemed an intimidating prospect, especially with the self-assured, confident Lee in the room. Who, after all, was Nathanael Greene to have a seat in such a council? Why, he was a Quaker; he was self-educated; he had never fought a battle in his life!

Washington asked his generals for their advice. Around the room they went. Gates said the proposed attack on Boston was improper. Lee said he was not familiar enough with the men and so considered the plan too risky. Sullivan thought winter would offer a better opportunity. Heath and Thomas said the plan was impracticable. Putnam said he disapproved, at present. Ward was solidly against it.

All were opposed, except for the most junior, most inexperienced general in the room—and the one most eager to impress the commander in chief—Nathanael Greene. Actually, Greene hedged his views, saying that while he regarded the plan as impractical, if the Americans could land ten thousand troops in Boston—Washington's plan did not specify the size of the assault force—he would support an attack.

The attack did not take place. But a frustrated Washington could not help but notice that with all the military genius, experience, and leadership ability assembled around him, only the junior brigadier general from Rhode Island seemed at all willing to take a chance. Only Nathanael Greene seemed remotely and ever so cautiously on George Washington's side. Events would soon prove that Washington had taken careful notice of the young general with the slight limp and the earnest manner.

Greene's assessment of their chances with a landing force of ten thousand was far too optimistic, as he would implicitly concede a few months later, in February, when Washington again pressed for agreement on an assault. Then, Greene would contend that "an attack upon a town garrisoned with 8,000 regular troops is a serious object," which is exactly what the senior generals had said. He would add, somewhat disengenuously, "I always thought an attack with 20,000 men might succeed," which not only contradicted his position in October but was more than a little wishful thinking, since the Americans had no more than eighteen thousand troops at the time.

If he seemed a little too eager to please, and if he seemed to contradict himself from time to time, it was perhaps understandable, for he was very much a work in progress. Henry Knox, the young bookseller who was now an artillery officer, said of Greene, "[He] came to us the rawest, the most untutored being I ever met with." In less than a year, however, Knox said Greene "was equal, in military knowledge, to any General officer in the army, and very superior to most of them."

But he was more than just a general; he was a rebel, fighting not for territory or for conquest but for ideas—revolutionary ideas. This raw, untutored forgemaster had put on a uniform to help cast aside the old order and create something new and bold. The long siege allowed him time not only to learn about leadership and supplies and tactics but also to reflect on America's political struggle. And he was not shy about offering his opinions.

To Samuel Ward Sr., an increasingly influential figure in Congress, Greene vented his frustration with what he regarded as the tedious and irrelevant political wrangling in Philadelphia. In October 1775, an impatient Greene told Ward that "people" in camp "heartily" supported "a Declaration of Independence." The notion of a complete break with Britain was, even at this late hour, hardly commonplace. Many political leaders still believed a peaceful resolution to the conflict was possible, and still regarded themselves as loyal subjects of King George III. Only two months before, Thomas Jefferson confessed he was in favor of reconciliation with the British. Maryland's lawmakers were on record as opposing independence. And even George Washington referred to Britain's troops in Boston as the "ministerial" army—meaning that they represented not the king, who still commanded the loyalty of many American patriots, but the corrupt and oppressive cabinet.

Greene, however, seemed to realize that separation was inevitable.

Why not make the declaration now? he wondered. And while Congress was at it, why not crack down on the traitors who continued to do business with the enemy? Facing the armed might of the British army, with troops preparing for winter, Greene lashed out at merchants who carried on normal trade with Britain. "I would make it Treason against the state to make any further Remittances to great Britain," he wrote to Ward. "Stop all supplies to the Ships throughout America. . . . The Merchants in general are a body of People whose God is Gain, and their whole plan of Policy is to bring Publick measures to square with their private interest."

Greene saw himself, and his fellow officers and soldiers, as the embodiment of republican virtue, sacrificing everything for the sake of liberty. He was none too patient, then, with civilians who seemed less enthusiastic about the cause, and they were numerous. Again, to Ward, he complained about his fellow Americans who put profits ahead of patriotism.

> This is no time for geting Riches but to secure what we have
> got. Every shadow of Oppression and Extortion ought to
> disappear, but instead of that we find many Articles of
> Merchandise multiplied four fold their value. . . . The
> Farmers are Extortionate where ever their situation furnishes
> them with an Opportunity. These are the people that I
> complain mostly of; they are wounding the cause.

In other letters to Ward, Greene showed a grasp of how the rebels in America fit into the larger picture of clashing empires. He urged Ward and Congress to "embrace" France and Spain "as brothers" in the fight against the common enemy, Britain. "We want not their Land Forces in America; their Navy we do," he wrote.

As the memorable year of 1775 entered its final months, however, Greene and the other American commanders were faced with issues more pressing than extortionate prices and foreign alliances.

Their citizen soldiers were preparing to go home.

With enlistments among the New England soldiers due to expire on December 1, Congress dispatched Benjamin Franklin, Benjamin Harrison, and Thomas Lynch to Cambridge to meet with Washington and his generals. They arrived on the night of October 15 and immediately were briefed on the perilous situation. Greene sat in on the somber discussion between the delegates and Washington, and he found himself paying careful attention to the legendary Franklin, who years before had fallen in love with and vainly pursued Caty's aunt, Catherine Ray. Of Franklin, Greene wrote, "Attention watched his Lips and Conviction closed his periods," and he assured Ward that he and the other generals would pay the delegates "every mark of Respect and Attention during their stay." They remained for four days, during which they heard unpleasant truths. The army was about to melt away, and Washington, the colonies, and Congress would have to recruit and pay for a new army. Otherwise, the siege of Boston would end in a British victory.

The politicians and the generals talked about the very prosaic details of fighting a war: the size of a new army, the costs of feeding, clothing, and supplying the troops, the length of new enlistments, even the size of food rations. They agreed on a sweeping reorganization plan for a new army consisting of twenty thousand troops divided into twenty-six regiments. Greene's three Rhode Island regiments were melded into two new regiments, the 9th and 11th Continentals. Congress, based on the recommendations of Franklin, Harrison, and Lynch, authorized Washington to begin recruiting new soldiers for one-year enlistments, which would expire on December 31, 1776.

Greene and other generals argued that Washington should offer bounties to troops already on duty who agreed to stay with the army for another year. But Washington refused, arguing that the soldiers already were well paid. Many political leaders sided with Washington, but for different reasons. Offering bounties seemed like a step toward the creation of a professional, standing army. And that smacked of oppressive, militaristic Old World tradition, and not the republican ideal of a citizen army.

Greene, in this case, was very much Old World. He pleaded with Washington for bounties, especially as the new year approached and recruiting yielded disappointing results. He believed bounties would help build an army of seventy thousand, a highly unrealistic number. But without bounties, by early December only a few thousand men had signed up for service beyond New Year's Eve. And only a small number of those recruits came from Rhode Island, to Greene's intense mortification. He regularly harangued the Rhode Islanders to put the cause ahead of self, but with disappointing results, even among the officer corps. Of the sixteen second lieutenants in Rhode Island's regiments, none reenlisted. Rhode Island had been assigned a quota of fifteen hundred recruits, but so few came forward that Greene plunged into despair. To Ward, he wrote: "I fear the Colony of Rhode Island is upon the decline. I was in hopes . . . that ours would not have deserted the cause of their Country. But they seem to be so sick of this way of life, and so home sick that I fear the greater part and the best part of the Troops from our Colony will go home." He told his brother Jacob that civilians at home ought to "make it disgraceful for any of the [soldiers] to return home."

In the midst of these anxious weeks, Greene had an opportunity to relax and perhaps even entertain some memories of his increasingly distant youth. A delegation of Quakers from Rhode Island, led by the influential Moses Brown, visited Washington's headquarters in mid-December, asking for permission to deliver relief for civilians trapped in Boston and running low on food and fuel. Washington was sympathetic but reluctant, explaining that Bostonians fleeing the city reported that smallpox was epidemic. They agreed that Brown should write to General Howe, the British commander, to effect a meeting between the delegation and several Quakers from Boston. Perhaps with a knowing smile, Washington urged Brown to consult with one of the camp's resident Quaker apostates, Nathanael Greene. (The other was Thomas Mifflin; Brown and his party later met with him, too.)

The Quakers and Greene dined together on the night of December 14. In a journal he kept of his visit, Moses Brown wrote that Greene graciously handled what might have been an awkward occasion. Greene told

Brown and the other Quakers that they should abide by their principles, notwithstanding that he had abandoned them, but he added that they should not take sides in the conflict between America and Britain. If they did, "they must Expect to suffer," he said.

The Quakers and the former Quaker parted on amiable terms, and the delegation went on to distribute assistance to the poor and hungry in and around Boston, with no regard for politics or political allegiances.

As 1775 drew to a close, some ten thousand men had enlisted to serve in 1776, half the troop strength Congress had authorized. Though Greene and other American commanders pleaded with their troops to remain with the army, they were betrayed by bitter conditions. The weather had turned cold, with snow piled in great white heaps on the ground, and firewood became increasingly scarce. Troops were eating their provisions raw because they had nothing with which to build campfires for cooking. Even wooden fences had been broken apart and burned. "Our suffering," Greene wrote, "has been inconceivable." In a humane gesture that was becoming one of the hallmarks of his leadership, Greene ordered that sentries be replaced every hour, rather than every two hours, to protect his men from the freezing, windy conditions.

There was news from across the Atlantic as the year drew to a close, and it was equally chilly. Only now were the Americans learning that King George III, in his speech at the opening of Parliament on October 26, had announced that more troops and ships would be sent to the New World to suppress what he called a "desperate conspiracy," and that he was receiving "the most friendly offers of assistance" to help put a "speedy end" to the revolt. The British navy already had bombarded and burned the town of Falmouth in Maine, a punitive action that shocked the Americans, and now the king himself was saying the rebels could expect more of the same. Those Americans who clung to the belief that somehow George would mediate the crisis rather than take sides against them were stunned. There no longer was any doubt that the king and Parliament were united.

American troops prepared to leave the snow and smoke and smells of their camps around Boston not knowing that yet another bitter blow was about to fall: American soldiers in Canada, suffering in even more extreme conditions, were about to launch what would prove to be a disastrous New Year's Eve assault on Quebec. The battle cost the life of the promising American commander Richard Montgomery and the freedom of Nathanael Greene's young friend Samuel Ward Jr., who was captured.

A despondent Greene retired to his tent on New Year's Eve to write a long letter to Samuel Ward Sr. Neither man knew, of course, that Sammy Ward was in such mortal peril on this frigid night. But Greene knew that first light would reveal a depleted American army, even though some newly arrived militia units from New England had been deployed to fill in gaps on the lines. He told Ward: "We never have been so weak as we shall be tomorrow when we dismiss the old Troops; we growing weaker and the Enimy getting stronger renders our situation disagreeable. However if they Attack any of our Posts I hope [they'll] be met with a severe repulse."

Such hopes were little more than wishful thinking. On the morning of January 1, 1776, Nathanael Greene had only seven hundred soldiers in his brigade. His authorized troop strength was more than double that number.

Washington chose to ignore what must have been a depressing sight that first day of the new year. His general orders that morning announced that the new army was, "in every point of View . . . entirely Continental."

> His Excellency hopes that the Importance of the great Cause we are engaged in, will be deeply impressed upon every Man's mind, and wishes it to be considered, that an Army without Order, Regularity and Discipline is no better than a Commission'd Mob; Let us there fore . . . endeavour by all the Skill and Discipline in our power, to acquire that knowledge and conduct which is necessary in War.

To commemorate the occasion, Washington ordered a new flag raised on the hills overlooking Boston. A replica of Britain's Union Jack decorated the upper left corner, but the flag also bore thirteen stripes on a background of white. From their redoubts guarding Boston, British troops saw the strange banner and cheered. They thought the Americans had surrendered. That, too, was wishful thinking.

Through the first days of January, the old army of provincial militias was replaced by and reorganized as a new Continental army in the midst of the siege. It was, Greene believed, an unprecedented achievement: "We have just experienced the Inconveniency of disbanding an Army within Cannon Shot of the Enimy and forming a new one in its stead, an Instance never before known." The British never attacked during the transition, which Greene attributed to their faulty intelligence, and recruiting improved dramatically through the first few weeks of the year. On January 4, Greene advised Samuel Ward Sr. that Congress should prepare for outright war, now that the new Continental army was in place.

> It is no time for Deliberation, the hour is swiftly rolling on
> when the Plains of America will be deluged with Human
> Blood; Resolves, Declarations and all the Parade of Heroism
> in Words will never obtain a Victory. Arms and Ammunition
> are as necessary as Men. . . . An Army unequiped will ever
> feel the want of Spirit and Courage but properly furnished
> fighting in the best of Causes will bid defiance to the United
> force of Men and Devils.

The new army was designed to be more stable and more professional than the undependable collection of militia that had borne the fight thus far. The one-year enlistment assured the generals that their regiments would not slip away one night or walk away from camp with weapons in hand. It went without saying that there would be problems on New Year's Eve, 1776, when the new enlistments were up, but Washington, Greene, and the other generals had their sights set on more immediate problems.

Greene continued to enforce strict discipline at the most minute level. He banned card games, which must have seemed like cruel and unusual punishment for bored soldiers working the interminable siege. His reasoning was simple: "[Playing cards] brings on a Habit of Drinking; and the Habit of Drinking [leads to] Disputes and Quarrels, disorder and Confusion which disturbs the Peace and Tranquility of the Camp, and often proves fatal to Individuals." The last phrase suggests that Greene's rigid discipline was necessary in a camp filled with well-armed men with little to do.

His days were spent among the men, his nights at his desk writing letters long and short to friends and colleagues. Greene had been in camp since April, and the effects of hard work, fatigue, and camp life were beginning to show. His stomach was constantly upset, and in late January he developed jaundice. He asked Washington for permission to return home to recuperate, but his request was denied. Washington once again was pressing his generals for their consent in an attack on Boston, before spring allowed the British to reinforce their garrison. So, instead of submitting himself to the comfort of his now very pregnant wife in Coventry, Greene rested, or tried to rest, in his quarters on Prospect Hill. "I am as yellow as saffron, my appetite all gone, and my flesh too," he told his brother Jacob. "I am so weak that I can scarcely walk across the room." When Caty got wind of her husband's illness, she immediately left Rhode Island and set out for camp on Feburary 20. While the precise date isn't known, she had just recently given birth to their first child, a boy they named George Washington Greene.

Caty had been to camp at least once before little George was born, so she was used to the sights and smells of an army of thousands camped in open fields. She had met, or would soon meet, some of the army's leading commanders, including His Excellency, the commander in chief. Not one to turn away from a pretty face, Washington teased young Caty about her "Quaker-preacher" husband and seemed completely charmed. Other officers were similarly taken with Caty's looks, high spirits, and almost scandalous preference for the company of men—and not, save for

Martha Washington, the wives of other generals. The women in camp took note that General Greene never seemed to go to church when his wife was in camp, and wasn't that so very interesting?

Under Caty's care, Greene recovered quickly, and soon the yellow drained from his face. The American army was recovering, too. Troop strength approached eighteen thousand, but its hue was unchanged. Still green, Washington's new troops were about to attack Boston, or at least that was the plan until more cautious generals advised against it. An exasperated Washington devised another plan: if he couldn't attack the British, he could at least make the British attack him. Artillery from New York's Fort Ticonderoga soon rolled, a miracle made possible by Henry Knox's men. Washington decided to put the artillery to immediate use: the Americans would seize Dorchester Heights, overlooking the British positions from the south. General Howe would have no choice but to attack, a prospect Washington welcomed. Greene and his fellow generals Israel Putnam, John Sullivan, and Horatio Gates were ordered to devise a plan to take the heights.

On the night of March 4, American artillery opened fire on Boston for the third night in a row. Amid the smoke and sound, some two thousand American troops moved on Dorchester Heights, spending the overnight hours digging and fortifying. By dawn on March 5, Washington's men had built two forts and four well-armed strongholds. The British position in Boston was no longer tenable—the Americans could bombard them at will.

Howe had spent the last few weeks making plans to end the siege unilaterally by evacuating the smallpox-ridden city. But Washington's display of aggression infuriated him, and he ordered his troops to prepare to storm the heights. Before they could, however, a late-winter storm blew in, and Howe changed his mind. After negotiations with Washington carried out under a flag of truce, the British began their leave-taking, sailing out of Boston in mid-March, with the last troops leaving on March 17. The long siege was over; the Americans were victorious.

Washington entered the city on March 18, and two days later, he named his youngest general, Nathanael Greene, as military commander of the city. Showing that he certainly had learned practical lessons about military life during his short career as a general, Greene ordered the deputy quartermasters to "draw Beer for the Troops."

Nathanael Greene's first campaign was over.

5 | The Dark Part of Night

There was little time to savor the recovery of battered Boston. Those thousands of British troops who had sailed out of the harbor in mid-March were heading somewhere, and Nathanael Greene believed he knew the final destination: New York City.

It was a hunch, but it made sense. A glance at a map was all the evidence Greene needed. An army in control of New York could control the Hudson River—or, as it was called at the time, the North River—the most strategic waterway in the thirteen colonies. An army that mastered the Hudson could master America, because the river neatly divided New England, the seat of the rebellion, from the remaining colonies. Months earlier, Greene anticipated that the British eventually would make a move on the city. New York, he wrote, was of "Vast Importance to the Enimy" because it allowed the British waterborne access to Canada via Lake George and Lake Champlain in northern New York. For that reason, Greene said, keeping New York out of British hands was vital to the "General success of our Arms."

So Greene knew his command in Boston would be short-lived. But for a few days at least, he allowed himself a few distractions. Caty still was with him, after rushing to camp when he was ill with jaundice. The couple dined with several prominent Bostonians in late March and joined Washington and the other American generals for a banquet at the Bunch of Grapes—a famous patriot gathering spot—on March 28. Life suddenly was a good deal more pleasant that it had been in the hills overlooking the city, and Caty delighted in the socializing and the attention of His Excellency and all the other Continental officers in their fine dress uniforms. The parties and dinners offered Caty a fleeting glimpse of life as it might have been, before the war, before her husband left home for the battlefield. Reality, however, was just outside the door. The suffering city of Boston, ravaged by smallpox, occupation, and siege, stared at Caty with hollow eyes.

Her husband would make sure that his troops did not add to the city's burdens, as he once again showed that he had little patience with disorder and lack of discipline. On March 27, he issued a sternly worded order promising to punish not only those troops found guilty of plundering the city but even those who condoned such misbehavior with their silence or inaction: "If any should be base enough to commit any Acts of Plunder and attempt to conceal the Effects, their messmates . . . will be considered an accessary to the Crime and . . . will be punished accordingly." Greene also lectured the troops—not for the first time— about indecent language, "it being ungenerous, unmanly and unsoldier like." Victory had added a swagger to the step of the American soldiers, and they deployed all manner of colorful phrases to harass Bostonians who had remained in the city during the siege. Many of them were Tories or neutral, and Greene saw them not as enemies but as fellow Americans, however misguided. He forbade his soldiers to insult "any of the Inhabitants with the Odious Epithets of Tory." Such sensitivity would become a hallmark of Greene's relations with loyalist or neutral civilians.

His tenure as Boston's commander ended on March 29, when Washington ordered him to march toward New York at sunrise on April 1 with a brigade of five regiments. Washington was determined to get to New

York before the British did, and when he received word from Rhode Island governor Nicholas Cooke that the British fleet had been spotted off Newport, he told Greene to move as quickly and as unencumbered as possible. Greene dutifully dispatched word to his troops that no "Tables, Chairs, or Useless Luggage is to Go on board the Waggons that may Impede" the march.

The urgency was not necessary; Cooke's information was wrong. The fleet carrying Howe's troops actually was sailing to Halifax, Nova Scotia, to refit. Cooke's informant had thought he saw sails in the distance off Newport; in fact, he saw rolling banks of clouds and fog. Armed with the new, and correct, intelligence, Greene slowed the pace of his march, arriving in Providence on April 4. The following day, Greene's brigade turned out to welcome and salute General Washington as he passed through the city on his way to New York. Greene's troops were conspicuously well dressed and well groomed for the occasion; Greene had instructed them "to be Washed . . . [with] their hair combd and powdered, and their arms Cleand." Greene rode beside the commander in chief as the citizens of Providence cheered the troops and their generals.

After delivering Caty to Coventry, Greene resumed his journey to New York, boarding a troopship in New London that took him to Long Island on April 17. The British were nowhere in sight; the Americans had won the race for the city. Now, however, they would have to defend it. A few weeks after their arrival, Washington showed just how impressed he was with the young general from Rhode Island. He named Greene as commander of the American forces on Long Island, across the East River from Manhattan. With barely a year's experience in uniform, Greene was given the task of preparing for an invasion they all knew was coming. It was a telling display of Washington's confidence in him.

Greene inherited a series of fortifications laid out earlier in the year by his eccentric friend Charles Lee, whom Washington had sent to Long Island even before Boston fell. The hills in the area of modern-day Brooklyn Heights offered a commanding position over the East River and New York City, concentrated then in what is now downtown Manhattan.

Properly fortified, that position would be the key to protecting the city. An invasion from the west, from the Hudson River, was unlikely because the shoreline's rocky palisades would make a landing difficult. Even if the British were to run the gauntlet of American defenses on the heights and take possession of Manhattan, Lee wrote, "they will find it almost impossible to subsist" if the Americans continued to possess Long Island.

Still, even the usually confident Lee found himself at wit's end trying to defend an area so vulnerable to naval assault. "What to do with the city, I own, puzzles me," he told Washington. "It is so encircled with deep, navigable water, that whoever commands the sea must command the town." Left unsaid was the sad but undeniable fact that the Americans had no navy to speak of.

Before he could complete the works, Lee was transferred to Charleston, South Carolina, the target of an early British thrust in the South. Lee believed the civilians in Congress had sent him in the wrong direction; he was, he told Washington, better suited to the ongoing American effort in Canada. After all, he noted, "[I am] the only General Officer on the Continent who can speak and think in French."

Another eccentric American officer, Colonel William Alexander, replaced Lee and continued the work until Greene took over. Alexander was a debt-ridden aristocrat from New Jersey who preferred to be called by another, decidedly unrepublican name: Lord Stirling. Years before, Alexander had claimed the title through his father, a lawyer from Scotland. Ironically, the British House of Lords refused to recognize Alexander's claim to an earldom. His friends in the American army, however, were happy to accord him the title, and so he was referred to as Lord Stirling in all army correspondence.

The American defensive line on Long Island extended from Red Hook to Brooklyn Heights, looking out on Flatbush and much of today's south Brooklyn. To the rear was the East River, and across the river on Manhattan was Washington's headquarters. Thrilled to be given such weighty responsibility, Greene immersed himself in the details of his new command. His orders during the early weeks of May reflected the array of responsibilities that went beyond merely supervising the work of building trenches and fortifications. The mastery of detail that would serve him well throughout the war was evident in the flow of paper from his headquarters. He instructed his quartermaster to find more straw for the troops' bedding; he ordered three hundred spears and a grindstone (the spears were handed out to men whose weapons were under repair); he reminded the troops to observe a day of fasting and prayer on May 16 in accordance with the will of Congress; and he ordered that when his men gave the day's password to sentries, they should do so "softly," as if "the Enemy was Encamped in this Neighbourhood." The enemy was nowhere near the neighborhood, of course, but Greene noted that such discipline was necessary in order to avoid "bad habits" when the invasion finally took place.

Added to these time-consuming but necessary responsibilities was the never-ending chore of maintaining order in camp. Local residents complained to Greene that the troops were ruining their "Meadow Grounds" in their search for food, and so the general told his men to "gather Greens" elsewhere. Even more provocative were civilian complaints that Greene's men were often spotted swimming nude in a nearby pond. Greene dictated an order so filled with prudish rage it's hard to imagine that he wasn't smiling as he spoke.

> Complaints Having Been made . . . that Some of the Soldiers . . .
> Come out of the Water and Run up Naked to the Houses with a
> Design to Insult and Wound the Modesty of female decency . . .
> the General finds Himself under the Disagreeable Necessity of
> Expressing His disapprobation of such a Beastly Conduct. . . .
> Where is the Modesty, Virtue and Sobriety of the New England
> People for which they have been so Remarkable? Have the
> Troops Come Abroad for No Other Purpose than to Render
> themselves both Obnoxious and [Ridiculous]?

Greene was not one to take civilian opinion lightly—in a previous order, he had told the men to "behave themselves toward the Inhabitants"—but if he never followed up on the complaints of naked soldiers offending female decency, it may have been with intent. Many of the civilians on Long Island were suspected of loyalist sympathies so their sensitivities would not have been Greene's top priority. That was true in New York as well; in fact, Greene's friend Henry Knox had made note of the city's political views during a visit there several months before. In a letter to his wife, Lucy, Knox condemned not only the "profaneness" of New Yorkers (it was "intolerable," he said) but also "their Toryism, which is insufferable, and for which they must repent in dust and ashes." The royal governor of New York, William Tryon, still commanded the loyalties of many influential New Yorkers.

What a contrast between the citizens of New York and those of Greene's native state. On May 4, the Rhode Island legislature and Governor Cooke renounced their allegiance to King George. Although the lawmakers did not necessarily declare Rhode Island independent of Britain, that is how many people, Greene included, interpreted their action. To Governor Cooke, Greene wrote: "Tis nobly done. God prosper you, and crown your endeavours with success."

New York was not an easily defended city. There were enemies within, including the city's mayor, who was implicated in a Tory plot to assassinate Washington. And before long, the Americans could expect to see a mighty armada sailing into New York Harbor, with ships filled with thousands of His Majesty's best troops. It was hard to believe the Americans could somehow prevail. Nevertheless, Washington and his generals, along with the civilian leadership in Congress, agreed that such a vital city could not simply be conceded to the enemy.

Greene continued to fortify Brooklyn, supervising construction of five forts along the line. One of them, on the American left flank, was christened Fort Greene, a Brooklyn place-name that has survived to this day. In early June, Greene crossed the East River by ferry to join Henry Knox for a tour of northern Manhattan to inspect the army's prospective line of retreat. Greene and Knox, already friendly, grew closer during these weeks of frantic preparation. Their wives joined them in New York, and the two couples spent several evenings in each other's company, often at Knox's headquarters at the southern end of Broadway in Manhattan or in the uptown quarters of George and Martha Washington. There were times when Knox must have wondered what his friend Greene saw in Caty, other than her undeniable beauty. A man of books who was as devoted to self-improvement as Greene, Knox had trouble hiding his distaste for his friend's twenty-one-year-old wife, who seemed unserious and light. It's less certain how Lucy Knox felt about her frequent companion; their relationship apparently blew hot and cold through the years of war and winter camps. Lucy was nearly as portly as her stout husband, in contrast to Caty, whose beauty and figure continued to beguile Greene's colleagues.

If Caty noticed Knox's disapproving glances, she didn't let it interfere with her fun. The drudgery of domestic life and her suffocating in-laws were miles away, and that suited her just fine. She was very much at ease in this highly masculine world, all smiles and light patter, an incorrigible and vivacious flirt. Other wives whispered about her disregard for convention—who did she think she was, daring to flirt with His Excellency? But her husband stood by her, enjoying her company as much as she did his (and that of his friends). One afternoon in mid-June, Greene brought Caty along for a tour of the Long Island shore, where they looked through a telescope out into the vast reaches of New York Harbor and the Atlantic Ocean. One day soon, the horizon would be filled with masts and sails, and it would be time for Caty to leave.

Though Henry Knox didn't see it, Caty Greene must have had a serious side, for she became fast friends with Martha Washington, who certainly possessed a sense of propriety. Twice Caty's age, dowdy but more confident and self-assured than the young woman from Block Island, Martha took a motherly interest in Caty Greene after they met in Boston during the siege. They renewed their acquaintance in New York until Caty suddenly left in late June, after learning that her son, George Washington Greene, was ill. Frantic, she sailed back to Rhode Island to be greeted with wonderful news: young George was recovering nicely.

Mother and son enjoyed a warm reunion, but soon Caty's thoughts drifted away from hearth and home. She longed for the company of her husband and his friends, and the excitement of New York. She quickly returned to the city, much to the surprise and annoyance of her husband. Henry Knox told Lucy, who had returned to Boston, that his friend would "have rather lost his arm than to have seen [Caty] here at this time." The British buildup had begun.

As he awaited the enemy onslaught, Greene renewed an acquaintance with John Adams, whom he had met during the siege of Boston. The timing of this new and potentially useful relationship was not entirely accidental. In early spring 1776, just after Boston was taken, Greene's friend and ally Samuel Ward Sr. died of smallpox. Ward was Greene's conduit to Congress, a fellow Rhode Islander, the father of his friend Sammy, the father-in-law of his brother Christopher. Greene counted on Ward to keep him informed of the latest intrigues in Philadelphia and to make sure that Greene's views did not go unheeded in the capital.

At the time of his death, Ward had become a well-respected leader and a voice for independence. Greene mourned the loss of his friend but also seized on his meeting with Adams to cultivate a new ally in Congress.

Greene, who had grown up in a colony where there was little difference between political and personal loyalties, understood the importance of having an ally in Congress. Amazingly, for a man so conscious of his lack of formal education, he was secure enough to approach one of the Revolution's least approachable figures, John Adams, a Harvard graduate and lawyer. It was becoming clear that although he remained extremely sensitive to criticism, Nathanael Greene did not lack for nerve, a trait that would serve him well in the battle to come.

Greene's correspondence with Adams constitutes a fascinating colloquy between two headstrong individuals representing often-clashing interests: the military and the political wings of the American revolutionary movement. That larger conflict informed their debate over who should control promotions, with Greene arguing that Washington—as the commander in chief—ought to make those decisions, and Adams countering that only Congress, as the representative of the people, should have that power. Greene said that Adams's policy was bound to be "dangerous, often injurious and sometimes very unjust" because occasionally an inferior officer "may get promoted over the superior [officer] if a single instance of bravery is a sufficient reason for . . . promotion." Adams replied that giving Washington sole power of promotion was no guarantee of justice and was likely to be "more dangerous to the public liberty."

Greene may have argued from principle, but he also had a selfish motive. He lusted for higher rank and figured his best chance for advancement lay with Washington, not Congress. He already was lobbying for promotion to major general, and his campaign was neither subtle nor flattering. "As I have no desire of quitting the service, I hope the Congress will take no measures that lay me under the disgreeable necessity of doing it," he told Washington. In other words, if he didn't get the promotion he sought, he would quit the army. These were not necessarily the sentiments of a pure patriot and dedicated republican. But Greene simply couldn't help himself; still insecure, still fearful that others might be whispering about his limp or his lack of education, he monitored the horizon in search of impending insult.

No insult was forthcoming. When Congress announced the names of new major generals, Greene was on the list.

Other exchanges between Greene the soldier and Adams the politician continued to reflect the tensions of a democracy at war, tensions that did not end with the Revolution. At one point, Greene accused Adams, and Congress, of playing a "desperate game" because they refused to recruit and pay for a large regular army, preferring to rely on part-time militia. But the concerns Greene expressed in these letters were not always so cosmic. Just as often, he badgered Adams about pay increases for officers (Adams was not sympathetic) or government pensions for the families of soldiers killed or maimed in action (this argument made better headway than the pay issue).

These debates, filled with passion and sound arguments, soon seemed a good deal less important. Beginning in late June, great events overshadowed academic disputes between friends over the salaries of American officers.

On the morning of June 29, an American rifleman in New York on his way to an outhouse chanced to look out on the city's glorious harbor. In the distance, where Staten Island and Long Island reached out toward each other, he saw something that took his breath away. "I spied, as I peeped out the bay, something resembling a wood of pine trees trimmed," he wrote. "I could not believe my eyes . . . when in about ten minutes the whole bay was as full of shipping as ever it could be. I do declare that I thought all London was in afloat."

It was not all of London. It was merely the advance guard of General William Howe's invasion force, sailing in on more than a hundred ships to do battle with the impudent rebels of America. As more ships sailed into the harbor, the invading force grew to nearly thirty-two thousand men. Warships under the command of General Howe's brother, Admiral Lord Richard Howe, assembled off Staten Island to support the army. There would be no more embarrassments, like those that had disgraced His Majesty's forces in and around Boston. Overwhelming force, applied vigorously by land and by sea in New York, would end the rebellion once and for all. The British, together with German mercenaries, set up camp on Staten Island and awaited their marching orders.

Opposing this vast British force were just nineteen thousand men, most of whom were inexperienced, and many of whom were sick. As he continued to supervise the defensive works on Long Island, Nathanael Greene also diagnosed the illness that was plaguing the American camp. The soldiers' health, he proclaimed, suffered from eating too much fried meat—an assertion that no doubt puzzled many fellow officers, given Greene's utter lack of medical knowledge. Showing himself to be a man well ahead of his times, Greene ordered the commissaries to serve more vegetables and fruit, and that meat, if it had to be consumed at all, should be roasted rather than fried. ("Vegetables," he told Washington, "would be much more wholesome" than meat.) He also reemphasized the importance of hygiene, ordering extra supplies of soap and again demanding that latrines be properly maintained—the old ones filled up and new ones dug every three days—and that "all Filth and Putrid matter" be buried. "The General Also forbids in the most Positive Terms the Troops easing themselves in the Ditches of the Fortifications, a Practice that is Disgracefull to the last Degree," he wrote.

This sick, undermanned, inexperienced army seemed to be ripe for the taking in early July, save for the fact that on July 9, the troops heard stirring words that reminded them of why they were gathered under arms in New York. At six o'clock on that summer's evening in New York, brigades of men from New England and Pennsylvania and Virginia—men who would have believed, even a year ago, that they had nothing in common—gathered by order of George Washington on their respective parade grounds. They grew silent as they were read the words drafted in Philadelphia and approved on July 4. Washington said he hoped those words would "serve as a fresh incentive to every officer and soldier to act with Fidelity and Courage."

The men cheered, and later that evening, the local Sons of Liberty made quick work of a fine lead statue of King George III in the city's Bowling Green. The statue showed George dressed as a Roman emperor, majestically astride a noble steed. By the time the Sons were finished with George, he was headless and otherwise in pieces.

Then it was back to reality.

The Americans expected an attack at any moment. Nervous sentries on night patrol near Greene's headquarters fired into the darkness when they heard footsteps or saw a sudden movement. Greene confessed to Adams that he was worried that he had too few troops to oppose the mighty force encamped across the Narrows on Staten Island. He could see his opponents gathering strength by the day; one morning he rose before dawn and rode to Red Hook to monitor the British fleet in the distance. It's hard to imagine what private thoughts passed through his mind as he spied this huge armada assembling to test the defenses that he—Nathanael Greene of Rhode Island, late of Nathanael Greene & Company—was building on the hills above the East River. The finest soldiers in the world were drilling across the harbor on Staten Island, and one day soon, they would attack in force. How would he react? Would they make a mockery of his forts and fences and other defensive works? Would he panic as the sun caught the glint of the bayonets? Would he die, leaving little George fatherless, leaving Caty a widow? She was back home now and pregnant again.

What had he gotten himself into?

Doubts about his troops troubled his days. He told Adams he wished he had been given more time to discipline his men before they faced the inevitable onslaught. He may well have been wondering about his own discipline. Although he had witnessed death and destruction in Boston, and although he had heard the screams of the wounded and the dying, he had not yet experienced the full force of His Majesty's fury. What would it be like? He could not know, and perhaps it was better simply to dwell on duty rather than fear. He told Adams, "What falls to my lot I shall endeavour to execute to the best of my ability."

What fell upon his lot was paperwork. Administrative duties were ceaseless, and Greene resented these burdens as they piled high on his beloved mahogany desk. With only minimal secretarial help, Greene was signing passes, dictating orders, presiding over court-martials, mulling requests for discharge from the service, and, of course, keeping up a lively communication with political leaders. He complained to Washington that the flow of paper was interfering with more important work.

> [It] is impossible for me to attend to the duties of the day,
> which in many instances prejudices the service. . . . The
> science or art of War requires a freedom of thought and
> leisure to reflect upon the Various incidents that [daily]
> occur, which cannot be had where the whole of ones time is
> engrossed in Clerical employments. The time devoted to this
> employment is not the only injury that I feel, but it confines
> my thoughts as well as engrosses my time.

Still inexperienced, Greene didn't understand that paperwork and logistics were part of any commander's burdens—as a similarly burdened Washington might have told him. When he imagined himself on the battlefield, he saw glory, not chores. Caesar, after all, didn't write about his bureaucratic duties in Gaul, and Marshal Saxe hadn't offered instruction in managing paperwork.

Greene also didn't understand that it was his mastery of details that made him all the more invaluable as a member of the American high command. Washington had no way to judge Nathanael Greene as a battlefield commander, at least not yet. Instinct, however, told him that here was a competent and earnest leader of men, a self-taught general who kept his troops well drilled and reasonably happy, and one who, incidentally, kept the paper flowing. What more could one ask of a general on the verge of his first combat?

Greene's complaints did achieve some measure of relief: Washington, noting that "General Greene being particularly engaged at present," allowed a lieutenant to sign passes that previously had required Greene's signature.

July passed without an enemy move on Greene's position. On the night of August 1, Greene rode to the Narrows after hearing a report that still more British ships were anchoring off Staten Island. He told Washington that he spotted thirty-six new vessels with troops aboard. Greene didn't know it, but the new arrivals were part of a British fleet that had attacked General Lee on Sullivan's Island, near Charleston, South Carolina, on June 28. The battle had ended in a British defeat and a hasty retreat.

Still, the British waited, causing Washington to observe that there was "something exceedingly mysterious in the conduct of the enemy." The enemy's conduct was not only mysterious but scandalous. Lord Rawdon, a young and particularly smug officer who would cross paths with Greene years later in the South, was among the troops idling on Staten Island. He described to a friend, the earl of Huntington, how His Majesty's troops were keeping themselves entertained as they awaited their marching orders. "The fair nymphs of this isle are in wonderful tribulation," he reported. "A girl cannot step into the bushes to pluck a rose without running the most imminent risk of being ravished." Rawdon noted, with jolly irony, that the island's young women took exception to wanton assaults; "they don't bear them with the proper resignation," he said. As a result, "we have most entertaining courts-martial every day."

As the hot, humid summer passed, hundreds of American soldiers came down with what Greene called "putrid fever"—probably typhoid. The army was woefully unprepared to treat so many sick soldiers, about a third of the army. Disease was, and remains, as much a part of war as mangled corpses and burned flesh, but Greene was unwilling to shrug his shoulders and leave the ill and the wounded to the fortunes of war. "Great humanity should be exercisd towards those indisposd," he told Washington on August 11. "Kindness on one hand leaves a favorable and lasting impression; neglect and suffering on the other is never forgotten. . . . Something is necessary to be done [speedily] as many sick are in a suffering condition."

Four days later, on August 15, Greene was among those "in a suffering condition."

The weather that morning was wet and foggy, which screened the Americans' view of British movements on Staten Island. But reports of stepped-up activity had been coming into Greene's headquarters for several days, suggesting final preparations for a move across the Narrows onto Long Island. Greene was impatiently awaiting a new complement of militia companies that were a day late as of August 15. He told Washington the laggards would soon regret their tardiness. They would soon "feel my Resentment by vigorous and spirited Exertions of Military Discipline," he said.

Greene never received the chance to make good on this grim promise. Soon after writing to Washington, he was confined to his bed with what he called a "raging Fever." He sent word to Washington, across the East River on Manhattan Island, that he hoped to be back in his saddle soon, but his illness only became worse. Within two days, one of his two aides-de-camp, Major William Livingston, informed Washington that Greene had suffered through a "very bad night" and "cannot be said to be any better this morning than he was yesterday." His temperature was dangerously high; he had little appetite and almost no energy. He could sit up in bed for no longer than an hour at a time.

Washington had a crisis on his hands. After months of preparation, the defense of Long Island was in the hands of a sick, bedridden man just as the enemy was expected to unleash a powerful assault. Greene sought to reassure his commander by dispatching an optimistic message on August 18, reporting that he was feeling better and, while still weak, he believed that he would be out of bed "in a few days."

The enemy, however, could strike at any moment. Washington acted swiftly, although perhaps not decisively: he ordered Greene to sail across the river to Manhattan to complete his recovery. In Greene's place as commander of Long Island, Washington at first named General John Sullivan, a lawyer from New Hampshire, but then reconsidered and sent a more senior general, Israel Putnam. The new commander was competent enough but had not been privy to Greene's strategy and his preparations. As reports came into headquarters of British troops boarding transport ships, Washington increased troop strength on Long Island from four thousand to nine thousand.

Greene was still weak and in bed, in a private home near the present intersection of Broadway and Ninth Street in Manhattan's Greenwich Village, when the British finally launched their assault on the defenses he had built and the troops he had commanded. The British landed unopposed on the southern shoreline of modern-day Brooklyn, near Gravesend, on August 22, and under cover of night on August 26 the main British force moved toward the virtually undefended Jamaica Pass on the American left while other units assailed the American right and center. In heavy fighting on the twenty-seventh, the Americans were outflanked and badly mauled. Washington, who had crossed the East River to take personal command of the battle, found himself trapped with the river to his back. That river, however, offered a desperate chance for salvation: on the foggy night of August 29, with the British asleep but prepared to finish off the rebels the next day, Washington withdrew his force across the river to the temporary safety of Manhattan.

Would the Battle of Long Island have turned out better for the Americans had Greene been in charge, and not the inferior Putnam? Probably not. The British had twenty thousand crack troops; the Americans had less than half that number, including undependable militia. Still, Greene quietly cursed his fate, and on August 30, as the Long Island defenders stumbled through the streets of New York City, Greene poured out his frustrations on paper.

> Gracious God! to be confined at such a time. And the
> misfortune is doubly great as there was no general officer who
> had made himself acquainted with the ground as perfectly as I
> had. I have not the vanity to think the event would have been
> otherwise had I been there, yet I think I could have given the
> commanding general a good deal of necessary information.
> Great events sometimes depend on very little causes.

The loss of Long Island made the defense of New York City untenable. The British army commanded the high ground across the river; the British navy would rule the rivers surrounding Manhattan Island. On September 5, Greene, now recovered, sent a grim and clear-eyed analysis of the precarious American position to his commander in chief. He noted that the entire main army risked capture and destruction in New York because of the enemy's ability to land troops anywhere on the island, and that fate was to be avoided at all costs. "I give it as my oppinion that a General and speedy Retreat is absolutely necessary and that the honnor and Interest of America requires it," he told Washington. As for the city itself, Greene was surprisingly cold-blooded. Let it burn, he said.

> Two thirds of the Property of the City of New York and the
> Suburbs belongs to the Tories. . . . I would burn the
> City and Suburbs. . . . It will deprive the Enemy of an
> oppor[t]unity of Barracking their whole Army together. . . .

> It will deprive them of a general Market. . . . All these
> advantages would Result from the destruction of the City.
> And not one benefit can arise to us from its preservation.

Washington agreed, but Congress did not. The politicians expressly forbade Washington to carry out Greene's wishes. "This in my judgment may be set down among one of the capital errors of Congress," an exasperated Washington wrote to his cousin, Lund Washington. Greene then contended that the army should retreat from the city anyway, but nobody else shared his view. At a council of war on September 7 in Washington's headquarters, Greene's colleagues, including Washington, decided on a compromise plan that combined withdrawal and defense of the island. Nine thousand troops were ordered north to Harlem Heights in upper Manhattan, a dozen miles from the settled part of the city and south of an American strongpoint dubbed Fort Washington, which was perched on the high ground along the North River palisades. Five thousand Americans were left within the city itself, and another five thousand or so were stretched in positions between the city and Harlem Heights to guard against a British invasion from the East River.

This was a dubious evasion of a difficult decision. Instead of either withdrawing completely, as Greene argued, or fortifying the city, Washington and the other generals spread the American army thinly along the length of Manhattan Island. Greene stubbornly continued to press for a general retreat from the island. He was convinced that Washington was on the verge of a catastrophic miscalculation. With boldness that bordered on impudence, Greene addressed a petition to Washington, begging that a new council of war reconsider the decision to defend New York. Greene was the highest-ranking officer, and only major general, to sign the petition.

A new council of war took place four days later, on September 11, in the headquarters of General Alexander McDougall. Greene made an impassioned and effective argument in favor of withdrawal from the city. The army's youngest major general carried the day, and the vote was reversed. The troops in the city began moving north, toward Kings Bridge, and Washington moved his headquarters to Harlem Heights to supervise the retreat. Left behind in the city, because of a lack of wagons, was about half of the army's cannons and other vital equipment and food supplies.

The British arrived even as the withdrawal was under way. They landed in force on a sultry morning, September 15, in Kip's Bay, along Manhattan's East River waterfront near present-day East Thirty-fourth Street. The American defenders, most of them militiamen, ran away. Their performance so embarrassed Washington that Greene would later say that his commander was "so vext at the infamous conduct of the Troops that he sought Death rather than life."

The British halted their northward advance that day without assailing Harlem Heights. Other British troops had turned south, to take the city itself. As if to confirm Greene's assessment of their allegience, hundreds of New Yorkers turned out to greet the British forces. The following morning, September 16, Greene and his three-thousand-man division were deployed south of the heights, near where today's West 125th Street approaches the Hudson River, when gunfire signaled a skirmish nearby. An American patrol had stumbled upon British light infantry units operating north of the main British line. The Americans fired several volleys and then began withdrawing back toward the main American position. The British followed, and one of their buglers taunted the retreating rebels with a fox-hunting call used when the quarry disappeared into a hole. The American commanders flushed with embarassment and anger.

The British were far too eager to complete the rout. Their contingent numbered only about three hundred, and they had moved far in front of their lines. Washington seized a chance to redeem the previous day's dishonor; he told Greene to send a hundred and fifty men forward to distract the British from an encircling movement under the command of Colonel Thomas Knowlton.

The British spotted Knowlton before he could complete his maneuver, forcing the Americans to attack from the flank rather than from behind. The British buckled and began to retreat as Greene pressed from one side and Knowlton from the other. The Americans saw something new and startling: the back of a British redcoat.

Major General Nathanael Greene had never been in battle before. The siege of Boston, though hardly casualty-free, was static and almost predictable, a waiting game. This was something else again. Men shouted and screamed to unhearing comrades; smoke covered the field; young, healthy men dropped in their tracks, dead before they hit the ground if they were lucky; if not, their youth and lives seeped away slowly, horribly, and they would scream until they could scream no more.

For Nathanael Greene, war no longer consisted of words on a page. It was happening all around him. He rode among the suddenly emboldened American soldiers, shouting orders and encouragement. The Americans continued to rally. After nearly two hours of intense fire, the British retreated again, and the Americans were prepared to pursue. Washington, however, dared not risk a general engagement, so he judiciously ordered his men to cease firing and return to their defenses.

The Battle of Harlem Heights was hardly an epic. The Americans suffered about sixty casualties; the British, about a hundred and seventy. Numbers aside, it was the sight of those redcoats in retreat that gave the battle significance. As Greene noted, at Harlem Heights the British had "met with a very different kind of Reception from what they did the day before."

Still, there was no denying the disaster that had befallen the Americans. New York City was lost to the enemy. The day after the Battle of Harlem Heights, Washington dispatched Greene across the river to New Jersey to take command of that state's defenses, including a strategic fortress across from Fort Washington called Fort Constitution—later renamed Fort Lee. Greene's new assignment was critical. New Jersey offered a path from New York to Philadelphia; defending that path suddenly was of the utmost importance. Long Island and New York already had fallen. Could the cause survive the loss of Philadelphia, too?

Greene was given the task of guarding against the unthinkable. It would require all of Greene's organizing skills and strategic vision. But

Washington, whose faith in his troops remained shaken despite Harlem Heights, had decided that this young major general was fit for important work. Washington's secretary wrote that "Greene is beyond doubt a first-rate military genius, and one in whose opinions the General places the utmost confidence."

Three days into Greene's new command, his wish for New York City came true. On the night of September 20, a series of fires erupted along the waterfront, and within hours, a third of the city was in flames. British soldiers summoned to perform the work of firefighters discovered that buckets and other firefighting equipment were either disabled or nonexistent. The fires became an inferno, and from his headquarters on Harlem Heights twelve miles to the north, Washington saw an orange glow in the sky. "Providence, or some good honest fellow, has done more for us than we were disposed to do for ourselves," he said as he watched the lost city burn. A good honest fellow who had nothing to do with the fire, but who was arrested in a roundup of suspected patriots that night, was Nathan Hale, an American spy. He was hanged the next morning.

If Greene felt some sense of satisfaction as he watched the flames from his post in New Jersey, he was discreet enough to keep such thoughts to himself. But there was no disguising his optimism, even in the face of disastrous defeats. "I apprehend the several retreats that have taken place begin to make you think all is lost," he wrote to his brother Jacob. "Don't be frightened; our cause is not yet in a desperate state." But Greene was not so sanguine about members of Congress who continued to believe the war could be won with part-time soldiers. That, Greene believed, was frightening.

> The policy of Congress has been the most absurd and
> ridiculous imaginable, pouring in militia men who come and
> go every month. A military force established upon such
> principles defeats itself. People coming from home with all

the tender feelings of domestic life are not sufficiently
fortified with natural courage to stand the shocking scenes of
war. To march over dead men, to hear without concern the
groans of the wounded, I say few men can stand such scenes
unless steeled by habit or fortified by military pride.

Greene continued to insist that the nation needed a regular army to
defeat the professionals of Britain and the mercenaries purchased from
German princes. But until Congress came around to his (and Washington's) view, he would do his best to turn these militia outfits and inexperienced regulars into a fighting force. A corporal in New Jersey, John
Adlum, quickly noticed a difference almost as soon as Greene arrived:
There was, he wrote, "a great change with respect to the discipline of the
troops, which before was lax." As if to acknowledge Greene's complaint
about the dangers of relying on militia, Congress soon authorized the
raising of eighty-eight more regiments for the Continental army.

One of Greene's tasks in New Jersey, in addition to strengthening
Fort Lee and overseeing the construction of a new barracks, was the
reorganization of the army's hospitals, which he found in a wretched
state. He wrote directly to John Hancock, the president of Congress, demanding more medicine for suffering soldiers who "exhibit a Spectacle
shocking to human feelings." Hospitals were too small for the number of
sick and wounded, and some regimental surgeons "[couldn't] be trusted
with the necessary Stores"—it was rumored that they were using the
army's supplies for private purposes. As was the case in Boston and
Long Island, Greene continued to look after his sick and wounded
troops, not only out of humanity but because he understood that their
suffering brought down morale among healthy soldiers.

Greene also spent time studying maps of New Jersey, the vital link between New York and Philadelphia. Anticipating the worst, a march
through the state toward the capital, he organized supply depots in several towns, including Princeton and Trenton, along a possible line of retreat. This was precisely the kind of foresight and organization that so

impressed Washington. Other generals had leadership abilities, other generals understood strategy and tactics, but Greene knew how to get things done.

His diligence brought him into the interior of New Jersey, where Continental soldiers stood guard over vital bridges and scoured the countryside looking for deserters. During one such trip, Greene sought to cross a bridge on the Hackensack River in the New Jersey Meadowlands but found his journey blocked by a Continental soldier named Kilpatrick. An Irishman who had been serving in the British army in Boston until he defected to the American cause, Kilpatrick was singularly unimpressed by the stranger with a slight limp. The soldier summoned Corporal Adlum. "Here is a gentleman who says he is General Greene," Kilpatrick said, gesturing toward the gentleman and sizing him up. Kilpatrick reminded Adlum that they had orders to stop anybody "that had the appearance of a soldier." Kilpatrick didn't realize how flattered Greene must have felt to be judged as having the appearance of a soldier—a far cry from what his colleagues had said about him in the Kentish Guards! Greene amiably produced a letter attesting to the fact that he was, indeed, General Greene, and an embarrassed Kilpatrick allowed him to pass. Greene seemed to appreciate the soldiers' professionalism, even more so when they stood at attention and presented arms when he returned during several other excursions. Greene became so familiar with the guards that he soon was asking them about local conditions: Were there loyalists in the neighborhood? Were supplies readily available in case of an emergency? Unlike the aristocratic generals across the Hudson River, Nathanael Greene did not consider the troops below his station. Many years later, Adlum recalled that Greene remembered him when they crossed paths in camp, and often spoke with him.

Greene's command expanded in mid-October, when Washington was forced to withdraw from Harlem Heights after a British landing at Throgs Neck, in what is now the Bronx, threatened to trap the Americans on Manhattan. With Washington headed for White Plains, Greene inherited the garrison at Fort Washington, just across the river from Fort Lee.

The American generals believed Fort Washington was unassailable, even with the rest of the army to the north and west. The fort's two thousand troops could disrupt British communications from one end of the island to the other and could menace British warships attempting to sail north up the Hudson River. What's more, with Fort Washington in American hands, the British would have to leave sizable forces on Manhattan, rather than throw their whole might in pursuit of the retreating Washington. And if the American troops were threatened, Greene believed the garrison could easily be evacuated across the river to New Jersey.

Greene saw Fort Washington as a second Bunker Hill. If the British attempted to attack this strongpoint built more than two hundred feet above the river, they would be punished as they were punished on that bloody day in June in Charlestown. He was not alone in this view. In late October, the fate of Fort Washington became the topic of much discussion and controversy among Washington's generals. Among those who believed the fort should be held was General Charles Lee, recently arrived from his victory in Charleston. Washington himself wasn't much help: though his instincts suggested that the fort's troops could be better used elsewhere, he hesitated. Greene convinced him that he could sell the British another hill at great expense.

Greene crossed the Hudson River regularly through late October and early November as an attack on Fort Washington seemed likely. He alerted Washington to one potential problem at the fort: if the Americans were forced to withdraw from the fort's extensive outer defenses to make a stand inside the fort itself, it wasn't large enough to accommodate all the troops. Nevertheless, Greene reinforced the fort and its outer defenses with a thousand more soldiers, increasing troop strength to nearly three thousand.

The possibility of an assault increased after the British attacked Washington in White Plains and, after an indecisive standoff, General Howe withdrew back to Manhattan.

The guns of Fort Washington opened fire on the night of November 5 as three British warships attempted to slip past the American defenses.

While the ships were damaged, they managed to get upriver, mocking the American defenses. When Washington received this disturbing news, it awakened his reservations about defending the fort named in his honor. Although he had told Greene, "Pay every attention in your power and give every assistance you can" to Fort Washington, now he dispatched quite another message. "If we cannot prevent Vessels passing up," he asked, "what valuable purpose" could Fort Washington serve? "I am therefore inclined to think it will not be prudent to hazard the Men and Stores at [Fort] Washington, but as you are on the Spot, [I] leave it to you to give such Orders as to evacuating [Fort] Washington as you judge best."

But Greene had no intention of ordering an evacuation. The fort's commander, Colonel Robert Magaw, told Greene that if the British tried to besiege the fort, he could hold out until December. Greene decided to hold his ground and tempt the British into disaster. "I cannot conceive the garrison to be in any great danger," Greene wrote to Washington. "The men can be brought off at any time."

Nevertheless, after marching south from White Plains, Washington arrived at Fort Lee on November 13 and was surprised to discover that Greene had not acted on his suggestion to evacuate the fort. Still, Washington hesitated as he heard reassuring words from Greene, prompting Washington's aide Joseph Reed to complain of his commander's "indecisive mind."

In White Plains, where Washington had left him with more than five thousand troops, General Charles Lee seemed anything but indecisive. He wrote to Reed that defending Fort Washington would be a huge mistake. He made no mention of his arguments in favor of the fort's defense several weeks before. And, in a letter to Greene on November 11, Lee said nothing about his new doubts about the fort. Instead, he simply asked that Greene return the horse and sulky he had borrowed; more remarkably, Lee boldly asserted, "My friend Howe has lost the Campaign." A few days later, however, Lee adopted an entirely different tone in his letter to Reed: "I cannot help expressing my concern that General

Greene has reinforced [the fort]. I should have been rather pleased had he called off a considerable part of the garrison."

Lee issued his warning on November 16. It was too late.

General Howe sent ten thousand troops forward to attack Fort Washington's three thousand defenders. Greene and the Americans had not anticipated that the British commander would hurl such a large force at the garrison. At about one o'clock on the afternoon of November 15, a British officer carrying a white flag marched toward the American defenses with a drummer at his side. He had a message from Howe: surrender or die. Colonel Magaw said he was prepared to fight to the last man. When Greene received word of the ultimatum, he crossed the river for an urgent conference with Magaw and other officers. He recrossed the river late at night and kept his thoughts to himself.

The following morning, Greene, Washington, and two other officers were climbing into rowboats that were to take them from Fort Lee to Fort Washington when they heard a tremendous roar from the opposite shore. The British assault on Fort Washington had begun. The fort's outer defenses came under a fierce bombardment by land and by sea. The generals hurried across to the scene of the action, landed at the foot of the craggy palisades upon which the fort was built, and were escorted to the top. They found themselves in what Greene would later call "a very awkward situation." Awkward, indeed—the British already were pressing in on all sides. Shells were blasting great gaps in the American defenses, and British and Hessian troops were advancing from three directions. Washington, Greene, and Generals Israel Putnam and Hugh Mercer were caught in the middle of this impending catastrophe.

Amid the smoke, noise, and chaos enveloping the American position, Greene urged Washington to leave immediately and volunteered to remain behind to command the desperate defense of Fort Washington. Putnam and Mercer did likewise. Washington was in imminent danger of death or capture; either one surely would have ended the Revolution.

Washington agreed, but he persuaded his generals to come with him. They made their way down to the shore by an old path, and they were rowed away as the British pressed forward.

They left behind nearly three thousand men. Within a matter of hours, nearly all of them were made prisoners—the rest were dead or wounded—and most of the prisoners would later die terrible deaths in foul, suffocating prison ships anchored off present-day Brooklyn. Fort Washington surrendered. It was the worst defeat of the war so far.

And it was, to a large extent, Nathanael Greene's fault.

Ultimately, Washington had to take the blame, for he had arrived at Fort Lee in plenty of time to overrule Greene and order an evacuation before the British attacked. But he didn't. And while Washington accepted responsibility, the loss was so bitter he could not help but remind Congress that he had taken bad advice, advice given him by Nathanael Greene. Neither man knew that days before the attack, an American officer had deserted to the British and told them all he knew about the fort's defenses.

Washington had to break the disastrous news to Congress in a letter the morning after. In it, he did not spare Greene, noting that he had instructed the young general "to govern himself by Circumstances. . . . General Greene, struck with the Importance of the Post, and the Discouragement which our Evacuation of Posts must necessarily have given, reinforced [Colonel] Magaw."

Greene was distraught. Had Washington fired him on the spot, historians very likely would have judged the action understandable and perhaps even necessary. Greene was, after all, little more than an amateur playing at war, and Fort Washington had shown the danger of taking advice from such a man. Nobody was quite sure why he was a general in the first place; he had no experience, no expertise, and little more than a schoolboy's enthusiasm for the idea, although not the reality, of war. It had been a mistake to place him with such a trust. Yes, his intentions were good, and he was competent enough as an administrator, but as a strategist?

Nobody rose to Greene's defense. In fact, the duplicitous General Lee heaped scorn on Greene's injured reputation. "Oh, General," Lee wrote to Washington, "why would you be overpersuaded by men of inferior judgment to your own?" Lee tersely informed Washington that he would not honor Greene's recommendations for promotions among the Rhode Island troops under Lee's command. He claimed that other officers accused Greene "of partiality to his connections and townsmen, to the prejudice of manifestly superior merit." Some of those Greene recommended, Lee said, "were wretched."

If Greene believed he no longer had a friend in the world, he was not entirely mistaken. Washington's aide Joseph Reed, a presumed ally of Greene's, joined the whispering campaign against him, telling Lee that the fort's loss was Greene's responsibility. Greene poured out his heart to Henry Knox, one officer who most certainly had not abandoned him, in a letter the day after Fort Washington fell: "I feel mad, vext, sick and sorry. Never did I need the consoling voice of a friend more than now. Happy should I be to see you. This is a most terrible Event. Its consequences are justly to be dreaded." Characteristically, he asked Knox to tell him "what is said upon the Occasion." If Knox knew what was being said, one can only hope that he spared his friend. His reply to this heartrending letter has not been found.

Washington, although eager to make it clear that he was simply listening to bad counsel, did not fire Greene. To his credit, he kept the young general at his side, understanding that there were more battles to fight, knowing he would need every good man he could find. He did not protect Greene from criticism, but he declined the chance to make him a public scapegoat.

With Fort Washington in enemy hands, Fort Lee was useless. In addition to three thousand men, the fort held enormous stores of ammunition, foodstuff, tools, and muskets. All would have to be removed to some other place in New Jersey. A lethargic evacuation, hampered by a lack of wagons, was under way on the morning of November 20 when Greene was awakened from his sleep with electrifying news. General Charles Cornwallis, a brilliant young officer, and six thousand troops had landed in New Jersey about six miles north of the fort. Their orders were to finish off Greene.

In Lord Cornwallis, Nathanael Greene was about to meet an antagonist who was everything the Rhode Islander was not, a symbol of the Old World of privilege who now sought to crush troops under the command of a New World general who represented the triumph of merit over blood. Cornwallis was a graduate of Eton, the English finishing school for highborn military officers, a politician, a onetime aide to King George III, and a veteran of Britain's campaigns on the Continent.

A liberal, at least by the standards of his class, Cornwallis had mixed feelings about the men he now sought to crush. He believed the Americans had valid complaints, but when mere discontent degenerated into outright rebellion, he put politics aside and returned to his first career, the military. If nothing else, he shared with Nathanael Greene a love of country and a sense of duty.

Now the graduate of Eton was hot on the heels of the unschooled general from Rhode Island.

Greene had posted troops along the New Jersey cliffs overlooking the Hudson River, anticipating the British offensive. But Cornwallis had exploited a gap in Greene's patrols and had crossed the river at night, undetected. News of the British advance set the American camp into motion and chaos. Greene sent for Washington, who had ridden to Hackensack, and quickly ordered the troops to evacuate the fort. There was no time to douse the campfires, no time to eat breakfast, and, worst of all, no time to collect all the supplies, tools, and weapons in camp. Luckily, Greene already had removed much of the fort's ammunition. Washington later estimated that the army lost more than two hundred cannon (a terrible loss), along with "a great deal of baggage, between two and three hundred Tents—about a thousand Barrels of Flour and other stores."

Cornwallis nearly had them. His advance guard arrived in Fort Lee even as the abandoned campfires burned and some of Greene's slow-moving troops—they moved slowly because they were drunk—were lingering in camp. Greene joined Washington for a sullen march through the meadows outside of Newark. The race through New Jersey was on.

Greene's terse summation of the retreat did little justice to the suffering of this ragged, dispirited army: "We retreated to Hackensack. From Hackensack to Equacanock [present-day Passaic]; from Equacanock to Newark; from Newark to [New] Brunswick; from [New] Brunswick to this place"—meaning Trenton, where they arrived on December 2. They marched eighty miles in less than two weeks, along muddy roads, in dirty clothes, through towns that offered no parades, no smiles, no friendly waves, and certainly no new recruits to add to an army that had suffered such grievous losses since the Battle of Long Island. Local residents were quick to take a British offer for pardons providing they reaffirmed their allegience to the king. The soldiers, fighting, sacrificing, and dying for the liberty of their fellow Americans, were disgusted. Ebenezer Huntington, a Continental captain who was on the march through New Jersey, wrote: "Our people, instead of behaving like brave men, behave like rascalls. . . . People join them almost in captains' companies to take the oath of allegiance." Washington called up the New Jersey militia; most of the militiamen ignored him. They were not about to risk their lives, fortunes, and sacred honor in a lost cause. Members of Congress, fearing the approach of the pursuing British, fled from Philadelphia—just after assuring Washington they would do no such thing.

Lord Rawdon, the arrogant young British officer who had been so amused by reports of Staten Island women resisting British rapists earlier in the year, assured a friend that the American army "is broken all to pieces, and the spirit of their leaders . . . is also broken." He concluded that "it is well nigh over with them." When Charles Lee, marching ever so slowly south toward Washington's column, was taken prisoner in the New Jersey town of Basking Ridge, the end certainly seemed in sight. He was a professional soldier, as opposed to the amateurs who followed Washington through the snows of New Jersey, and many believed he, not Washington, was the man best suited to lead the rebels. Certainly he thought so. Not long before his capture, he shared his opinion of his commander in chief with another British officer turned rebel general, Horatio Gates. "Entre nous," wrote the man who bragged of his ability to speak and think in French, "a certain great man is most damnably deficient." But now Charles Lee, who considered himself the answer to the American army's deficiencies, was in His Majesty's custody, and that damnably deficient commander in chief was leading his men to God knows where.

It was along this terrible, demoralizing march that Thomas Paine found new words to move his fellow patriots. Paine had joined Greene's staff several weeks earlier as a civilian aide, and now he shared the army's suffering as it slogged along, underfed and underclothed. He looked into the hollow eyes of those few troops—only about three thousand now—who remained with Washington. He wrote at night in Greene's camp, often, no doubt, after long conversations with Greene and other American officers. From these observations came a brilliant pamphlet, *The Crisis.*

"These are the times that try men's souls," Paine wrote. "The summer soldier and the sunshine patriot will, in this crisis, shrink from the service of their country; but he that stands it now deserves the love and thanks of man and woman."

The winter soldiers of the American army, shoulders stooped, heads down, defeat written on their faces, gloomily crossed the Delaware River into Pennsylvania on December 8. They were barely across when their British pursuers entered Trenton, just missing a chance to finish off the campaign with a crushing victory.

On December 16, Greene wrote a letter to Caty that had some of his friend Paine's eloquence and, amazingly, much of his own optimism. The march, trying though it was, at least allowed him to put some distance—physically and otherwise—from the disaster at Fort Washington. He told Caty: "Fortune seems to frown upon the cause of freedom; a combination of evils are pressing in upon us on all sides. However, I hope this is the dark part of the night, which generally is just before day."

Those words were not simply empty encouragement to a worried and, thanks to her visit to New York in June, pregnant wife. As Greene awaited the army's next move, he established his headquarters in a private home along the Delaware River. There, above a mantle, he added a personal bit of decoration: a painting of a rising sun.

6 | Victory or Death

On a cold Christmas Eve about three miles west of the icy Delaware River, Nathanael Greene hosted dinner for George Washington, his staff, and other top American officers. The officers drifted in after a hard ride through the rolling, frozen fields leading to Greene's quarters, a private house owned by the Merrick family. While the house was made of stone and so was sturdier than the hastily built huts nearby, it also was unfinished and drafty. But the condition of the house hardly mattered. Neither, in fact, did the festive night itself. The American generals gathered not to celebrate but to discuss a surprise attack planned for the following day. Christmas was a time when lonely soldiers based in a faraway land—such as, say, the Hessian mercenaries who occupied Trenton—might be expected to have their guard down. The freezing weather certainly didn't help morale, but at least the snow and ice made it highly unlikely that George Washington would risk his ragged band with a surprise attack.

On this cold Christmas Eve, the only Americans with reason to be festive were those who were counting the days to New Year's. On that eagerly awaited day, their military obligations would expire and they would be free to leave their wretched camp and return to their homes. Those expiring enlistments were very much on the minds of the American generals as they gathered in Greene's headquarters. If they did not act now, they would be doomed to inaction when the bulk of the army—thousands of troops, most of them from New England—retired on January 1. Thanks to a stream of reinforcements, the army now numbered more than ten thousand, although only six thousand were healthy enough for duty. But Washington had to make use of this expanded force by January 1.

On the other side of the river, a Hessian force of only about fifteen hundred guarded Trenton. Numbers alone suggested a glorious opportunity for the Americans after months of defeat and loss, and Greene was eager to take advantage. "I hope to give the Enimy a stroke in a few days," he wrote on December 21.

On Christmas Eve, from his place at Greene's dining table, a somber Washington reviewed his plans for the following day's action with his officers. The men would be issued a three-day supply of cooked rations. The operation's countersign, or password, would be "Victory or Death." One detachment under General James Ewing would cross at Trenton Ferry and seize a bridge over the Assunpink Creek, blocking a Hessian retreat to the south. Meanwhile, another detachment of more than two thousand men under Colonel John Cadwalader would cross the river to the south to create a diversion. The main attack force of about twenty-four hundred men with Henry Knox's artillery would cross the river at McKonkey's Ferry, north of Trenton, and then march toward the town in two columns. General Sullivan would command the column on the right, following the river road into town. Greene would command on the left, along Pennington Road, with Washington himself marching with Greene's division. All these moves would have to be coordinated carefully, because surprise was essential. After overwhelming the garrison, the Americans would press forward against Princeton and perhaps even the critical British outpost in New Brunswick.

The generals went over the details of the complicated plan and then bade one another good night, leaving Greene to his thoughts. The next few days truly would bring them victory or death.

The dreadful weeks leading to this decisive moment had brought him closer still to Washington. When he heard that critics were complaining that he had been slow to evacuate Fort Lee before Cornwallis forced his hand, he noted with "satisfaction" that his conduct was "approved by the General" under whom he served. And when nervous politicians in New England asked Washington to send Greene to his home state after the British captured Newport in early December, the commander in chief refused. The general, Greene told Caty with some obvious pride, "would not permit me to go." Benedict Arnold was dispatched to Rhode Island instead of Greene.

Washington's loyalty to Greene was repaid a hundred times over. Grateful that he was not publicly humiliated for the loss of Fort Washington, happy that he had so quickly regained Washington's confidence in this hour of peril, Greene became Washington's earnest champion and stouthearted defender. On December 21, Greene wrote to John Hancock, urging the nation's political leaders to give Washington greater powers over the conduct of the war: the appointment of officers, the recruitment of new regiments, the power to arrest those who refused to sell merchandise to the army. The good New World republicans in Congress had been reluctant to grant what were described as "dictatorial" powers to a military officer, but Greene argued that in Washington, Americans had a general who would not abuse the powers given him in an emergency. Showing off his self-taught erudition, Greene noted that he ordinarily would be "no advocate for the extention of Military Power." It was, however, necessary. He wrote:

> Remember the Policy of the Romans (a People as tenacious
> of their Liberties as any on Earth), when their State was
> invaded they [delegated] full Powers to exert their whole
> Force. The Fate of War is so uncertain, dependant upon so
> many Contingencies. A Day, nay an Hour, is so important in

the Crisis of publick Affairs that it would be folly to wait for
Relief from the deliberative Councils of Legislative Bodies.

He assured Congress that there "never was a man that might be more safely trusted" with such broad powers as Washington. Thanks in part to Greene's argument, Congress approved a measure giving Washington the powers he needed to preserve the army and so the Revolution.

The Americans began moving out of their camp toward the river at two o'clock on Christmas Day. Washington thought he could have everybody into New Jersey by midnight, but as the hours passed along the cold river's banks it became clear that the crossing would take a good deal longer. It was an awful night, with wind and sleet whipping against far too much bare skin, and ice floes interfering with American boats. The men were not completely across until four o'clock, just a couple of hours before sunrise—a potentially disastrous development. Even worse, although Washington and Greene didn't know it, the crossing at Trenton Ferry under Ewing never materialized, and Cadwalader's diversionary landing to the south had been aborted.

Cold and nervous, the Americans assembled on the Jersey side and marched about three miles, and then, after a short break for rest and a fast meal, they split into the two columns for the final five miles to Trenton. Conditions offered no mercy; two soldiers froze to death as they rested along the march. Greene's troops, some of them without shoes, marched in silence through the snow. Conditions remained horrendous, and Greene would later describe the weather as "one of the severest" storms he had ever witnessed. A wind from the northeast blew snow and hail into the soldiers' faces, making them all the more miserable. Progress was far slower than Washington had planned—Greene's column still was two miles from its objective as the sky lightened.

By the time Greene's column neared the town, morning had broken. Hessian pickets deployed in a cooper's house about a half mile outside

Trenton spotted the Americans, and both sides opened fire. The Germans retreated and shouted alarms: *"Der Feind!"* The enemy!

Greene's men raced toward the pickets, overcame them, and moved into position, bringing their artillery into action as the stunned Hessians stumbled out of their barracks and into withering fire. Washington and Greene heard drums and a bugle to the south, near the river; Sullivan's men had arrived on cue. The plan had worked. The Hessians would be squeezed between the two American columns.

The Hessian commander, Colonel Johann Rall, was asleep when the Americans attacked. Still groggy, he ordered his troops to move against Knox's artillery at the head of Queen and King streets, near Greene's position at the north end of town. The cannons put a bloody end to that attempted advance. Sullivan's men were advancing from the south, and a detachment from Greene's column was squeezing in from the west. As the Hessians tried to regroup amid the roar of the cannon and the staccato crack of musket fire, their unit's band struck up martial music to inspire resistance. Rall, in a blue uniform and on horseback, tried to rally his men but was cut down by American fire. A couple of soldiers scurried to his aid, but his wounds were mortal. The Hessians put down their weapons and surrendered.

The Americans, their cause seemingly hopeless only days before, had won an astonishing victory and showed the world and their countrymen that they were not finished. A happy Nathanael Greene accompanied Washington to a church on Queen Street, where Colonel Rall was dying. The two Americans offered some polite, comforting words through an interpreter and then assured Rall that his men, now prisoners, would be treated fairly. Rall was in terrible pain, struck twice in the side, and knew he had not long to live. (He died less than two days later.) After a few minutes, Greene and Washington left Rall to his fate.

It was a glorious day for the country, Washington said. But what next? As the Americans celebrated in the streets of Trenton, Greene urged Washington to pursue the Hessians who had managed to escape and were fleeing toward another enemy garrison some eighteen miles to the south, in Mount Holly. The Americans had emerged from Trenton with barely a scratch, just four wounded (including the commander's cousin, William Washington). Why not strike again?

Washington wisely decided against Greene and in favor of caution. Greene's enthusiasm and inexperience blinded him to the condition of his victorious troops. Many were drunk or feeling no pain (for a change) after relieving the Hessians of their rum. They also were exhausted after hours of hard marching in terrible conditions.

The clinching argument against pursuit was less tangible but critical all the same, for it would provide Greene with an invaluable lesson in strategy. Washington understood that he had won a notable victory, and in a single, bold stroke he had improved the morale of his men and the country. He risked that victory if he pushed too hard.

So the Americans withdrew from Trenton, marched back to McKonkey's Ferry, and crossed the Delaware again. But they had only two days to rest, for they soon were on the march again, crossing the Delaware for a third time on December 30, returning to Trenton to await another chance to attack the enemy. Conditions during this third crossing were even worse than on Christmas Day, but in one respect, the journey was easier, for there were fewer troops to move. Hundreds were leaving as their enlistments expired.

Greene was both apprehensive and optimistic as he faced, for the second time, the possibility that the army might dissolve. After joining Washington in New Jersey, Greene took time to write to Caty. "This is an important period to America, big with great events. God only knows what will be the issue of this Campaign, but everything wears a much bigger prospect than they have for some weeks past."

Another issue, however, weighed heavily on his mind. Caty would soon give birth, and although her letters to him have not been preserved, it's not hard to see that she was troubled. Her husband was at war, and she was about to have their second child. She was completely dependent on her husband's family in Rhode Island, and relations between Caty and some members of the Greene family were less than ideal. Greene did his best to provide his wife with some comfort, based on an unrealistic prospect. "Should we get possession of the Jerseys perhaps I may get liberty to come and see you. I pity your situation exceedingly. Your distress and anxiety must be very great. . . . By the blessing of God I hope to meet again in the pleasures of wedlock."

There was no chance that Greene would receive liberty to return to Caty anytime soon. The bulk of the Continental army had but a few hours of service remaining. Men without shoes, whose bloody feet had traced a red trail through the snows of New Jersey, had had enough of war and sacrifice. One soldier recalled that the troops "had their hearts fixed on home and the comforts of the domestic circle."

George Washington, ordinarily reserved and distant, appointed himself to the position of the Continental army's chief recruiting officer. After asking for volunteers to stay past their expiration date and finding few takers, he chose to make a speech—a sure sign of his desperation, for he avoided such demonstrations. On horseback, where he displayed such an impressive sense of command, he spoke personally to several regiments whose men were about to go home. They gathered in the snow they had become all too familiar with, men in ragged, pathetic clothing, men who were dreaming of a warm fireside, civilian clothes, and the comfort of friends and family. Continued service promised more deprivation, more violence, more suffering. They could hardly be blamed for staying put when a drumroll summoned volunteers.

Washington's voice now broke the silence. The men, most of them anyway, had never witnessed this side of their legendary commander; indeed, few armies in the world would have heard their commander in chief address them as fellow countrymen, as equals. "My brave fellows," he said to a unit from Pennsylvania, "you have done all I asked you to do, and more than could be reasonably expected; but your country is at stake. . . . You have worn yourselves out with fatigues and hardships, but we know not how to spare you."

With the new powers Congress had given him just days before, Washington unilaterally offered soldiers who reenlisted a bounty of ten dollars—almost double their monthly pay of six dollars. His eloquence or his generosity, or both, had the intended effect. "God Almighty [inclined] their hearts to listen to the proposal and they engaged anew; happy for America," Greene wrote. More than three thousand troops remained with the army, while just over twenty-five hundred left. Troops from New England were conspicuous among the volunteers, which gladdened Greene's heart. "This is the greatest evidence of NE virtue I ever saw," he told Rhode Island governor Nicholas Cooke. "Let it be remembered to their eternal honor."

The crisis was averted.

In Washington's new Continental army, Greene was given command of a division consisting of about fourteen hundred soldiers in four brigades. But many of those units were far below their fighting strength. Lord Stirling's brigade, for example, had no more than a few dozen men. Militia units, emboldened by the daring assault on Trenton, helped fill in some of the gaps.

On January 1, this new army bade farewell to departing comrades, some ill and some simply sick of war, and took up defensive positions outside Trenton. That very day, young Lord Cornwallis arrived in Princeton, just twelve miles from the American position. He had been scheduled to sail home from New York to attend to his ailing wife, but General Howe canceled his leave after the unexpected American victory at Trenton. Cornwallis was given eight thousand men and the assignment of crushing the Americans on the banks of the Delaware. Greene had some inkling that the British were eager to make amends for Trenton. On New Year's Day, he delivered a warning to the head of the Pennsylvania militia, John Cadwalader: "[We] have great reason to Apprehend the Enemy are in motion, and I Apprehend they are meditating an attack."

They were more than mediating. Leaving behind some twelve hundred men to guard Princeton, Cornwallis led a force of seven thousand troops out of the small college town before dawn on a dreary, wet January 2. Their progress was slow as they slogged through mud, and they did not move in secret. Washington had placed skirmishers along the road leading from Princeton to Trenton. When word reached the American camp that Cornwallis was advancing, Greene quickly moved up to reinforce the forward defenses. As a unit from Rhode Island marched to meet the enemy, Greene shouted: "Push on, boys! Push on!" The skirmishers successfully delayed Cornwallis's arrival until sunset.

More than five thousand Americans were deployed south of the city on ridges along the banks of Assunpink Creek, with Greene's division on the left. They had no line of retreat, for behind them was the Delaware River. The British were just across the creek, a few hundred yards from the American lines. With a purposeful march and bold action, Lord Cornwallis had Washington trapped, and he knew it. So did some of the American troops, who understood that they were in an untenable position. "It appeared to me that our army was in the most desperate situation I had ever known it," wrote one soldier. If the Americans were defeated, nothing would stop Cornwallis from marching on Philadelphia.

Though his aides advised him to press forward immediately, Cornwallis decided that he had exhibited enough boldness for one day. Washington had nowhere to go; victory could wait until morning. Then, Cornwallis promised, the "old fox" would be his.

Across the creek, Greene joined other officers for a conference with Washington. Their choices were gloomy indeed. They could make a run for it south along the Delaware River, but that would expose Philadelphia to an attack. Somebody—accounts disagree on precisely who it was—suggested an audacious alternative: a quick march along a little-used road to Princeton, which, based on the size of Cornwallis's assault force, was likely to be lightly defended. From there, the Americans could march on the vital British supply center at New Brunswick, adding glories to glory.

The Americans seized on the bold—and only—alternative to disaster. Orders went out in the dark of night: prepare to march.

Amid whispered commands and muffled grumbling, the Americans moved out after midnight, with good fortune as their escort. The afternoon had been mild and rainy, which had stymied Cornwallis as he marched along the main road. Now, as the Americans made the opposite journey along the less-traveled Quaker Road in much colder weather, the mud froze, making the march somewhat easier than Cornwallis's ordeal. But only somewhat. Ice and frozen earth made the journey treacherous in spots, causing soldiers and animals to slip and fall. The column stopped and started for no apparent reason, like a particularly obstreperous mule. And when the march ground to a halt, already exhausted soldiers fell asleep standing up.

Greene and Washington marched through the darkness with the main American force. When they were just two miles outside of town, a small detachment under General Mercer moved to the left to secure the main road. Greene veered slightly to the right, onto the back road to Princeton. The march took him past a Quaker meetinghouse, near a stand of trees and overlooking a brook. Did the sight of the austere meetinghouse inspire a memory, however fleeting, of his Rhode Island childhood, and the long Sundays spent on wooden benches, listening to his father's stern admonitions? It's impossible to know. But his letters made clear his frustrations with the Quakers he encountered on both sides of the Delaware. He complained that most Quakers were, in essence, Tories by another name, in part because they refused to accept the Continental dollar as currency. "This line of conduct," he wrote, "cannot fail of drawing down the resentment of the People upon them."

Washington and Greene were marching near the rear of the American column at about eight o'clock when a British unit marching toward Trenton spotted the rebel columns. Mercer's detachment moved toward the British, who had assumed defensive positions; after furious fighting during which Mercer was fatally wounded, the Americans began falling back. Falling back, that is, until Greene and Washington charged forward with the bulk of the army. The Americans re-formed and moved toward the enemy; a volley rang out from both sides, with Washington in the middle. An American officer, Edward Fitzgerald, covered his eyes. Finally, he looked up to find the commander in chief still in the saddle, still urging his men on. "The day," Washington said, "is our own."

The Americans resumed their march on Princeton, where the British force was severely outnumbered. Many fled as the Americans approached, but a few hundred sought refuge in Nassau Hall. They gave up when a young officer named Alexander Hamilton began shelling the building.

The audacious gamble at Trenton had been matched by an equally daring victory at Princeton. Though he was and would remain a stern critic of the militia, Greene singled them out for praise. "Great credit is due to the Philadelphia Militia . . . who behaved exceeding well considering they were never in action before," he wrote. News of the rebel triumphs spread throughout the capitals of Europe, where princes and field marshals spoke in glowing, astonished tones of the rebel American army. "The achievements of Washington and his little band of compatriots between the 25th of December and the 4th of January, a space of 10 days, were the most brilliant of any recorded in the history of military achievements," wrote Frederick the Great, the Prussian military leader whose earlier writings had inspired a young Quaker boy named Nathanael Greene to put on a soldier's uniform.

The Americans lost only about thirty-five men, although one of them was the much admired General Mercer. British losses were about a hundred dead and three hundred wounded or captured. Greene was ordered to take a detachment north in pursuit of British troops fleeing Princeton, but the chase was called off. Rather than move on New Brunswick, Washington decided to march his men to Morristown, a small New Jersey town of some three hundred people and a fine, English-style village green. Months before, when he was in command of Forts Lee and Washington, Greene had sent small detachments near Morristown to secure the area. Now, thanks to Greene's foresight, Morristown and its vicinity would provide the exhausted but victorious American army with a necessary respite.

Though he would not have predicted it as recently as November, Nathanael Greene began the new year of 1777 a happy man. His loyal and effective service at Washington's side in the two battles, not to mention through the long march through New Jersey, had expunged the memory of the lost forts on the Hudson River. When Washington's adjutant, Joseph Reed, left the service to pursue a political career in Pennsylvania, Greene filled in for several weeks, assisting the commander in chief with paperwork and other chores. The long winter hours they spent together in headquarters, which was a former tavern on the edge of the village green, strengthened the bond between the two men, much to Greene's delight. His regard for Washington bordered on worshipful, and in a letter to Caty on January 20, he seemed like a schoolboy proud to have won the approval of his teacher: "I am exceeding happy in the full confidence of his Excellency General Washington, and I found [that confidence] to increase every hour, the more [difficult] and distressing our affairs grew. But thanks be to God they now are in a much better train but by no means as agreeable as I could wish."

His living conditions in Morristown certainly were agreeable enough. He was installed in the home of a man named Hoffman, whom he described as a "very good-natured, doubtful gentleman." The gentleman's doubts, as coincidence would have it, concerned religious dogma, which mortified his wife—"a great lover of the clergy"—but delighted Greene, whose own doubts were of long standing. He told Caty, "Major Clarke, one of my aides-de-camp, is eternally perplexing [Mrs. Hoffman] with doubts and difficulties, by dark hints and oblique insinuations respecting the purity of manners and principles of the Church of England."

Still, as pleasant as life with the Hoffmans (and with Washington) might be, Greene longed to be with his pregnant wife. She had been out of touch for some time, prompting a mild scolding. "I am unhappy in not hearing from you, not a line has come to hand for months past," he wrote. He again told Caty that he might be able to arrange a leave, if the enemy cooperated by fleeing New Jersey: "I wish to get the Enemy out of the Jerseys that I may get Liberty to come Home."

Reveling in the victories in Trenton and Princeton, Greene still believed the Americans could mount a winter offensive to reclaim the whole of New Jersey. He told his brother Christopher that he expected to be in battle again soon, perhaps in an attack on the British depot in New Brunswick. If successful, the assault surely would "get the Enemy out of the Jerseys," as he told Caty. It would also further discourage the considerable loyalist community of New Jersey, whose allegiance to the Crown had softened thanks to outrages committed against civilians—Tory and patriot alike—by British soldiers and Hessian mercenaries. Furious civilians "breath nothing but revenge" against the enemy, Greene reported in early January. The enemy's "ravages in the Jerseys exceeds all description. Many hundred women ravished," he wrote.

The plan to attack New Brunswick, however, soon was abandoned as Washington, Greene, and the other American generals turned their attention to rebuilding their army for the second time. Those soldiers who agreed to serve an extra six weeks after the Battle of Trenton now were marking time until they could go home, and some of them had no intention of waiting for the magical day. They deserted in droves—the British estimated that three thousand Americans deserted in the first few months of 1777. That figure probably was too high, but there was no denying that the American army was in the midst of yet another manpower crisis. Only about three thousand soldiers remained in camp; even worse, there were but a thousand regular Continental soldiers—the rest were militia. And those lonely soldiers suffered through shortages of food and other supplies, and soon a far worse affliction, disease. In late February, Greene and the division he commanded moved from Morristown to Basking Ridge, some ten miles south of Washington's headquarters. There, he told Washington, he found that "Small Pox prevails amongst the Troops." Greene urged the risky but necessary step of a mass innoculation of the army, and Washington agreed. The innoculations worked wonders, annihiliating the disease within a matter of months. The army's recruiting efforts, however, were not nearly as successful.

If the British had realized how painfully weak the Americans were during the winter of 1777, they could have ended the rebellion with an aggressive attack on Morristown. But such an assault was out of the question. General Howe remained understandably shaken after the losses in Trenton and Princeton, and so chose prudence over boldness. Besides, he was having so much fun in New York, a city whose Tories were delighted to play host to the distinguished general.

Though the campaign season ended with Washington's decision not to attack New Brunswick, neither side hibernated much while in winter quarters. The British and particularly the Hessians near present-day Perth Amboy and New Brunswick continued to terrorize civilians in New Jersey. In mid-February, Greene heard a report that British troops had murdered "two of the Inhabitants . . . because they did not assist them with their Waggons to carry off their dead. One they shot through the Head, the other they kild with a Bayonet." Those dead British soldiers heaped on wagons offered mute testimony to the American strategy of harassing the enemy's vital foraging parties—groups of soldiers sent out into the countryside in search of food and supplies. A loyalist judge in New York, Thomas Jones, reported that not "a stick of wood, a spear of grass, or a kernel of corn could the troops in New Jersey procure without fighting for it. . . . Every foraging party was attacked."

Some of these small engagements did not lack for ferocity. One, in mid-April when the armies still were in winter quarters, broke out when Cornwallis attacked an American detachment under General Benjamin Lincoln in Bound Brook, north of New Brunswick. Greene raced from his post in Basking Ridge to Bound Brook, but all was quiet by the time he arrived. He summed up the ebb and flow of the battle by noting, with some humor, that he had had dinner that night in the home of a local merchant named Van Horne. Earlier in the day, in the same house, Van Horne had shared his breakfast with General Cornwallis. "This," Greene wrote, "is the State of the War." It was also the state of their burgeoning relationship, these two very different men thrown together by circumstance and destined to shadow each other for the rest of the war.

According to a letter among the papers of General Anthony Wayne, Greene was involved in a major skirmish on February 8 a few miles west of New Brunswick. An eyewitness to the fighting, a soldier named Craig, told Wayne that a detachment of about five hundred Americans under Greene ambushed a British patrol or foraging party, killing three hundred. That estimate was impossibly high, and there is no mention of the skirmish among Greene's own letters. It's possible, though, that a letter recounting the ambush was lost.

———

Most of Greene's work during the gray New Jersey winter was devoted to the prosaic tasks of pushing paper, a task he loathed, and supervising the health and well-being of his men and their horses. His desk was filled with reports from foraging parties who prowled the countryside in search of food for man and beast, and from skirmishing parties he deployed "not so much for the annoyance of the Enemy, as to get them acquainted with the Ground and to keep them employed." After long days spent in his headquarters in the village of Basking Ridge, candles by his desk brightening the winter darkness, he retired each evening to a room in the home of his friend Lord Stirling, who owned a fine mansion surrounded by a magnificent estate, kept neat and lovely thanks to the hard work of Lord Stirling's slaves.

He also devoted time and energy to army politics, keeping a careful watch over who was promoted to what rank and making sure that his friends received justice. Relations between the army and Congress and state legislatures were tense that winter over such issues as recruitment, promotions, and military strategy. Congress passed a resolution calling on Washington to "totally . . . subdue" the British "before they are reinforced." The commander in chief stewed over this presumptious and utterly unrealistic request and replied tersely, "Could I accomplish the important objects so eagerly wished by Congress, I should be happy indeed." He included with his letter a roster of the army, showing that he had but three thousand men to "subdue" the British.

Greene's turn to be outraged came when he heard a report, which turned out to be false, that Rhode Island was recruiting men for its militia instead of raising new regiments for the Continental army. Greene dispatched an angry letter to Rhode Island governor Cooke that testified to his vision of a strong American union guided by national, rather than regional, interests. "There is not a State upon the Continent whose interest and happiness depends so much on a union with the others as yours," he lectured Cooke. "You are the most exposed and the least capable of making a separate defence, consequently 'tis your interest to cultivate every measure that may tend to form the union of strength. . . . Where is the State that's able to withstand the Enemies collective force?"

With political machinations very much on his mind as winter dragged on, Greene took advantage of the lull in combat to renew his correspondence with John Adams. While the letter he wrote to Adams mostly concerned itself with negotiations between the British and American officials over the release of General Charles Lee, who had been taken prisoner by the British, Greene used the occasion to show off his knowledge of military history, hoping either to impress or perhaps even to intimidate the better-educated Adams. In a flourish that spoke more to Greene's profound insecurity than his self-taught erudition, he told Adams:

> I am sensible you have not the most exalted oppinion of your
> Generals. Who is in fault? Every one would wish to be an
> Epaminondas, Sertorius or Turenne if they could, but if
> Nature has refused to crown the sons of America with such
> choice Gifts, who is to blame, either she or we? We cannot be
> blameable only as we stand in the way of better men.

Epaminondas was an ancient Greek general; Sertorius, an ancient Roman; and Turenne, a French general from the seventeenth century. Greene, very much aware that he lacked the formal education of his colleagues and peers, went out of his way to show the Harvard-educated Adams that he had read a book or two in his day. In his reply, Adams upped the intellectual ante by saying that he certainly did not expect to find the likes of Epaminondas in the American army because, after all, "in the opinion of Dr. Swift [the famed Irish writer] all the Ages of the World have produced just Six such Characters, which makes the Chances much against our seeing any such." It's unlikely Adams knew that Swift was one of Greene's favorite authors.

The two also sparred, again, over congressional control of promotions. Congress had recently promoted five brigadier generals to the post of major general and had named ten new brigadiers. Greene told Adams,

"Your late Promotions will give great disgust to many." One of those disgusted officers was an ambitious brigadier named Benedict Arnold of Connecticut, who was denied a promotion to major general because his small state already had two such officers. Adams countered by reminding Greene that the "officers of the Army ought to consider that the Rank, the Dignity, and the Rights of whole States are of more Importance than this Point of Honour, more indeed than the Solid Glory of any particular officer." While Adams's point was undeniable, it also was unrealistic. Promotions would continue to be a sore point in the American army. The politics of promotions eventually led to Arnold's infamous desertion and attempted betrayal of West Point in 1780.

In late March, Washington asked Greene to go to Philadelphia to consult with members of Congress personally, another sign of the commander in chief's confidence in the Rhode Islander. Washington explained to Congress why he had chosen Greene: "[because he] is so much in my confidence, so intimately acquainted with my ideas, with our strength and our weaknesses, with everything respecting the army." Washington hastened to point out that he could "ill spare so useful an officer at this time." But spare him he did.

Part of Greene's assignment was to smooth over some of the resentments that had developed over the winter between the two arms—political and military—of the Revolution. But he also had more specific duties: Washington told him "to impress strongly upon Congress . . . the necessity of keeping the Paymaster regularly supplied with the article of Cash; without it, every thing moves slowly on, and many and great disadvantages flow from the want of it."

Greene had never been in Philadelphia before, nor had he met very many members of Congress. He spent two hours in front of the entire body, answering questions about a range of topics, including the never-ending talks about arranging a prisoner exchange aimed at freeing General Lee from captivity in New York. He then spent two evenings in the company of a committee of congressional delegates, including Samuel Adams. This firsthand view of politics in action was not to his taste. "There is so much deliberation and waste of time in the execution of business before this assembly that my patience is almost exhausted," he told Washington, who must have allowed himself a brief smile of recognition. The image of the political leaders spending their days debating while his soldiers were hungry, tired, and all too few in number remained with Greene. Several weeks later, he complained that "Congress have so many of those talking Gentlemen among them that they tired themselves and every body else with their long, laboured speeching that is calculated more to display their own talents than promote the publick interest."

To break up the monotony of politics during his short stay in Philadelphia, Greene allowed himself a tour of the capital's fortifications; he was alarmed to find them "insufficient." More satisfying was the sight of the city's young women. When he returned to Morristown on March 30, he dashed off a letter to his wife, reminding her that it had been "eight long months" since he "tasted the pleasures of domestick felicity." To further drive home the point, he added: "The young ladies of Philadelphia appear angelick. A few months Seperation more will put my virtue to a new tryal. If you don't wish to put my resolution to the torture, bless me with your company; that is, providing your health and other circumstances favors my wishes." While well-intentioned, it was not the most sensitive letter a husband could send to a wife, particularly a wife who, though Greene didn't know it, had given birth just a couple of days earlier. Greene received the good news soon afterward: he was the father of a baby girl. He and Caty named her Martha Washington Greene.

Pleased though he was by this "second pledge of conjugal affection," Greene couldn't erase the memory of those "angelick" young women in Philadelphia. In a letter congratulating Caty on the birth of Martha, Greene casually mentioned that he once again was staying in Lord Stirling's house, in the company of three young women: the daughters of Stirling and of New Jersey governor William Livingston. He felt duty-bound to inform Caty that these young women were of "distinguished merit: Sensible, polite and easy." Being in their presence made him long for Caty all the more: "I never wisht more ardently to see you in my life than now. The hours grow tedious and the heart impatient. Fortune is rather unfriendly to afford but a few months enjoyment for several years Marriage. However, I hope fortune has something better in store."

It did, but not for several months and not until after Caty recovered from a frightening bout of pneumonia, which led to weeks of bedrest. None of Greene's family members saw fit to inform him of his wife's condition, leading him to conclude that she was ignoring his letters.

The coming of spring brought mystery. What were the intentions of General Howe, now that the snow and ice had been replaced by budding trees and green grass? Through winter, Nathanael Greene had insisted that the British would be drawn, inevitably, to Philadelphia. They had been so close to the capital at the end of 1776, so close that they sent Congress fleeing to Baltimore. They still had two posts in New Jersey, New Brunswick and Perth Amboy. Moving troops from New York, perhaps across Staten Island, to join the New Jersey garrisons for a march toward the rebel capital seemed like a logical move.

Howe was not without other options, however, as the Americans knew all too well. The Hudson River remained a tantalizing prize. A joint offensive from Canada and New York City retained its potential to split the states in half and allow the British to isolate New England while moving against the mid-Atlantic region.

The Americans had little choice but to wait upon events. Although Greene, at Washington's request, devised a plan for an attack on New Brunswick, he actually voted against implementing it (as did every other general) during a council of war with Washington on May 2, 1777. The generals agreed that they could not afford to risk an attack against a well-fortified position. While recruitment had improved during the winter, increasing Washington's troop strength by early spring to slightly more than seven thousand fit for duty, they still were not strong enough for offensive action. So the Americans remained in New Jersey even as the air grew warmer and the days longer. Greene couldn't understand why the enemy remained listless, just as he couldn't understand why so few of his fellow countrymen were willing to defend their infant nation. "It is to be regretted," he said, "that the cause of freedom rests upon the shoulders of so few." To Caty, he wrote of British delay and American reluctance.

> What has kept them in their Quarters we can't imagine. We
> have got together a small force although by no means equal to
> our expectations. . . . O that the Americans were but Spirited
> and resolute! How easy the attempt to rout these
> miscreants. . . . I am sure America will be Victorious finally,
> but her sufferings for want of Union and publick Spirit may
> be great first.

It was Caty's sufferings, however, that commanded his attention through the spring. He finally learned how sick his wife was in a letter, which has been lost, from Caty herself. On May 3, he wrote:

> I was almost thunderstruck at the [receipt] of your letter.
> How different its contents from my wishes: a lingering
> disorder of five Weeks . . . and from the present symptoms a
> confinement of two months longer. Heaven preserve you and
> bless you with patience and fortitude to support yourself
> under the cruel misfortune. . . . Oh that I had but wings to
> fly to your relief. The healing balm should not be wanting to
> mitigate your pain.

Greene feared that her illness would keep her away from camp until the start of the campaign season, which would put off a reunion until winter, eight months away. He applied a little tenderness—"my Heart mourns the Absence of its counterpart"—and, just for good measure, he tried to arouse a little jealousy. He again mentioned the daughters of Lord Stirling and Governor Livingston, who, as Caty didn't need to be reminded, shared Lord Stirling's mansion with the general. Greene told Caty, "You never was among a more agreeable set of young Ladies in your life."

In mid-May, Greene rode with Knox and several other officers from

Morristown to Peekskill, New York, to examine American defenses along the Hudson River south of West Point. He had a hard time keeping his mind on the task at hand—Caty, or more to the point, Caty's absence, continued to weigh on his mind. After the generals pronounced their dissatisfaction with the river's defenses and recommended that they be made stronger, Greene set out for Morristown. He wasn't riding long before he fell from his horse, slicing open his lip and otherwise bruising himself. In that condition, he rode to the New Jersey home of a friend, Abraham Lott, a patriot merchant. There, he heard that Caty had arrived in Morristown. He could hardly believe it! "O, how my heart lept with joy!" he later recalled. Bruised and battered, he got back on his horse and rode to Morristown, only to discover no trace of Caty. He was the victim of faulty intelligence; his wife, in fact, still was home in Rhode Island.

He wrote to her twice the following day, May 20, and told her once again how much he missed her. With soft words and sweet language, he made it clear he wanted desperately to see her, but only if she felt she was well enough for the journey. If she was ready for camp, well, she ought to treat herself to new clothes for the occasion. And if she wanted something in Boston, why, she ought to write to Lucy Knox, who would be happy to send the items to camp.

Had Greene stopped there, Caty no doubt would have been charmed back to full health, especially after reading the line about the new clothes. But Greene could not help himself; he was self-conscious about not only his own lack of education but Caty's as well. Lucy Knox was a formidable figure, and not simply because she was almost as big as her prodigious husband. Greene told Caty: "But remember when you write to Mrs. Knox you write to a good scholar; therefore mind and spell well. You are defective in this matter, my love, a little attention will soon correct it. . . . People are often laught at for not spelling well but never for not writeing well."

For Nathanael Greene, few things in life were more dreadful than the prospect of being laughed at. Whether Caty was similarly insecure at this stage in her life is uncertain. But her husband's admonition may not have served history well; Caty's letters to Nathanael, apparently filled with even more spelling errors than her husband's, have never been found. She may have seen to it that nobody would laugh at her spelling.

At the time, however, Greene's willingness to pay for a new wardrobe outweighed his criticism of her spelling. She arrived in his new camp in Middlebrook in June, dressed no doubt in something fine and new, and her husband reacquainted himself with the "pleasures of domestick felicity."

Caty Greene's arrival coincided with a first-class row between the Continental army and Congress, a nasty, hasty, ego-driven, and ultimately foolish argument that cost Nathanael Greene his friendship with John Adams and nearly cost him his career.

Tension between the Revolution's military and political leaders was hardly new, but by late spring, relations were beginning to become even more disagreeable. Greene did nothing to help matters when he sent an undeservedly blunt letter to Adams on May 29 protesting rumors that gout-ridden General Philip Schuyler of New York was about to be elected president of Congress while still holding his commission in the army. That information turned out to be false—Schuyler, who was a delegate to Congress while serving as a general, was not elected president— but Greene's letter showed how passionately he believed in the separation of politics and the military. Not for the first time, however, his passion was inflamed by bad information, and he did not have the patience or the wisdom to check his facts before launching a misdirected tirade. To Adams, he wrote:

> No free people ought to admit to a junction of the Civil and
> the Military; and no men of good Principles, with virtuous
> intention, would ask it or ever accept . . . such an
> appointment. . . . I have no objections to General Schuyler as
> a General, neither have I to his being President of the
> Congress if he is thought to be the most suitable person for

that important post. But he must cease to be a General before he commences [to be] a member of Congress.

Adams certainly did not need such a lecture, as he politely assured Greene several days later. He, too, thought it was "utterly improper" for General Schuyler to serve in Congress, never mind become its president. Nevertheless, Schuyler resigned neither his commission nor his seat in Congress. Would that he had. Several months later, he was removed from command of the army's Northern Department after he bungled the defense of Fort Ticonderoga.

More troublesome was another complaint. A French military officer, Phillippe Tronson du Coudray, had received a commission to serve as a major general in charge of artillery for the Continental army. An American agent in France, Silas Deane, had arranged for du Coudray's appointment. Greene, protective of his allies as ever, saw du Coudray not only as an unreliable outsider but as a rival to his friend Henry Knox, the army's current commander of artillery. In the same letter to Adams, Greene condemned the "impropriety of putting a [foreigner] at the head of such a Department" and noted that such a move "will deprive the Army of a most valuable Officer," meaning, of course, Knox. Once again, Adams was on Greene's side, echoing his concern about the "danger of entrusting so many important Commands to foreigners" and assuring Greene that du Coudray would have "few advocates" in Congress.

Greene, ever watchful for the slightest sign of disrespect, was not satisfied. He told his brother Jacob, "Congress and I do not agree in politics; they are introducing a great many foreigners." He thought such officers would be far more susceptible to "British gold," never anticipating, of course, the treachery of his native-born friend Benedict Arnold.

Greene's grumbling turned to a piercing cry of rage when he learned that du Coudray's commission had taken effect on August 1, 1776. That meant the Frenchman would be senior to Greene, who had been promoted to major general on August 9, 1776.

Nathanael Greene, the man who nearly quit the Kentish Guards when soldiers whispered about his limp, was not about to suffer such a slight in silence. And there was no question in his mind that the du Coudray appointment was, in fact, a deliberate personal slight. He instantly dispatched a message to John Hancock, the president of the Continental Congress.

> A report is circulating here at Camp that Monsieur de
> Coudray, a French Gentleman, is appointed a Major General
> in the service of the United States, his rank to commence
> from the first of last August. If the report be true it will lay
> me under the necessity of resigning my Commission as his
> appointment supercedes me in command. I beg you'll
> acquaint me with respect to the truth of the report, and if
> true inclose me a permit to retire.

Greene was not alone in his rage. In separate letters that indicated close collaboration, Generals Henry Knox and John Sullivan also vowed to resign. The three generals apparently did not consult their commander in chief before issuing their threats, which made matters even worse.

The members of Congress were furious. In fact, they had not approved du Coudray's appointment, and as Adams already had indicated, many shared Greene's belief that a foreign officer should not be given such a high-level command. The deal had been struck between Silas Deane, America's slippery agent in Paris, and du Coudray, but Adams insisted that Congress believed Deane had overstepped his authority in offering the commission. Deane wasn't much of one for rules anyway. He saw the war, and the secrets he knew, as an opportunity to make money, and so intent was he on this pursuit that he never realized that his business partner, George Bancroft, was a British spy.

Even though Congress and Greene essentially agreed that the du Coudray appointment was inappropriate, months of suppressed tension between the politicians and the generals exploded in Philadelphia. On

July 7, Congress passed an angry resolution directing Washington to tell Greene, Knox, and Sullivan that their letters were "an invasion of the liberties of the people," indicating "a want of confidence in the justice of Congress." The politicians demanded that the three generals "make proper acknowledgments" for their "dangerous" interference with congressional powers. The scolding concluded with an invitation to Greene, Knox, and Sullivan to make good on their threats: "[If] any of those officers are unwilling to serve their country under the authority of Congress, they shall be at liberty to resign their commissions and retire." Adams hoped the generals would take Congress up on the offer, without pausing to consider what such a loss would mean for the struggling army. What's more, this guardian of republican principles said that if he had his way, there would be "a new election of general officers annually." A noble sentiment, no doubt, but perhaps not the most efficient way to win a war.

Adams then wrote a long, sad, and angry letter to his occasional correspondent from Rhode Island. "I never before took hold of a Pen to write to my Friend General Greene without pleasure, but I think myself obliged to do so now upon a Subject that gives me a great deal of Pain," Adams wrote. He told Greene that Congress had not approved the contract between du Coudray and Deane, and that, like Greene himself, Congress was perplexed that such an offer was made to a foreign officer. But now, he wrote, it "is impossible for Congress even to determine that Deane had no authority to make the Bargain without exposing themselves to the Reflection that their own officers intimidated them into it."

Adams properly pointed out that Greene could have written a private letter to himself or any other member of Congress to express his concerns, instead of sending a public letter threatening resignation. Greene indeed was guilty of Adams's charge of "Rashness, Passion and even Wantonness in this Proceeding." Adams urged Greene to apologize and declare publicly that he had full confidence in Congress. Otherwise, he said, "I think you ought to leave the service."

Greene's reaction to this dressing-down can be deduced by simply noting that he did not write again to Adams until 1782. Du Coudray eventually entered the Continental army as a captain and, just two months after the controversy, drowned in the Schuylkill River in Pennsylvania.

As Greene, Knox, and Sullivan issued their threats, the American army remained hostage to the unknowable intentions of His Lordship, General William Howe. Greene remained watchful for a move on Philadelphia. When he heard the British were pulling out of Amboy, he alerted Sullivan, posted in Princeton, that the "Phylistines are upon thee, Samson. Take care of thyself." In fact, they made no move toward the capital.

In early July, American troops in northern New York evacuated Fort Ticonderoga rather than fight British forces moving south from Canada under General John Burgoyne. It was a humiliating defeat and led to the dismissal of Generals Schuyler and Arthur St. Clair from command of the Northern Department. Greene thought he was the obvious choice to replace Schuyler or St. Clair. "I can plainly see the General wants me to go but is unwilling to part with me," Greene told his wife, who was staying with Abraham Lott in his mansion near Morristown. Greene told Caty that he was prepared to go if ordered, but preferred not to because the transfer would separate them once again. Instead of Greene, Horatio Gates and Benedict Arnold were sent north.

Rumors and speculation led Washington to march, countermarch, and march again through New Jersey as the Americans tried to anticipate either a British expedition up the Hudson River or an all-out assault on Philadelphia. Convinced in early August that the capital was, in fact, Howe's target, Washington marched the army toward Pennsylvania. Greene understood the symbolism of Philadelphia but questioned the strategy. Philadelphia, he wrote, "must be perserved at all events . . . but in my opinion [it] is an object of far less importance than the [Hudson] River."

General Howe did not agree. He set sail from New York for the capital but confounded the Americans by sailing into Chesapeake Bay and landing at Head of Elk for an overland march toward Philadelphia from the south. Finally, with summer nearly over, the campaign season of 1777 would begin.

On August 24, the Continental army marched through Philadelphia. Greene, having left Caty in New Jersey with Abraham Lott, marched with the division he commanded, made up of two brigades under the command of Generals John Muhlenberg and George Weedon. It took two hours for the army's eleven thousand soldiers to parade past citizens and politicians alike.

Greene didn't stop marching until he reached Wilmington, Delaware, where he monitored the British landing in Maryland. He was eager for the fight he knew would come soon. "I am in hopes Mr. How will give us a little time to collect," he wrote, "and then we don't care how soon he begins the frolick."

Mr. Howe gave the Americans two weeks. The "frolick" followed.

7 | The Cries of the People

Though he could be petulant and sensitive, Nathanael Greene also was an optimist. And that trait, along with his unquestioned loyalty and unrelenting competence, endeared him to George Washington. It was Greene who was eager to support Washington's plan to assail Boston in 1775 when other generals gravely shook their heads and grumbled their objections. It was Greene who was determined to learn from his mistakes—like Fort Washington—rather than excuse them or blame them on somebody else. And now, as the American army prepared to meet the British as they moved north from Maryland, it was Greene who declared that the troops were in "good health and high Spirits," prepared to give General Howe "a deadly wound." Those were the sentiments Washington needed to hear. He had had his fill of dire predictions and gloomy assessments.

As the Americans set up camp in Wilmington in early September, Greene and Washington and their aides rode forward to have a look at the enemy landing force miles away. Joining them was a young, enthusiastic teenager from France with the unwieldy name Marie Joseph Paul Yves Roch Gilbert du Motier. He became better known by his title, the marquis de Lafayette. Congress had given him another title, that of major general in the Continental army.

Greene already had made it quite clear what he thought of foreign officers, particularly those with grand titles like major general. The tensions over the du Coudray affair had cost Greene his friendship with John Adams and other allies in Congress. Yet he uttered not a word of protest when the teenage Lafayette showed up in Washington's camp—as a general! Perhaps Greene believed now was not the time to raise objections to yet another foreign officer. Or perhaps he, like Washington, simply was taken with the young Frenchman's idealism, enthusiasm, and utter lack of guile. It no doubt helped that Lafayette deferred to Greene, treating him as a mentor rather than as a rival for Washington's attention.

Washington, Greene, and Lafayette rode to within two miles of the British lines, but they learned little from their mission. They decided to head back to Wilmington, taking careful note of the terrain between the two camps. The coming battle might well be fought on this unfamiliar ground, so the generals examined its hills, valleys, ravines, and other natural features. While they were absorbed in their inspection, the sky darkened, the winds began to blow, and a storm settled in, forcing them to take shelter in a private farmhouse. There, far from the American lines, Washington, Greene, Lafayette, and a small guard were forced to spend the night—as lightning streaked the sky—hoping no British scouts would stumble upon them.

After a restless sleep, they returned to Wilmington. Washington immediately gave Greene the task of scouting the countryside for a good defensive position from which to challenge Howe. Greene spent hours in the saddle through the first week in September, reconnoitering, ordering stores to be moved away from the enemy's anticipated line of march, and trying to keep his temper as he came upon local citizens, some of them Quakers, who clearly and sometimes openly supported the British. The pacifist Quakers, clinging to the dogma that had stunted his intellectual development and deprived him of the education he so sorely missed, especially infuriated him. It was bad enough that they refused to fight for their country; worse, they supported their country's oppressor. That was unforgivable. Summoning the frustrations of his youth, he fiercely condemned the "villinous Quakers" who, he said, were "employed . . . to serve the enemy." Some Quakers were placed under arrest. Greene thought more should be.

Furious as he was with his coreligionists, his heart went out to ordinary citizens, many of them supporters of neither army, whose lives became intertwined with the war despite their neutrality. He passed them as they fled the no-man's-land between the two armies—dozens of families fleeing their homes and farms, wearily traveling the back roads in search of refuge from war and looting. To Caty, he wrote: "Here are some of the most distressing scenes immaginable. The Inhabitants generally desert their houses, furniture [moving], Cattle driving and women and children traveling off on foot. The country all resounds with the cries of the people." Looters from both armies added to the distress of these bewildered war refugees. Greene singled out the British, who, he said, "plunder most [amazingly]." In truth, the enemy had no monopoly on lawlessness; Washington's aide Joseph Reed noted that civilians of all persuasions, Tory, patriot, and neutral, "dreaded the appearance of either army." To the shame of their officers, American soldiers exploited American citizens, leading a frustrated Washington to issue orders demanding that the troops respect the property of the locals.

The British began their advance on September 8. When it became clear that they were marching not directly toward the American position but to the west, hoping to turn the rebels' right flank, Washington roused his army in the dead of night and marched north toward Brandywine Creek in Pennsylvania, a better defensive position. Greene's division was deployed in the center of the new American line at Chadd's Ford on the east bank of the creek. The Brandywine was not easy to cross—calling it a creek was an injustice—and Chadd's Ford, where the water was only knee-deep, was a logical place to expect a frontal attack. Behind Greene's division was the main road to Philadelphia. The rest of the army was strung out along the Brandywine, protecting other fords. Divisions under the command of Generals John Sullivan, Lord Stirling, and Adam Stephen were to Greene's right, while a militia unit guarded the American left. A small detachment under General William "Scotch Willie" Maxwell, known for his prodigous drinking, was dispatched across the creek to keep an eye on enemy movements toward the American defenses.

Greene spent nearly two days without sleep as he prepared his defenses. "I am exceedingly fatigued," he reported to Caty on September 10. "Last night I was in hopes of a good nights rest, but a dusty bed gave me [asthma] and I had very little sleep the whole night."

The morning of September 11 brought a reminder that summer had not retreated from these Pennsylvania fields. It already was hot and muggy when, just after breakfast, word reached the American lines that the British were on the move, headed for Chadd's Ford under the cover of a smothering fog. Maxwell's men, directly across from Greene's position, skirmished with troops under the command of Baron Wilhelm von Knyphausen before falling back across the river. Greene prepared his men for what figured to be a massive frontal assault with the full weight of Howe's army.

Morning dragged on, the sun became stronger, but the British did not attack Greene. He rode to Washington's headquarters to discuss what, if anything, they ought to do. While they were conferring, a messenger arrived with news that British troops had been spotted marching north on the west side of the river, seemingly headed for a crossing above the American right flank. The tactic was familiar enough: Howe had won the Battle of Long Island with precisely the same move—a feint to the center and a massive attack on the flank. Last time, however, Howe surprised the Americans. This time he had been spotted.

The British commander had divided his army in the face of an enemy that was roughly equal in numbers, a violation of one of the most basic rules of warfare. His risky plan called for a detachment of eight thousand troops under his command to march fifteen miles up the Brandywine, turn the American right, and get behind Washington; then, when the Americans redeployed to face the threat to their rear, Knyphausen would move across Chadd's Ford with his five thousand troops, squeezing the rebels between the two detachments.

The Americans, however, had a chance to destroy that strategy by gathering their army quickly and attacking the undermanned Knyphausen across Chadd's Ford. Washington put that very plan in motion. Greene rode back to Chadd's Ford and began preparing not the defensive action he had envisioned but an all-out assault. But even as word filtered down to the troops that they were about to cross the river, Greene and the other American generals received new orders from Washington. The assault was off. Headquarters had received contradictory reports about Howe's movements, and Washington decided he could not risk an attack without precise information. Could Howe have marched along the riverbank to fool the Americans but then retreated back to Knyphausen? Washington had to consider the possibility.

The Americans stayed in place under the hot sun. All the while, Howe was leading his troops along the river and crossing at an undefended ford above the American line. Early in the afternoon, Washington finally received definitive word that not only was a flanking movement in progress, but the British already were across the Brandywine and ready to assault the American right.

As Washington moved to counter the threat, Greene was ordered to stay in place in case Knyphausen made a move to support Howe. The battle was joined at about four-thirty in the afternoon. Greene could do nothing but listen to the distant report of musket fire and the bellow of artillery as he stood guard over Chadd's Ford.

After forty-five minutes of intense combat, troops under the command of General John Sullivan were in disarray. Greene received an urgent order from Washington: he was to march with one of his brigades to reinforce Sullivan. Greene fairly leaped into action, ordering General Weedon's brigade of Virginians to follow him and leaving General Muhlenberg's Pennsylvania brigade to keep watch at Chadd's Ford. Greene and his men marched four miles in forty-five minutes, arriving at the battlefield at about six o'clock and just in time to prevent Sullivan's retreat from becoming a rout. He later told a friend, Henry Marchant:

When I came upon the ground I found the whole of the
troops routed and retreating . . . and in the most broken and
confused manner. I was ordered to cover the retreat, which I
effected in such a manner as to save hundreds of our people
from falling into the enemy's hands. Almost all of the park of
artillery had an opportunity to get off. . . . We were engaged
an hour and a quarter, and lost upwards of a hundred men
killed and wounded. I maintained the ground until dark, and
then drew off the troops in good order.

While Greene's account is short on humility and self-deprecation, it
squared with other accounts of the battle's climactic sixty minutes.
Greene's arrival and the cool, competent manner in which Weedon's
troops covered Sullivan's retreat and effected their own stopped the
British from possibly enveloping the American army. Opposing Greene's
men were troops under the command of Lord Cornwallis. His Lordship
and Greene were getting quite familiar with each other.

The Battle of Brandywine ended with the Americans falling back on
the road to Chester after suffering about twelve hundred casualties. (One
of them was the marquis de Lafayette, who was wounded.) The British
suffered about ninety dead and nearly five hundred wounded. The
Americans surely had been beaten, but they had not been destroyed. Indeed, they had fought hard and well, and by doing so denied Howe the
crushing victory he had hoped to earn.

Greene saw nothing in this defeat to temper his enthusiasm. Even as
the Americans retreated, he was eager to strike the British. The performance of the troops, particularly those of his division, convinced him
that another battle with Howe would have quite a different result, and the
sooner, the better. "I expect the next action to ruin Mr. How entirely," he
told Caty. "You may expect to hear of another Action in a few days. Our
troops are in good health and high Spirits and wish for action again."
Their high spirits may have had something to do with a reward from
Congress: fresh rations of rum.

Privately, Greene was nursing a grievance. Washington had not seen fit to mention him or his division, particularly Weedon's brigade, in the accounts of the battle he sent to Congress. Had Washington not noticed how well Greene's men had fought? Still very much the limping private scorned by the Kentish Guards back in Rhode Island, Greene was ever wary of the comments, or silences, of his colleagues. After moping about and feeling sorry for himself, he finally asked Washington to explain himself.

The burdens piled upon Washington's shoulders were weighty enough as it was. He surely did not need to suffer a petulant Nathanael Greene, who had once before threatened to resign over a personal slight. Instead of reminding Greene of his priorities, Washington offered him the balm of flattery. "You, sir, are considered my favorite officer," he told Greene. "Weedon's brigade, like myself, are Virginians; should I applaud them for their achievement under your command, I shall be charged with partiality; jealousy will be excited, and the service injured."

Washington phrased his answer in the passive voice: he noted that Greene was believed to be his favorite officer; he was not, however, saying it himself. Others didn't doubt it, although at least one prominent American had a more cynical view of the relationship. Dr. Benjamin Rush, a physician and a signer of the Declaration of Independence, complained that Washington was little more than a cipher for Greene, Knox, and a young aide named Alexander Hamilton. He denounced Greene as "a syncophant to the General, speculative, without enterprise."

What this army needed, Rush decided, was a new commander in chief.

He was not the only American who thought so.

Near the pleasant village of Morristown where she continued to enjoy the hospitality of Abraham Lott and his family, Caty Greene followed news of the defense of Philadelphia with increasing anxiety. While the Lotts were convivial hosts who arranged for parties and dances—just the sort of thing Caty enjoyed—she was lonely, still ailing, and worried about her husband. The children, toddler George and infant Martha, were far away in Rhode Island, and she missed them, too. Her mood can be deduced through one of her husband's letters.

> My sweet Angel how I wish, how I long to return to your soft embrace. . . . How happy should I be could I administer consolation to you in a distressing hour. Rest assured my dear, nothing but the great duties of my station, the loud wails of my Country, the peace, liberty and happiness of [millions] should keep me from [you].

He promised he would soon return to her, if "kind fortune" carried him "through showers of leaden deaths unhurt."

Before they could reunite, there indeed would be more showers of leaden death, just as mid-September brought dark skies and rain showers to the fields of Pennsylvania. The defeated but unbeaten Americans spent the last two weeks of September on the march as Washington tried to anticipate Howe's next move. After Brandywine, a British occupation of Philadelphia seemed inevitable. Congress certainly thought so, as members soon fled for safer quarters, eventually finding a temporary home in York, Pennsylvania. The American generals, however, were confident they could make Howe pay dearly for a city that had only minor strategic value.

The British were ready to unleash a follow-up assault on September 16—four days too late, in the view of some of Howe's junior officers. The Americans took up defensive positions near the town of White Horse Tavern, about twenty miles northwest of Philadelphia. Greene was dissatisfied with the deployment, complaining that the troops occupied low, muddy ground. Behind the American center and the left wing was a soggy valley that would force the Americans to abandon their artillery during a retreat. Both Greene and another officer, Timothy Pickering, told Washington of their concerns. As they conferred, they could hear musket fire in the distance, signaling the start of the British advance. "Let us move," Washington said, at last.

As the Americans began to fall back to higher ground, a providential deluge bogged down the British so badly that they abandoned their attack. The Americans slogged their way eleven miles to a new position at Yellow Springs, and then marched again, through more rain and mud, finally crossing the Schuylkill River at Parker's Ford. They began moving toward Philadelphia, always trying to remain between Howe and the capital. In late September, however, Washington reversed himself and ordered a countermarch away from Philadelphia when he fell for a British feint aimed at the American supply depot at Reading.

For the first and last time, Greene muttered what others were saying openly about His Excellency George Washington. As they marched and marched and countermarched, Pickering told Greene that before he joined the army, he had "entertained an exalted opinion of General Washington's military talents." But after observing the commander in chief during the defense of Philadelphia, Pickering said, he had become disillusioned.

Greene, according to Pickering, replied, "The General does want [for] decision. For my part, I decide in a moment."

The Philadelphia campaign had become exasperating, almost as tedious as the previous summer, when Washington marched the army up and down the length and breadth of New Jersey. Greene and the army's other top generals, including Lord Stirling and Knox, met with Washington for a council of war on September 23 to discuss what, if anything, they could do to prevent the fall of Philadelphia. Howe had outfoxed Washington: his feint toward Reading succeeding in drawing the Americans nearer their depot and leaving the road to Philadelphia open. After completing the feint and doubling back, Howe now was moving closer to the capital. But Washington had to concede the obvious: he told his generals that "the Troops were in no condition to make a forced March as many of them are barefooted and all excessively harrassed with their great Fatigue."

The British marched into Philadelphia unopposed on September 26.

Lord Cornwallis led several hundred troops along Second Street as hundreds of civilians waved from the streets and rooftops. The capital was in enemy hands. Washington's barefoot soldiers could do nothing about it.

Three thousand British troops occupied Philadelphia. Nine thousand more remained outside the city, most of them camped in the nearby village of Germantown.

Greene and sixteen other major generals and brigadiers were summoned to a council of war at Washington's headquarters in Pennypacker's Mills, Pennsylvania, on September 28. Earlier that day, word had arrived in camp of a major engagement near Saratoga, New York, during which Americans under the command of General Horatio Gates inflicted heavy casualties on a sizable British force. (The decisive battle near Saratoga would not take place until more than a week later.)

With this news to cheer them, Greene and his colleagues heard Washington explain why another dramatic victory was within their grasp. Howe and the bulk of his army were camped in Germantown, about five miles north of the capital. Washington's informers reported that Howe had done nothing to fortify the town. With militia and Continental reinforcements heading for the American camp, Washington asked his generals if "it was prudent to make a general and vigorous attack upon the Enemy."

The matter was discussed and then put to a vote. Washington, though he had been given nearly dictatorial powers over the army when Congress fled Philadelphia, continued his practice of putting such matters before his general officers. Greene soon wearied of these deliberations, for they seemed to serve little purpose other than to delay urgent decisions. Of course, they also served to provide Washington with the cover of consensus when decisions went awry.

On this occasion, Greene joined nine other generals in voting against an immediate attack—a sign that while he was eager to please and ready to fight, he was not blind to hard facts. But this majority advised Washington to move the army to within twelve miles of Germantown to await the expected reinforcements and "be in readiness to take advantage of any favorable opportunity."

The American movement toward Germantown began almost immediately. Somewhere along the march, Greene lost a brass pistol that his friend Henry Knox had given him—carved into the barrel were the initials *H. K.* Greene posted a twenty-dollar reward for the pistol's return. There is no indication he ever got it back.

Once again, Greene was summoned to join his fellow generals in a council of war, this one on October 3. Washington informed them of intelligence reports indicating that Howe had weakened his main force, sending a detachment to attack an American fort on the Delaware River. By Washington's calculations, the British had between eight and nine thousand troops in their still unfortified camp in Germantown. The Americans, thanks to reinforcements since Brandywine, numbered about eleven thousand, including roughly three thousand militia.

Greene and the generals were unanimous—the time had come for an attack. Washington had a daring but extremely complicated plan that brought back memories of the Christmas raid on Trenton. The army would march overnight toward Germantown in four columns; like the Trenton scheme, the plan called for a surprise simultaneous assault on the garrison before dawn. At Trenton, a similiarly coordinated and closely timed attack went wrong almost immediately, which should have argued against an even more complex and far more dangerous assault against Germantown. But the Trenton battle plan, even in its improvised form, had worked. Washington believed a simliar attack could work again.

Washington placed Greene on the left wing of the advance, with Generals Stirling, Sullivan, Wayne, and Thomas Conway joining the commander in chief in the center and a militia force under General John Armstrong on the right. The fourth column, on the extreme left, would be made up of Maryland and New Jersey militia. The length of each column's march varied, depending on its starting point: Greene would have to march nineteen miles, while the other columns had only fifteen miles to travel. Each column was to reach its staging area at two o'clock, pause for two hours, then make its final push. The assault was to begin at four o'clock. To help distinguish friend from foe in the darkness, the troops were to be given white pieces of paper to wear on their hats. While the movement was under way, messengers on horseback would try to maintain communications between the columns, which were separated at their extremes by nine miles.

It's hard to imagine a more complicated plan of attack. But nobody raised any serious objections at the time.

A great deal depended on Greene. Washington gave him command of three divisions, comprising more than half the assault force's Continentals—nearly five thousand men. Greene's target, the British right flank, was reported to be the camp's strongest aspect. Once in position, Greene was to sweep in from the left at Lucken's Mill on the British right.

After the council of war, Greene returned to his division to put his men in motion. Thomas Paine, his friend from the march through New Jersey in 1776, had rejoined him in camp and was eager to march once again by Greene's side. But the general persuaded the master polemicist that he could best serve the cause by remaining in camp, out of harm's way until morning. Paine remained behind but was awake before dawn and on his way toward Germantown by five o'clock.

Greene's men began their march to the staging area at seven o'clock. Not surprisingly, given the recent history of such movements and the particular circumstances of this complex plan, things began to go wrong almost right away. The columns fell behind schedule. Messengers lost contact with the advancing troops. Greene's three divisions made a wrong turn in the darkness and lost time retracing their steps for four miles. Nobody knew where the militia was. Worse yet, General Howe soon knew where Washington—or, more generally, his army—was. British scouts or sympathizers had spotted the American movement and sent word to Germantown. Howe was out of bed at four o'clock.

Sullivan and Washington, in the American center, managed to stay close to schedule. They had no way of knowing Greene had gotten lost and had fallen dangerously behind. Before sunrise, Sullivan's men overwhelmed British light infantry outside Germantown. Many fell victim to American steel, but some escaped and fell back as fast as they could. More than a hundred outnumbered British reinforcements took shelter in a stone house outside the town. Known as the Chew House—the owner was a judge named Benjamin Chew—it became a formidible obstacle between the town and Sullivan's rear guard, commanded by Stirling. Rather than simply bypass the house, the Americans chose to invest it after Sullivan and Wayne advanced toward their objective. That decision delayed Stirling's men, who soon found themselves pinned down by British sharpshooters. Henry Knox brought up artillery, but cannonballs bounced off the house's stone walls. And time slipped by.

Meanwhile, Nathanael Greene was somewhere off on the American left, trying to make up for lost time through a predawn mist. As at Trenton, the Americans still were not at their objective by morning's light. Even worse for the attackers, on this day the fog of war was more than just a metaphor. A gray, misty blanket covered the battlefield, enveloping the Americans and turning confusion into chaos.

Forty-five minutes late, Greene's divisions approached the outskirts of town along the Limekiln Road. They had made up some time after recovering from their wrong turn, but also had met unexpected resistance in the form of a light infantry unit a mile outside of town. And when the commander of one of Greene's divisions, Adam Stephen, heard gunfire on his right, he ordered his men to march through the fog toward the sounds of battle. Stephen was operating in a fog of another sort: he was drunk. Unknowingly, his men were heading for the siege at Chew House when they saw ghostly figures in the distance. They opened fire—but the figures were American soldiers, under the command of Anthony Wayne. Startled by an apparent enemy unit they hadn't accounted for, Wayne's men fired back, and both units quickly fled in opposite directions, adding to the chaos and halting Wayne's advance on the town.

With visibility no more than thirty yards in places, Greene continued his move toward Lucken's Mill under heavy British fire. He stayed off the road, marching instead though woods and foggy fields. Somewhere along the march, a brigade under General Alexander McDougall lost its way. The careful timing, the complex coordination, the element of surprise, the predawn assault—all of Washington's plans were in ruins. Greene knew he was late, and he obviously realized that his attack on the British right would no longer be a surprise. So he improvised, turning his column to the right before reaching Lucken's Mill. One of his brigades, under General Muhlenberg's command, used their bayonets to attack British defenders near the town's meetinghouse. Their advance was impressive, and one of Muhlenberg's units took a hundred prisoners. But Greene was undermanned, thanks to Stephen's drunkeness and McDougall's disappearance. When the British counterattacked, Greene had little choice but to order his men to fall back. Washington, too, ordered a retreat. Lord Cornwallis brought up fresh troops to pursue Greene, but, in the words of Thomas Paine, "the enemy kept a civil distance."

The battle had raged for close to three hours, and despite the chaos and the fog and the failed coordination, the Americans had put up another impressive fight. As usual, casualty figures varied, with the Americans suffering more than a thousand killed, wounded, or taken prisoner, and the British about half that number.

As at Brandywine, there was little doubt about which side won the battle. And, as at Brandywine, the Americans left the battlefield in curiously good spirits. But for bad luck here and there—the fog, the friendly fire, the siege at Chew House—they believed they could have beaten not a detachment of Hessians, as at Trenton, but General Howe's main army. General Wayne described the battle as a "glorious day."

Some of Washington's colleagues, along with several members of Congress, saw nothing glorious about the defeats at Brandywine and Germantown and the British occupation of Philadelphia. Their whispered complaints about Washington and the men around him increased in volume and in vehemence when, just three days after Germantown, Horatio Gates's northern army defeated the British at Bemis Heights near Saratoga in upstate New York. Dr. Rush, the influential physician, gave voice to what many others were thinking when he praised Gates in a letter to John Adams. Gates, Rush said, had planned his campaign in northern New York with "wisdom and executed [it] with vigor and bravery." What a contrast with Washington, who had been "outgeneralled and twice beaten." Adams hardly needed to be reminded of Washington's failures. After Brandywine, he had vented in his diary: "Oh, Heaven! grant us one great soul! . . . One active, masterly capacity would bring order out of this confusion and save this country."

Nathanael Greene heard the grumbling. He may not have heard specific complaints about Washington, but he knew that Horatio Gates was being touted as the new great hope of the Continental army. Greene and Gates had gotten along well enough in the war's early months, but when Gates quietly emerged as a possible rival to Washington, Greene turned against him. He insisted that Gates was not, in fact, the hero of Saratoga—an assessment historians would later share. It was General Benedict Arnold who had turned the tide of battle with reckless and inspiring courage, despite, incidentally, having been relieved of command several days before by none other than Horatio Gates. Greene snarled that Gates was a "mere child of fortune." His bitterness and anger were clear in a letter written about a month after Germantown, as complaints about Washington intensified. He conceded, not very graciously, that Gates had won a great victory. But the credit, he said, belonged to others, including Gates's not particularly competent predecessor, General Schuyler.

> [The] foundation of all General Gates' successes were planned
> under [General] Schuyler's direction. . . . General Gates came
> in just timely to reap the laurels and rewards. Great credit is
> due to all the Northern Army, but that army has been much
> stronger than ours and a far less force to contend with.

Defensive as always in the face of real or imagined criticism, Greene complained that Gates's good luck even extended to his militia. They were, he wrote, much more "spirited and gallant" than the militia he and Washington were stuck with in Pennsylvania.

If the Southern Militia had lent the same aid to his
Excellency that the Northern Militia did to General Gates
Mr. How never could have got possession of the Rome of
America. We have had two severe and general actions. . . .
Our force has been too small to cover the country and secure
the city. The Inhabitants, so very unfriendly, [have] render'd
the task still more difficult.

Washington was not the only general whose flanks were exposed to
the grapeshot of congressional and collegial criticism. Greene was, too,
and he knew it. "I have been . . . told there has been some insinuation to
my prejudice respecting the Germantown battle," he wrote. Indeed there
was; critics in the army and in Congress were saying that his late appearance on the battlefield had led to the American defeat. It was unfair and
uninformed criticism, but then again, Greene himself was not particularly fair to Horatio Gates, either.

Greene made inquiries among his friends to find out what was being
said about him and by whom. He learned that critics—among them General Thomas Mifflin, another fallen Quaker and the army's quartermaster
general—believed he had had too much influence over Washington during the Philadelphia campaign. For the remainder of the war, Germantown remained an especially sensitive subject with Greene, and he never
tired of explaining and justifying his actions that day.

The British were in command of Philadelphia, but they did not rule the
Delaware River. The Americans controlled two strategic forts along the
river, about five miles south of the city. Along with Washington's continued presence in the area, the forts presented General Howe with a problem, for he needed the river clear of an American presence to secure his
lines of supply and communications. From the American perspective, if
the forts could be sustained and Washington could block some of the
roads leading to Philadelphia, the British might have to withdraw for
want of supplies.

Fort Mifflin, named for Greene's fellow Quaker and critic, was on Mud Island in the river itself, and Fort Mercer, named for the general killed at the Battle of Princeton, was on the New Jersey riverbank. Like Forts Lee and Washington on the Hudson River, Forts Mifflin and Mercer were across from each other and offered the Americans command of the narrow river. Adding to the hazard were the remains of ships sunk to further block the river, and a small American fleet operated just north of the forts.

Colonel Christopher Greene, a cousin of Nathanael Greene's, commanded the garrison at Fort Mercer. With him was Nathanael Greene's young friend Sammy Ward, who had been taken prisoner during the Canadian expedition two years before but had since paroled and returned to service.

The British and Hessians attacked the two forts in late October and found them well defended. Christopher Greene's four hundred Rhode Islanders beat back a Hessian force of some two thousand, to the delight of his cousin. "Honor and laurels will be the reward of the garrison," Nathanael Greene told Christopher. A siege ensued, which Greene monitored closely for both professional and personal reasons. Not only did the forts hold out hope for a much needed victory, but his kinsman and his friend Sammy were among the besieged.

Greene and the rest of the army moved to within a dozen miles of Philadelphia in early November, hoping to draw Howe's attention—and some British troops—away from the siege along the Delaware River. The new camp at Whitemarsh provided Greene with an unexpected distraction, which he was pleased to describe in a letter to Caty, still living with the Lott family in New Jersey.

> [Close] in the Neighbourhood of my quarters there are several
> sweet pretty Quaker girls. If the spirit should move and love
> invite who can be answerable for the consequences. I know
> this won't alarm you because you have such [a] high opinion
> of my virtue. It is very well you have. You remember the prayer
> of the Saints, tempt me not above what I am able to bear.

Caty no doubt found this letter terribly reassuring. She might have smiled just a bit to learn that not long after her husband entertained her with his thoughts of infidelity—and with Quaker girls, no less—his horse reared up and threw him ten feet. He landed just inches away from a nasty encounter with a stone wall. "One foot farther," he said, "would have given me a passport." He was lucky to walk away with just a sprained wrist.

After days of bombardment, Fort Mifflin, on Mud Island, fell to the British on November 15. Washington immediately ordered Greene to cross the Delaware into New Jersey to reinforce Christopher Greene and the other Rhode Islanders at Fort Mercer. General Cornwallis also crossed the river with quite the opposite assignment: to put an end to Christopher Greene's stubborn resistance. Cornwallis was first to arrive near the fort, and he soon had his victory. Christopher Greene decided that the fort was doomed, so he ordered his troops to set the place ablaze and then make good their escape. Nathanael Greene learned of the fort's loss while marching through Burlington, New Jersey.

His mission in New Jersey was moot, but Greene was eager for a fight anyway. He would try to get a sense of how many troops Cornwallis had with him. And then, he told Washington, "If it is possible to make an attack upon 'em with a prospect of success it shall be done." In his reply on November 22, Washington told Greene that an attack "would be a most desireable judgment." Later that day, Washington sent Greene another message, this one more adamant. He told Greene he was "inclined" to have him attack Cornwallis "as much in force as possible." Washington was determined to salvage some victory, however small, from this long and frustrating campaign.

While Greene was eager to show Washington's critics, and his own, that Horatio Gates had no monopoly on bold action, he tempered his enthusiasm when he learned that Cornwallis had been reinforced and now had five thousand troops. Greene had only about three thousand Continentals, and his militia force of about eight hundred was shrinking as militiamen drifted away from camp. He sent a long message back to Washington, explaining why he believed he could not carry out the general's wishes. "I cannot promise myself Victory, or even a Prospect of it, with Inferior Numbers," he wrote. "The Cause is too important to be trifled with . . . and your Character too deeply interested to sport away upon unmilitary Principles." Having, at some length, explained his reluctance to attack, he also assured Washington that he would do otherwise if given the order: "For your Sake, for my own Sake and for my Country's Sake, I wish to attempt every thing which will meet with your Excellency's Approbation." As he read this message, Washington must have appreciated his loyal lieutenant Greene all the more.

Greene's forces skirmished with elements of Cornwallis's force, but Greene never did launch the attack he and Washington had discussed. Greene recrossed the Delaware on November 29 and joined Washington in camp in Whitemarsh, Pennsylvania. Almost immediately, Washington asked him to meet with his army's other generals to decide what they ought to do next. An unorthodox winter campaign was not out of the question, in fact, Congress was all for it, and, perhaps not coincidentally, the commander in chief seemed eager to take on General Howe one more time. Amid rumors that the British were preparing to attack, Washington told Greene on November 28, "I shall not be disappointed if they come out this Night or very early in the morning."

There was no British assault, and Greene joined with the vast majority of Washington's generals in advising a retreat to winter quarters. But where? Greene, in a long memo to Washington dated December 1, advocated the area in and around Wilmington, where they had encamped before marching to defeat at Brandywine and Germantown. He told Washington that winter quarters ought to be located as close to the enemy as reasonably possible to prevent the troops from losing their edge. "If we retire so far back as to be totally out of danger, pleasure and dissipation will be the consequence," he told Washington. "Officers of all ranks will be desireous of visiting their friends. The men will be left without orders, without government—and ten to one but the men will be more unhealthy in the spring than they now are and much worse disciplined."

The issue of winter quarters or winter campaign remained unsettled.

A committee from Congress arrived in camp on December 3 to talk about prospects of renewed assaults on the British. It was clear the politicians were not prepared to see the army retire for a few months, allowing the British a comfortable winter of balls and parties in the city that had given birth to American independence. Washington asked Greene and the other generals to put their views in writing. Greene wrote long into the night, producing a well-written analysis that showed yet again just how far his self-education had taken him.

> However desirable the destruction of General Howe's army may be and however impatient the public may be for this desirable event, I cannot recommend the measure. I have taken the most serious View of the subject in every point in which I am able to examine it and cannot help thinking the probability of a disappointment is infinitely greater than of Success. We must not be governed in our measures by our Wishes.

Greene's argument carried the day. He was an optimist, it was true, but he was no fool. He was eager for battle, but he knew there was no point in risking the army. There would be no renewed attack on Philadelphia. General Howe's troops would be free to enjoy the winter respite among the Tories and Quakers of the former rebel capital.

The Continental army soon broke camp and marched from Whitemarsh to winter quarters in a place near Philadelphia named Valley Forge.

8 | Low Intrigue

The march toward Valley Forge, twenty-five miles northwest of Philadelphia, signaled a temporary halt in the war, but a battle within the Continental army itself raged all the same. Exhausted American soldiers trooped into camp on December 19 and began building log huts to shield themselves from the cold, yet nothing could protect them from political maneuvering and a scandalous lack of supplies. Intrigue would not keep them clothed, they could not live on whispered plots, and the heat of dissension in Congress did nothing to keep them warm in Valley Forge.

Nathanael Greene's most formidible opponents in the winter of 1777–78 were not snow and ice, not Howe and Cornwallis, but some of his putative colleagues and fellow patriots. The defeats at Brandywine and Germantown, the fall of Philadelphia, and the loss of the Delaware River forts inspired a movement against not only the commander in chief but one of the men accused of manipulating him into bad decisions: Nathanael Greene.

His sternest and most powerful critic was, ironically enough, the army's only other Quaker general, Thomas Mifflin, Washington's one-time aide-de-camp and a respected warrior, businessman, and former member of the Continental Congress. The defeats of autumn 1777 left Mifflin distinctly unimpressed with Washington's military skills and with his choice of intimate advisers. He was not alone in this judgment, but he was uncommonly open about his opinions. Mifflin especially loathed Greene, believing he was both incompetent and too cautious. The fall of Philadelphia, where Mifflin had been based as the army's quartermaster general, only increased his complaints and criticisms. Philadelphia might have been saved, Mifflin said, but for Washington's indecisiveness and Greene's timidity. Greene, ever watchful for criticism—whether intended or not—was well aware of what Mifflin was saying behind his back. "General Mifflin and his creatures," he wrote, "have been endeavouring to wound my reputation. It is said that I govern the General and do every thing to damp the spirit of enterprize."

That was precisely the criticism of the moment: Washington was weak and indecisive—a pale imitation of a commander when compared with the great Horatio Gates of Saratoga fame—and he was unduly influenced by Greene's cautious strategies. Mifflin had complained that the "ear of the Commander in Chief" was "exclusively possessed by Greene," a development he deplored. Greene, Mifflin said, was "neither the most wise, the most brave nor the most patriotic of counselors."

Mifflin's dyspeptic view of Washington and Greene had little trouble finding a friendly hearing within both the army and Congress. Benjamin Rush concluded that either Horatio Gates or the Irish immigrant Thomas Conway, a very junior brigadier general who had been at Brandywine and Germantown, ought to replace Washington. And the Adams cousins, John and Samuel, resented Washington's fame, which John Adams regarded as a danger "to our liberties." But no member of Congress was as openly hostile to Washington, and to Greene, as another delegate from Massachusetts, James Lovell. He referred to Greene and Henry Knox as Washington's "privy counsellors" and said he spoke for many "disgusted patriots" who had come to despise "the reigning

Cabal" around Washington. It was just a matter of time, he said, before the army "will be divided into Greenites and Mifflinians."

Even before the march to Valley Forge, tensions between Washington's supporters and his opponents worsened when Congress reorganized its moribund Board of War to reassert its authority over the army, which it had surrendered in late 1776 at Greene's urging. Thomas Mifflin won appointment to the three-member board, and he immediately resigned his position as quartermaster general. It was a scandalously selfish decision, for it left Washington without an officer in charge of supplies on the eve of winter. Mifflin soon persuaded Congress to expand the board to five members and just as quickly sponsored the nomination of Horatio Gates as the board's president. Gates now was well positioned to undermine Washington and establish himself as the heir apparent. Congress, in mid-December, further drove home a message to Washington and Greene by naming General Conway as the army's inspector general and promoting him from brigadier to major general. As inspector general, Conway was given power to periodically visit camp or the front lines and report his findings directly to Gates, Mifflin, and the other members of the Board of War. Greene regarded Conway as nothing less than a spy working on behalf of Mifflin and other anti-Washington forces, a sentiment the commander in chief seemed to share. When Conway complained to Congress that he had been "cooly received" when he showed up at Valley Forge, Washington replied in even chillier language. "My feelings," he wrote, "will not permit me to make professions of friendship to a man I deem my enemy."

And that enemy, Conway, and his sponsor, Mifflin, were now in a position to do more than merely criticize Washington and Greene. Mifflin, a talented and serious foe, had maneuvered brilliantly to find a prominent position for the very man he believed better suited to the job of commander in chief, Horatio Gates. Conway was in place as an independent auditor of Washington's army, answerable only to the board itself. And Gates, though not inclined to plot or conspire, seemed willing to entertain the idea of stepping into Washington's shoes.

Greene never doubted that there was a full-fledged conspiracy to overthrow Washington and replace him with Gates. A certain faction, he wrote, "is said to be forming under the auspices of General Gates and General Mifflin, to supplant His Excellency from the command of the Army and get General Gates at the head of it. How success swells the vanity of the human heart." Greene knew that if his commander in chief fell, he, too, would fall and be replaced by the likes of Conway or Mifflin. Historians have since suggested that the anti-Washington officers, members of what was called the Conway Cabal, never actually went beyond their pointed criticisms. Greene didn't believe it.

He treated Gates, Mifflin, and Conway not as colleagues but as enemies who must be crushed before they crushed him. He told other officers that Conway was a "very dangerous man," a general with "small talents" and "great ambition." Greene, of course, was not without ambition himself; ambition, in fact, had put him on this road to Valley Forge at the side of his commander in chief.

Through the early weeks of 1778, Greene unleashed a cannonade of letters designed to shred the reputations of his new foes, condemning Conway as "the greatest novice at war" and insisting, again, that Gates had been merely lucky at Saratoga. He wrote to the new president of Congress, Henry Laurens, to complain about Conway's promotion to major general, promising that in the future, "men of honor will decline the service," while "low intrigue will be the characteristic and genius of the Army."

Through his small number of friends and sympathizers in Congress, Greene monitored political gossip and debates about Washington's fate. A former aide named John Clark Jr. told him that Philadelphia was buzzing with rumors that Washington had written a letter requesting that Congress appoint Greene as commander in chief "if he fell." This would have been seen as an invasion of congressional prerogative, another weapon to use against both Washington and Greene. No such letter has ever been found, but the rumor made the rounds and still was circulating in 1780, at another low point in the war. If nothing else, the very fact that some people believed it to be true must have given Greene a measure of satisfaction.

But there was very little else to comfort him in this increasingly bitter battle. Clark told Greene that various "reports have been circulated . . . to prejudice the People against His Excellency and you." The strain of army politics, combined with the privations of winter camp, took a physical and emotional toll on Greene. An unexplained eye ailment prevented him from meeting with Washington in early January, and even Caty's arrival in camp did little to raise his spirits. In fact, Caty's presence may have exacerbated, rather than eased, the roiling tensions at headquarters. Lucy Knox, a frequent if often reluctant companion of Caty Greene's, observed that "all was not well with Greene [and] his lady" at Valley Forge. Some scholars have suggested that Caty Greene, fully recovered now and delighted to be free of the Lotts' smothering embrace in New Jersey, reveled just a bit too much in the attention paid her by French officers in camp, particularly the marquis de Lafayette. She also was plainly, perhaps far too plainly, attracted to General Anthony Wayne and the army's commissary general, Jeremiah Wadsworth. Wayne was a blunt, plain-speaking frontiersman trapped in an unhappy marriage. Wadsworth was a handsome and prosperous merchant from Philadelphia. Both men delighted in Caty's company, and years later, after Nathanael's death, they would become Caty's lovers.

Evidence of a strain between the Greenes crept into Nathanael's letters from Valley Forge. Their two children, George and Martha, were living in Rhode Island with Nathanael's brother Jacob and his wife. During the winter, however, Jacob fell ill, and Nathanael's children were taken to the home of another brother, Elihue. Martha soon was diagnosed with a case of rickets. The shuttling of his children from house to house and the news about Martha upset Greene, and in a letter to still another brother, Christopher, he lamented the fate of his "poor almost fatherless and motherless children." Caty had left the children more than six months earlier, when George was about a year and a halfold, and Martha three months. But if Greene suddenly was upset that his children were "almost . . . motherless," he had only himself to blame. He had, after all, begged her to join him, and when begging didn't work, he taunted her with fantasies of infidelity.

In joining their husbands at Valley Forge, Caty Greene, Lucy Knox, Martha Washington, and the wives of other generals bore witness to the terrible suffering that winter. While they were better off than the starving, half-naked soldiers huddled twelve to a hut, they breathed in the same acrid smoke, smelled the same foul camp odors, and shivered through the same long nights. Their very presence, however, and their willingness to endure a measure of discomfort offered the troops inspiration and at least a bit of distraction. A young soldier in camp later recalled how the generals' wives brightened their spirits: "In the middle of our distress, there were some bright sides to the picture which Valley Forge exhibited. . . . The lady of General Greene is a handsome, elegant, and accomplished woman [who] spoke the French language and was well-versed in French literature."

The new year of 1778 was only three days old when Nathanael Greene sent a foreboding letter to his brother Jacob. The army had been in Valley Forge fewer than three weeks, but already there were signs that this would be an awful winter. Eleven thousand men were gathered in camp, and it was up to Congress and the army's supply officers—the quartermaster general, the commissary general, and the clothier general—to see to it that this small city was fed, clothed, and otherwise equipped for the next several months. But supplies were low, and, not coincidentally, so was morale.

Greene told Washington on New Year's Day that the officers were complaining that they were "exposed to the severity of the weather, subject to hard duty and nothing but bread and beef to eat morning, noon and night, without vegetables or anything to drink but cold water." Several days earlier, fifty officers in Greene's division resigned because of low pay.

The troops, Greene wrote, were "almost worn out with fatigue and greatly distressed for want of clothing, particularly the articles of shoes and stockings." They still were in tents on New Year's Day, for they had not completed construction of the windowless log huts in which they would spent the rest of the winter. Although these early weeks of the new year were not especially cold or snowy, the troops suffered all the same. The work of building nearly a thousand huts was intense, their flimsy tents could hardly qualify as shelter, and food and other supplies grew scarcer with each day. Greene wrote to General McDougall, who had been with him at Germantown, of the dreadful breakdown in supplies.

> The Quarter Master General, Commissary General and Clothier Generals departments are in such a wretched condition that unless there are some very great alterations in those departments, it will be impossible to prosecute another Campaign. Our Troops are naked . . . and the men getting sickly in their Hutts for want of acids and Soap to clean themselves.

Of course, the former quartermaster general, Mifflin, had quit his job when he chose to devote himself to Board of War politics. The commissary office also lacked experienced leadership. Both departments quickly disintegrated thanks in part to congressional bungling, and it was the consequent breakdown in the supply system—more than the weather—that led to misery, illness, and death at Valley Forge. By mid-January, when the camp's huts finally were completed, some four thousand soldiers were so poorly clothed that they dared not venture outside. Some used pieces of their tents for shirts, coats, or footwear. All the while, fifty loads of clothing were in a warehouse in Lancaster, Pennsylvania, awaiting supply wagons that never arrived.

The army's staple food, morning, noon, and night, was a concoction called fire cake—bread, not of the best quality, baked on a stone over a fire. From the damp, grim huts came a muffled complaint: "No meat! No meat!"

Conditions worsened in early February, when the relatively mild winter turned bitter and a snowstorm further reduced the already limited flow of supplies into camp. Men and horses alike starved to death in the snow. The countryside already had been stripped clean of supplies for soldiers and forage for animals, so there was no relief in sight. Colonel James Varnum, Greene's friend from their younger days in Rhode Island, was despondent, and he warned Greene that the army seemed on the verge of collapse. He wrote that "the situation of the Camp is such that in all human probability the Army must soon dissolve." Varnum was a respected officer, not one given to complaints or panic. Greene brought the letter to Washington's headquarters on February 12. That very day, Washington issued an order authorizing the troops to move farther into the countryside and simply take what they needed from local citizens. Washington loathed this practice, believing it smacked of British and Hessian thuggery, but he had little choice. He told his officers to impress all "Cattle and Sheep fit for Slaughter" within fifteen to twenty miles of the Schuylkill River. The owners were to be given certificates that, Washington promised, would ensure them of payment for their lost livestock.

Nathanael Greene was given command of this massive foraging operation, upon which hundreds of lives and perhaps even the army itself depended. It was not a command for the faint of heart, because it would require brutal tactics when sweet persuasion failed. Even the most stouthearted friend of American liberty was bound to resent soldiers, however well behaved, hauling off livestock and crops at the point of a gun, tendering only a piece of paper promising payment at some future time. And it was, after all, winter for civilians, too. They had worked a fine harvest in the fall and had planned to enjoy the fruit of their labor through the hard months until spring. The requirements of the Continental army did not enter into their plans.

The forced impressment of private property figured to be a public relations nightmare for the starving American army. From the day he marched off to Boston with the Rhode Island Army of Observation, Nathanael Greene was sensitive to the importance of public opinion, especially in a war fought in the name of democracy. The army's virtues, he had often said, reflected the virtue of the cause. But now necessity collided with virtue, and Greene had no choice but to put aside his ideals and hope for the best. Much of the foraging operation would take place in areas known for their unenthusiastic Quakers and outright loyalists. At least the Americans would make no new enemies when they showed up at those farmhouses.

Greene and his party of several thousand soldiers moved out of camp and into the countryside almost immediately, and just as quickly he discovered the endless complications of supplying an army. There were not enough wagons to cart whatever they might find, and they were receiving little cooperation from their fellow Americans, who were concealing their wagons from Greene's men. Other farmers pleaded with Greene to leave them alone. He told Washington on Feburary 15, "[The] Inhabitants cry out and beset me from all quarters, but like Pharoh I harden my heart." His men had caught two civilians transporting provisions to the British; Greene ordered them whipped with a hundred lashes "by way of Example."

The example was not intended just for other civilians. He, too, sought to set an example for his subordinate officers. They had no taste for this cruel business, but Greene told them that they had little choice, that they too had to harden their hearts. He told his men that he would punish "the least neglect with the greatest severity." His instructions to Colonel Nicholas Biddle, the army's commissary general of forage, were equally blunt: "You must forage the Country naked," he wrote. Greene knew that stripping the countryside of forage for civilian horses and livestock would create a new set of problems for civilians. It was bad enough that the soldiers took their feed, but what of the animals left behind, doomed to starvation? Greene had a solution. He told Biddle that "to prevent [civilian] complaints of the want of Forage we must take all their Cattle, Sheep and Horses fit for the use of the Army."

When his men brought back little from their initial forays, Greene expanded the reach of the party, showing a command of details and logistics that clearly made an impression on the commander in chief back at headquarters in Valley Forge. Greene ordered a detachment to Lancaster County to round up a hundred wagons. He expanded foraging opera-

tions into Bucks County. Confronted with evidence that civilians continued to conceal stock and wagons from his soldiers, Greene promised
Washington that "examples shall not be wanting to facilitate the business." When patriotic appeals and promises of future payment failed, the
lash would have the final word. Greene took no pleasure in this work—
the "business I am upon is very disagreeable," he wrote—but he regarded it as a grim necessity. "God grant that we may never be brought
into such a wretched condition again," he wrote to Washington.

After five days of exhausting work, he was able to send a bit of good
news back to Valley Forge from Bucks and Chester counties, whose residents, he noted, were not the most cooperative.

> I sent on to Camp yesterday near fifty Head of Cattle. I wish
> it had been in my power to have sent more, but the
> Inhabitants have taken the alarm and conceal their stock in
> such a manner that it is very difficult finding any. They have
> done the same with their Waggons and Harness. Our poor
> fellows are obliged to search all the woods and swamps after
> them and often without success. I have given orders to give
> no receipts for everything they find concealed and to notify
> the people accordingly.

Greene's unsentimental, even cold-blooded, methods were having an
effect. By February 20, Colonel Biddle reported that he had forty wagons
filled with provisions. General Anthony Wayne, whom Greene dispatched across the Delaware into New Jersey, found a good supply of
livestock and also burned supplies of hay that seemed destined to fall
into the hands of British foraging parties from Philadelphia. The army's
improving fortunes apparently softened Greene's heart just a bit, for
when a civilian named Nathan Sellers pleaded for the return of his only
horse, a mare, Greene agreed, after Sellers promised to keep the horse
from the British.

Greene was back in camp in late February after eleven days of arduous and ruthless labor. The supplies he brought back eased the situation in Valley Forge a bit, but conditions still were appalling. Greene told Knox what he found when he returned.

> The troops are getting naked, and they were seven days
> without meat and several days without bread. Such patience
> and moderation as they manifested under their sufferings
> does the highest honor to the Magnanimity of the American
> Soldiers. The seventh day they came before their superior
> officers and told their sufferings in as respectful terms as if
> they had been humble petitioners for special favors. . . .
> Happy relief arrived from the little collections I had made
> and some others, and prevented the Army from disbanding.

Greene's contribution to the army's survival at a critical moment, and the unquestioned zeal with which he acted on Washington's orders, did not go unnoticed at headquarters. Washington, encircled by enemies even within the army itself, knew he had no more loyal general than Nathanael Greene, and surely none more capable of executing orders, no matter how distasteful. There was no issue more pressing at the moment than the army's ability to feed and clothe itself. Greene's foraging mission did, in fact, provide relief, but larger supply problems remained. Greene told Knox that the army was still in danger of starving.

The supply system had become bogged down in congressional and army politics, and the results were deadly. Soldiers continued to die—the body count at Valley Forge would reach twenty-five hundred—and others were deserting for want of food and clothing.

The army needed a quartermaster general, a man who understood the logistics of supply and who was tough enough to take on unpleasant assignments. The army did not need a quartermaster general like Thomas Mifflin, who was glad to rid himself of the dull work of supply to devote himself to the work of undermining the commander in chief.

Congress had been considering General Phillip Schuyler as the army's new quartermaster general, but a committee from Congress visiting the army at Valley Forge agreed with a conclusion Washington had reached: Nathanael Greene was the only man for the job. Washington had come to treasure Greene's competency, but that was not the only virtue that recommended him for the vital post. Greene also was devoted to Washington, and that loyalty was never more important than now, with other generals and politicians seemingly plotting against him. Greene's background as a businessman didn't hurt, either; he was a problem solver, a man who understood how to find supplies and move them from one point to another. And that, in a nutshell, was the job of a quartermaster general. He was responsible for purchasing, transporting, and distributing a breathtaking array of supplies, everything from tents to canteens to nails to saddles. Although the purchasing of food came under the power of the commissary general, and that of clothing was the responsibility of the clothier general, the quartermaster general was in charge of transporting those supplies as well. When the army moved, the quartermaster was in command of the march, which meant that he had to establish supply posts along the route, become familiar with the terrain (for the location of sources of water and forage, among other things), and scout possible sites for new camps.

Washington broached the subject of this immensely complex job directly with Greene, telling him that future supply disasters were inevitable unless somebody familiar with the army's needs accepted the unglamorous but urgent assignment. These were not words Greene longed to hear. He knew what Washington said was true, but he also knew that he had not joined the army to become a staff officer pushing paper behind the lines. He wished for fame on the battlefield. As he later told Washington, "Nobody ever heard of a quarter master in history." He told Knox that he had no desire to be "taken out of the Line of splendor." He had visions of his friends gaining the laurels he dreamed of. To his friend General McDougall, he complained, "All of you will be immortallising your selves in the golden pages of History while I am confined to a series of [drudgeries] to pave the way for it."

Besides, the job promised only frustration, as members of Congress conceded when they said the next quartermaster general would face "the

Confusion of the Department, the depreciation of our Money and the exhausted State of our Resources." One could hardly imagine a less attractive proposition.

The pressure from Congress and Washington at least offered Greene a chance to negotiate, and he took full advantage. He asked that he retain his title of major general, with a vague understanding that he would have a place on the battlefield, rather than behind the lines, when campaign season resumed. Congress agreed, although with the caveat that Greene would no longer command a division. He asked Congress to name two trusted friends, Charles Pettit and John Cox, as his top deputies. Pettit, a lawyer and an accountant in civilian life, would be in charge of the department's books. Cox, a merchant, would supervise the department's purchases and would monitor stores of supplies. Congress agreed to this request, too.

The obstacles fell, one by one. Ultimately, though, what mattered most to Greene was Washington's wishes. As he weighed his decision, seeking the advice of his many friends in the service, he consistently cited Washington's desire—his need—to have a competent, trusted friend as quartermaster. After all they had been through, with the war nowhere near victory, Greene simply could not say no to Washington.

So, in March, he said yes, although with great misgivings. He confessed, "[I am] vexed with myself for complying," but believed he had no choice, for Washington and civilian leaders were at him "Night and Day."

Until Nathanael Greene took the job, the quartermaster general of the Contintental army had worked not at Washington's side but in Philadelphia and, more recently, in York. Thomas Mifflin, who had served as quartermaster twice since 1775, had none of Nathanael Greene's prestige, access to the commander in chief, and field-level knowledge of the army's needs. From the moment when Greene accepted the job, the quartermaster general's office was transformed from a staff job to one of the army's most influential positions—simply because it was Nathanael Greene, confidant of Washington, who held it.

The post was not without its attractions. Although Greene had offered to work for his salary as a major general, his two assistants demanded much more, arguing that they were giving up private business interests and shouldn't suffer financially for their patriotism. Congress compromised by offering Greene, Cox, and Pettit a 1 percent commission, to be divided as they wished, on all goods or services they ordered for the army. Such an arrangement would never be allowed in a professional army of the twenty-first century, but it was quite legal and even customary in the eighteenth century. Greene's predecessor, Mifflin, also had received a commission on the department's purchases.

Greene, though he considered himself as pure a patriot as any American, was not above considerations of money and profit even in the course of performing his duty. He continued to maintain his interest in the family company and often sent his brothers business advice. He had concluded that the fledgling American nation valued money above all else, and if he were to make anything of himself in the new nation he was trying to create, he would have to be rich as well as a patriot. "Money becomes more and more the Americans' object," he told his brother and business partner Jacob. "You must get rich, or you will be of no consequence."

Nathanael Greene intended to be a man of consequence. But as he contemplated his new life as a quartermaster, he saw nothing that would help him achieve his ambitions, or his personal happiness. Quite the opposite, in fact. In another bout of his periodic self-pity, he complained to another brother and business partner, William:

> I have spent but a short hour at home since the
> commencement of the War. . . . I am wearing out my
> constitution and the prime of life. It is true I shall have
> the consolation of exerting my small abilities in support of
> the Liberties of my Country, but that is but poor food to
> subsist a family upon in old Age.

With no attempt to hide his bitterness, he added that he could hardly count on the thanks of his fellow countrymen; "publick gratitude," he wrote, "would be a novelty in modern politicks."

Those harsh words came from a man who had sacrificed everything for the sake of his country, and, admittedly, for a chance at fame and glory, a man whose marches through the American countryside took him to places where other Americans actively worked against him, or hid their supplies from him, or simply didn't care whether the cause lived or died. Time and again, in private moments as he wrote or dictated letters in his quarters, he spoke of his disappointment with his fellow countrymen. How could they not care about liberty? How could they spy for the British? How could they believe they had no stake in the stuggle of the army that fought in their name?

To his credit, though, he never let his doubts and his bitterness distract him from his duty. With his new title and new responsibilities, Quartermaster General Greene left the camp at Valley Forge and moved to bigger quarters in Moore Hall, the home of a nearby patriot. The work was urgent. But the immediate crisis at Valley Forge had passed.

The army's bitter civil war was over by the time the trees in southeastern Pennsylvania were in bloom, signaling the end of a terrible winter. The intrigue, which Greene took as evidence of a full-scale conspiracy, ended in a complete rout of his and Washington's critics. "General Conway is at last caught in his own trap," Greene wrote with evident delight. "He is a most worthless officer as ever served in our army." The Board of War was discredited and stripped of most of its influence; Conway and Mifflin were destined never again to play important roles in army affairs, while Gates escaped with his reputation because of Washington's conciliatory attitude toward the victor of Saratoga.

The soldiers themselves, while hollow-cheeked and dressed in rags, actually emerged from winter as a better drilled, more professional army, thanks to the arrival of a gruff but well-liked Prussian who called himself Baron von Steuben. He was not a baron at all, but he was a magnificent military instructor, even though he spoke no English. (Supposedly, he demanded that his swearing be translated into English for the benefit of his pupils.) Despite Greene's skepticism about foreign officers, Steuben, like Lafayette, became a friend and an ally. He also became Conway's replacement as the army's inspector general.

The Board of War's downfall came after its members recommended a wintertime invasion of Canada in mid-February 1778. Gates, Mifflin, and the other board members offered nominal command to Lafayette—he was French, after all—but they tried to name Conway as second in command and de facto commander. The expedition soon fell apart and was condemned as folly from the beginning. This was one disaster that could not be blamed on Greene's poor advice or Washington's flawed leadership. The blame lay squarely with the Board of War, whose members showed themselves even less adept at strategy than they were at politics. Conway assumed the pose of aggrieved party and submitted his resignation from the army. To his apparent surprise, Congress accepted it. Even more humiliation followed: Conway challenged one of Washington's subordinates, John Cadwalader, to a duel and was shot in the mouth. He survived and sailed to France in disrepute. Mifflin resigned from the Board of War, although he remained a major general. Gates avoided the criticism heaped on his two allies when Washington signaled that he bore him no ill will.

As the crucible of Valley Forge passed into history, there was more good news for Greene personally and the army in general. The early winter tensions between Greene and his wife had given way to the inevitable, and Caty was pregnant again. (Caty's biographers indicate that she may not have welcomed this development.) Congress approved an extra month's pay for every soldier in camp, along with an extra ration of rum to celebrate the end of winter. News arrived in camp that the British commander in Philadelphia, Lord Howe, was about to be sacked and replaced by General Henry Clinton—a sign of British discontent with the war. And, best of all, in late April the army in Valley Forge learned that the French had signed a treaty of alliance with the fledgling United States. Greene joined Washington in reviewing a grand parade in camp to celebrate the occasion. The troops, under Steuben's command, marched and drilled with more energy, discipline, and inspiration than ever before. It was hard to believe that only months ago they were starving, ragged, and seemingly beaten.

Still, though, this revived army would be only as good as its supplies. And nobody knew that more than the new quartermaster general. Greene and his two capable deputies, Cox and Pettit, circulated a flyer addressed to "the Inhabitants of the United States," in which they promised "punctuality in payment" for goods and services, "a proper deportment" when dealing with civilians, and an end to the "many irregularities" that had taken place under Mifflin's leadership, or lack thereof. The circular also informed civilians that because cash payments in exchange for goods or services would be "impracticable," civilians would be given printed certificates, which they could then exchange for cash at payment offices. That was more easily said than done, although there was little Greene could do about late or nonexistent payments.

With Cox and Pettit already in place, Greene gathered around himself other competent and creative problem solvers to oversee the department's cumbersome bureaucracy, which employed three thousand people, from deputy quartermaster generals to wagon masters to laborers to clerks. The quartermaster's agents operated in defined geographic districts and were responsible for purchases and supply within that area. They reported to a regional quartermaster's office, which employed clerks, messengers, and other support staff, which in turn reported back to the quartermaster general himself. The efforts of many of these agents and deputies, like Cox and Pettit, have been lost to history, but they achieved nothing less than the army's salvation. Washington did not exaggerate when he told Greene that all would be lost without a dependable supply system. They had barely survived Valley Forge. They could not survive a repeat.

Greene's work in reorganizing the quartermaster's department was just as critical, and in some ways just as astonishing, as Steuben's achievement in turning the stooped-shouldered soldiers of Valley Forge into a steel-spined fighting force. Through springtime, Greene assessed the department's most pressing needs, which included a severe shortage of wagons to transport supplies and the persistent need for feed for the army's horses and livestock. It was, as Greene knew it would be, unglamorous work, but vital all the same. He ordered hundreds of thousands of bushels of grain to be stored in strategically placed depots along the Delaware, Schuylkill, and Hudson rivers, in or near Reading, Trenton, and Lancaster, and throughout the strategic state of New Jersey. His command of detail was obvious in a letter dispatched to Colonel Biddle, the officer in charge of forage.

> In forming your magazines, give all sorts of grain the
> preference to wheat. Oats first, Corn next, Rye next and so on.
> You must get a number of Screws made to Screw all the Hay
> and employ Hands to do it either at the farmers barns or at
> the magazines. . . . There must be a number of forage carts
> provided to be employed in no other business.

All of this cost money, and Greene was not afraid to spend what he believed was needed. He said as much to the president of Congress, Henry Laurens. A "large Sum of Money is absolutely ncessary for the Quarter Master's Department to enable us to make due Preparation for the coming Campaign," he wrote. And because Congress seemed reluctant to concede this point, Greene informed Laurens that he had, in essence, written a check for fifty thousand pounds against the national treasury to pay for supplies gathered in Easton, Pennsylvania.

Among the beneficiaries of Greene's spending spree was a small, family-run business in Rhode Island whose proprietor, Jacob Greene, was familiar with the quartermaster general. Jacob was more than just the quartermaster's brother. He was the quartermaster's business partner, too. Jacob and Nathanael, along with their cousin Griffin Greene, were now the sole owners of the family business, renamed Jacob Greene & Company. The other Greene brothers had sold their interest in the firm just before Nathanael became quartermaster—unfortunate timing on their part. Jacob Greene & Company's appointment as a contractor for the quartermaster general was not one of Nathanael Greene's best decisions. The company was not a major vendor, but quantity didn't matter. The conflict of interest should have been obvious, for the Greenes did little to conceal their plans. Nathanael promised brother Jacob that he would provide him with "all the information" he could without departing "from the lines of honor." Of course, Greene himself would define where those lines were drawn.

Griffin Greene was not reluctant to ask his cousin the quartermaster for favors, even when they involved private business. He told Nathanael that the company needed a little help "to git our goods" through the states of Connecticut, New York, and New Jersey. States imposed duties on goods shipped across borders, but Griffin wanted cousin Nathanael to designate the company's private cargo as military goods and thus exempt from taxes. It's uncertain whether he did so.

Greene, convinced of his own patriotism and purity of motive, would later lash out at critics who deplored this cozy relationship with his brother and cousin. Greene certainly was not the only officer or politician who maintained private business interests that benefited from inside information, contacts, and the war in general. George Washington, for example, invested in private vessels that raided British ships, made off with whatever goods they captured, and then sold them. Jacob Greene & Company also invested in these vessels, called privateers, thanks to the profits they made off government contracts. And although there is no indication that the family company ever sold goods to the army at anything more than standard market rates, Greene must have believed he had something to hide. He told his brother Christopher that he made a practice of burning letters containing what he called "family secrets."

Luckily, however, enough letters escaped the pyre to offer a glimpse of how the Greenes worked the system. According to a letter from the barely literate Jacob to Nathanael, the family company had been paid to provide, among other items, fifteen thousand canteens to the army. But Jacob was perplexed: what kind of canteens did brother Nathanael require? "I am At A Loos To Know [whether] They Are to Be Wood or Tin," he wrote. Meanwhile Griffin Greene won a contract to supply the army with four hundred tents—although not before he wrote to cousin Nathanael to complain that another vendor was bidding against him.

Welcome as this business was for Jacob Greene & Company, apparently Jacob wasn't counting on much in the way of long-term profits. He told his brother, "I Fear Billy How [Lord Howe] is . . . preparing To Give you A Fatal Blow in the opening of the Campaign." As it happened, Billy How was soon setting sail across the Atlantic to explain why he had not already adminstered a fatal blow to the Americans. General Henry Clinton was now in command.

The army still was encamped in Valley Forge on June 17 when Nathanael Greene reported to General Washington's headquarters for a council of war. Five other major generals attended the conference, including none other than Charles Lee, whom the British finally had released nearly two years after his capture. With Lee were his beloved dogs, and even an ordinary wit might have suggested that the British considered themselves better off, and the rebels that much worse off, with Lee and his companions in Valley Forge instead of New York. Joining Washington and the major generals were nine brigadier generals. Greene's place at the table for these deliberations was a minor personal victory. His primary responsibility was the quartermaster's office, and although he retained the title of major general, he was now a staff officer with no frontline command. Staff officers generally were not invited to councils of war, where strategy and tactics—not supply routes—were discussed. Washington, however, still valued Greene's insights, and so he allowed his quartermaster to participate in strategy sessions.

The topic of their deliberations would have seemed far too fantastic only five months before: the possibility of an attack on the British in Philadelphia. Word had been filtering into camp for nearly a month that the British were showing signs of leaving the once and future rebel capital. Though the Americans didn't know it, the British had decided they could no longer hold Philadelphia with the French and their navy now in the war. In fact, even as the American generals were debating their course of action, they learned that the bulk of Clinton's army had crossed the

Delaware into New Jersey, headed for New York by land rather than sea. Ten thousand troops, loaded down with more than a thousand wagons and other encumbrances, would have to make the ninety-mile journey along rutted roads and in full view of the New Jersey militia.

Quartermaster General Nathanael Greene was ordered to put the army in motion immediately. A glorious opportunity presented itself on the plains of New Jersey, and the energized and well-supplied American army was determined to take advantage of it.

The army left Valley Forge on June 19, and as the troops moved out toward New Jersey, Caty Greene bade farewell to her husband. She had been away from Rhode Island, from her children, for a momentous and difficult year. She was a survivor of Valley Forge, a witness to suffering and deprivation as well as the heroism and sacrifice of the patriot soldiers. She had strengthened her friendship with Martha Washington, her only true friend among the officers' wives. And she had experienced both the highs and lows of marriage: the joy of her reunion with Nathanael the previous June, the tensions of a cold winter camp, and the flowering of renewed love in the spring. She was pregnant, as usual after winter camp, but at least the tension between husband and wife was just another bitter memory from winter. Soon, Nathanael was sending her affectionate and gossipy letters. "Mrs. Knox," he wrote in one, "is fatter than ever, which is a great mortification to her. The General [Knox] is equally fat and therefore one cannot laugh at the other." Greene's news no doubt brought a smile to Caty's lips. She was proud of her own appearance and well aware that her beauty and demeanor made her the envy of other women in camp, including Lucy Knox.

As they moved out for a rendezvous with the enemy, the Americans marched roughly parallel to the retreating British, who were to the south. Clinton's troops, bogged down with hundreds and hundreds of wagons, were very slow, at one point traveling just twenty miles in three days. The Americans could travel lighter and faster because Greene had established supply depots along the route. "It has been and will be very expensive," he noted of the depots, "but it is unavoidable."

At nine o'clock in the morning on June 24, as the smells of camp breakfast filled the air, Greene trudged to Washington's headquarters for another council of war. It already was a hot, muggy day.

Washington told the generals that the British march was so slow he suspected something was wrong. He wanted to attack with the whole of the American army against Clinton's entire force.

Charles Lee said he had never heard anything so ridiculous, and he argued that Washington should simply preserve the army until the French arrived, whenever that might be. As Greene listened to Lee's oration, he became increasingly bitter and angry. Most of the men in the room seemed to agree with Lee, except for Washington's aide Alexander Hamilton. Greene finally spoke up and gently suggested an alternative: send a detachment of two brigades to support an assault by light troops on the British rear and flanks. The rest of the army would be close enough to support the attack in case this limited battle became more serious.

The generals chose an even more limited engagement, advising Washington to send only about fifteen hundred men to attack the British flanks. Greene, with reluctance verging on disgust, agreed to the compromise and signed a document with the generals' recommendations. He believed he was powerless to formally object, as his friend Anthony Wayne did by refusing to sign the recommendation. Greene believed that as a staff officer, and not a field commander, he had no right to raise objections to a battle plan. But that night, still furious with Lee, he returned to his tent to write a personal message to Washington.

> I must confess the opinion I subscribed to . . . does not
> perfectly coincide with my Sentiments. I am not for
> hazarding a general action unnecessarily but I am clearly of
> opinion for making a serious impression with light Troops
> and for having the Army in supporting distance.

Greene believed the Americans had to seize the opportunity that presented itself just a few miles to the south, near Monmouth Court House. "If we suffer the enemy to pass through [New Jersey] without attempting anything upon them," he told Washington, "I think we shall ever regret it."

Greene was not the only one who held this view. That night, Washington received similar messages from Wayne and Lafayette. Their private arguments persuaded Washington to disregard the formal advice of the war council. The army would swing to its right and march south to move closer to Clinton at Monmouth. Then an American detachment, which grew to five thousand, would attack the British rear guard. Charles Lee would command the assault. Greene would remain with Washington and the main army, temporarily in charge of Lee's division and ready to move into action if the limited engagement became a general action.

The day of the assault, June 28, was insufferably hot. Lee's attack was in trouble after only a few hours, and by late morning, the Americans were in full retreat. Unknown to the Americans, Clinton had reinforced his rear guard with some of his best troops, under the command of the ubiquitous Lord Cornwallis. Though Lee's retreat may have been prudent, Washington was furious when he learned of it. According to legend, the commander in chief let loose oaths the likes of which his brother officers had never heard, at least not from Washington's mouth. "Delightful," said an American general named Charles Scott. "Never have I enjoyed such swearing before or since."

Even before Lee's retreat, Washington ordered Greene to put aside his paperwork and move forward to support the attack. But when Greene learned that Lee was in headlong retreat, he reversed course on his own accord and rejoined the main American line, now threatened by the counterattacking British.

Greene was deployed on the American right. Cornwallis was marching toward him. It was midafternoon, the temperature was nearly a hundred degrees, and the humidity was unbearable.

Seven thousand British soldiers charged twelve thousand Americans. What Greene had envisioned as a sizable battle between detachments had become a general action involving the whole of the American army and a large portion of Clinton's. The British unleashed a furious cannonade, and the Americans replied in kind. Greene and his men held their ground as Cornwallis deployed units from the famed Coldstream Guards along with battle-hardened Hessians and British light cavalry. They charged Greene's position twice, and twice they were driven back.

The American line stood firm. Here, during several hours of ferocious fighting under a terrible sun, Steuben's miracle at Valley Forge took shape in flesh and blood, courage and discipline. Only months removed from the horrors of Valley Forge, the Continental army stood its ground against some of the finest soldiers in the world. By five o'clock, the battle dissolved into sporadic exchanges of cannon fire.

The two sides had fought to a draw; the British were able to resume their march to New York the following day, and the Americans were too exhausted to pursue. But the Americans nevertheless considered Monmouth a victory, for they knew just how far they had come since those terrible days just six months earlier.

Once they were recovered and rested, the Continental army marched toward the Hudson River to watch over Clinton. Spirits were high, but conditions remained oppressive. "We have suffered considerably by the Heat," Greene later wrote. "We marched through a Country from Monmouth to Brunswick not unlike the Deserts of Arabia for Soil and Climate." During the march, Greene reverted to his duties as quartermaster general, scouting out campsites, making sure supplies kept up with the march, and attending to an unending stream of paperwork.

On July 4, the tired and thirsty army camped near New Brunswick, where the second anniversary of American independence was celebrated with a parade and cannon fire. The troops were given extra rations of rum, and there were shouts and laughter in the summer night. The gray, cold, and hollowed-out ghost of Valley Forge had been exorcised.

The Continental army, and the Revolution itself, were renewed.

9 | "It Wounds My Feelings"

In his short service as quartermaster general, Nathanael Greene had shown himself to be the right man for the job. The assignment required organization; he was organized. It required an understanding of logistics and supply; he was a businessman. It helped to have a field-level understanding of the army's needs; he had been in the field since the siege of Boston.

In one way, however, Greene was poorly suited to the position. Being quartermaster general of the Continental army was a thankless job. But Nathanael Greene liked to be thanked.

More to the point, Nathanael Greene wished to be recognized—for his service, for his sacrifice, for his competence. The slightest hint of underappreciation was likely to inspire waves of self-pity and occasional threats of resignation. Even while he was considering the quartermaster's job, when the army still was encamped in Valley Forge, he confided to his brother Jacob and his cousin Griffin that he might quit the army. "It would be agreeable to retire if no injury was to follow to the public," he told Jacob, "for the Splendor of the Camp is but a poor compensation for the sacrifices made to enjoy it."

Hardly the sentiments of a selfless, liberty-loving patriot. But Greene missed his wife; he missed the children he fathered but did not know; he missed the opportunity to make himself wealthy. He wished for recognition but believed he had received only slights. Most recently, he was disappointed that his role in the fighting at Monmouth had been overlooked, just as it had at Brandywine. And Washington had said little or nothing about Greene's heroic efforts in transforming the quartermaster's office. But although Greene may have taken this oversight to heart, he did not hold it against the man he worshipped. Often, when he was depressed or feeling sorry for himself, all Greene needed was an acknowledgment, even if unspoken, that he was useful and appreciated. When he felt that way, he rarely complained or indulged in flights of self-pity. There is no question that he was not happy in his new role as the army's quartermaster general. His duties truly were thankless: he would win no medals for keeping the supply wagons running; he would garner no praise for dealing with skeptical civilian merchants and farmers reluctant to accept Continental currency; he would find no laurels in supervising a sprawling bureaucracy.

Instead of plotting strategy in Washington's headquarters, he spent his nights squinting by candlelight at accounts that recorded, for example, the number of axes and blacksmith's tools and tables and blankets that were in the army's possession and which states had provided them. A more secure but less ambitious man might have have found this kind of work its own reward, for without such attention to detail, the army would collapse for lack of supplies. But Nathanael Greene—the insecure soldier who walked with a limp; the amateur general among professionals; the self-educated Quaker who corresponded with learned men in camp and in Congress—needed frequent affirmation. It was a quality that, like every other necessity in the Continental army, often was hard to come by.

The army continued its march toward the Hudson River after celebrating the Fourth of July in New Brunswick. With Clinton safely back in

New York City, the Americans once again had to defend against a British move up the strategic river that divided New England from the mid-Atlantic states. Washington's defensive strategy, however, began to change when he learned in mid-July that a French fleet was off Sandy Hook in New Jersey. Instead of simply guarding against a British offensive, the Americans now had a chance to lay siege to New York. Washington was eager to grasp the opportunity.

Greene was not at Washington's side after the army left New Brunswick. He was riding miles ahead of the troops, scouting out possible campsites across the Hudson. Caty, who was pregnant, ill, and at home in Rhode Island, apparently expressed some of her own thoughts on where the army ought to camp. This rare excursion into her husband's business prompted a reply from Nathanael on July 17.

> You express a strong desire to get the Army on the East side
> of the [Hudson] River and [you say that] you have political
> as well as private reasons for it. Your private reasons I can
> interpret; but your Political ones I cannot divine. You may
> rest assured that there must be something very very
> uncommon to prevent my coming home; you cannot have a
> greater desire to see me than I have you and the Children. I
> long to hear the little rogues prattle. . . . Although I have
> been absent from you I have not been inconstant in love,
> unfaithful to my vows, or unjust to your bed.

Washington caught up with Greene on the east bank of the river in mid-July, and the two men conferred in Haverstraw. Greene then returned to his assignment. His search was not easy, for the territory was unfamiliar and the weather remained brutally hot. When several days had passed without word from Greene, Washington sent a message to him complaining of "neglect" in the quartermaster's office. What's more, Washington wanted to speak with Greene personally before writing to the French admiral Charles d'Estaing about plans for a siege of New York. But he could not do so until Greene returned to headquarters.

Greene might have taken Washington's message as a sign of his value to the commander, who seemed to be saying that he could not make important strategic decisions without his favorite general by his side. Instead, he felt the sting of his hero's disapproval. The chip he carried on his shoulder never felt heavier.

On July 21, with the army camped, finally, in White Plains, Greene sent a long letter to Washington baring his insecurities and wish for approval in language he had never used before when addressing Washington. At times blunt, at other times self-pitying to the extreme, Greene's langage was as raw as his wounded ego: "Your Excellency has made me very unhappy. I can submit very patiently to deserved censure; but it wounds my feelings exceedingly to meet with a rebuke for doing what I conceived to be a proper part of my duty, and in the order of things."

He explained that he had been meticulous in trying to find the proper location to camp the army, to the detriment of his health. The weather was hot, he pointed out, and he was exhausted. "And here I must observe that neither my constitution or strength are equal to constant exercise," he wrote, making an observation that seemed to belie his long service at Washington's side, which if nothing else had been strenuous.

> Your Excellency well knows how I came into this
> department. It was by your special request, and you must be
> sensible there is no other man upon Earth could have
> brought me into the business but you. . . . I flatter myself
> when your Excellency . . . will do me the justice to say I have
> not been negligent or inattentive to my duty.

Well into the letter, after a long recitation of his truly extraordinary service to Washington and the nation ("I have never solicited you for a furlough to go home to indulge in pleasure or to improve my interest"), Greene picked at old scabs and unwittingly revealed what hurts and grievances lay behind this extraordinary exercise: "I have never been troublesome to your Excellency to publish any thing to my advantage altho I think myself as justly entitled as some others who have been more fortunate. Particularly in the action of Brandywine." Nearly a year after the battle, Greene's emotional wounds were bleeding still.

In closing, Greene reminded Washington, "[I have] always endeavored to deserve the public esteem and your Excellency's approbation." Since it was clear that his work left something to be desired, Greene offered his resignation: "As I came into the quarter masters department with reluctance so I shall leave it with pleasure. Your influence brought me in and the want of your approbation will induce me to go out."

Washington, a man not given to displays of private or public emotion, surely was pained to read this almost pitiful letter from a fellow general whose wisdom, dedication, and sheer competence had become so vital to the American cause. He had not meant to offend Greene; what's more, he hardly needed to read Greene's recitation of the sufferings and sacrifices he had endured for so long. Washington's own record on that score was somewhat impressive, too.

The leadership abilities of George Washington have won praise and admiration through the centuries, but even his fondest admirers will confess that he often seemed aloof and remote. On this occasion, however, Washington chose urgency and intimacy, and perhaps as he calculated, the combination had its intended effect. Greene's letter had been delivered to his headquarters by messenger; Washington replied to it immediately, even though he was surrounded by staff and had on his desk a pile of letters from the South that required his attention. To his wounded general, he wrote: "I can, and do assure you, that I have ever been happy in your friendship, and have no scruples in declaring that I think myself indebted to your Abilities, honour and candour, to your attachment to me, and your faithful services to the Public."

Having written words Greene wished so desperately to read, Washington then reminded him that their friendship "must not debar" frank discussion of the army's concerns. For several hot, humid July days on the banks of the Hudson River, Washington could find nobody from Greene's department, nor, in fact, Greene himself. He was not happy and believed he was right to bring this to Greene's attention. "But let me beseech you my dear Sir not to harbor any distrusts of my friendship, or conceive that I mean to wound the feelings of a Person whom I greatly esteem and regard," he wrote.

A little more than two weeks later, on August 3, Washington sent Congress a letter filled with praise for Greene's transformation of the quartermaster general's office. "[In] justice to General Greene," Washington wrote, "I take occasion to observe that the public is much indebted to him for his judicious management and active exertions in his present department. When he entered upon it, he found it in a most confused, distracted and destitute state." But now, Washington said, the department "has undergone a very happy change, and such as enabled us, with great facility, to make a sudden move with the whole Army and baggage from Valley Forge." Thanks to Greene's "method and System," the army no longer suffered from lack of supplies and organization.

Greene returned with enthusiasm to his work. Washington had decided not to lay siege to New York, but to launch an assault on a place Greene knew well: Newport, Rhode Island, which the British had seized in December 1776. Greene was given the job of collecting wagons, teams, and boats to move reinforcements to his home state, where his friend General John Sullivan was in command. The attack would be the first joint Franco-American operation of the war, for the French fleet and its four thousand marines agreed to sail from Sandy Hook to Rhode Island to cooperate with Sullivan's forces.

Communications were paramount, and Washington was not happy with the slow speed of messages to and from Rhode Island. Greene, the army's problem solver, devised a system relying on express riders stationed in four outposts between White Plains and Providence. The problem was fixed.

Greene's bruised feelings were on the mend, but he still had a hard time reconciling himself to solving prosaic supply problems while his friend Sullivan was preparing for battle—and in Greene's home state, no less. Greene believed his place ought to be in Rhode Island, not in White

Plains arranging for wagons and for express riders. He lobbied Washington, who by now realized how brittle Greene could be, for a place on the line with Sullivan. It is impossible to know whether Greene's previous outburst influenced Washington, but the commander in chief suprisingly did not rule out the possibility of Greene leaving his duties as quartermaster general for a chance at glory in Rhode Island. In a letter dated July 23, Greene told Sullivan:

> You are the most happy man in the World. What a child of
> fortune. The expedition going on against Newport I think
> cannot fail. . . . I wish you success with all my Soul and
> intend if possible to come home and . . . to take a command
> of part of the Troops under you. I wish most ardently to be
> with you.

Washington granted his wish the following day. After an absence of three years, Nathanael Greene was going home to help liberate Newport—and home was precisely where he was going first. His deputy Charles Pettit took over the quartermaster's department during his absence. He left camp and rode one hundred and seventy miles in three days, arriving at home in Coventry at nine o'clock at night on July 30. For the first time in the young lives of the Greene children, the family was together.

Young George was now four; Martha, who was nicknamed Patty, was three. Neither of the children knew their father except through stories from Caty and other Greene family members. Caty herself was in the eighth month of her third pregnancy, uncomfortable, often not well, and always anxious. They spent several days reintroducing themselves to each other and socializing with relatives and friends before Greene turned his attention to the coming Franco-American movement on Newport. "I am . . . as busy as a Bee in a tar barrel," he told a friend.

He made an appointment to visit the count d'Estaing aboard his flagship in Narragansett Bay but was unable to keep it. "Accidents of the day" and uncertain winds prevented their meeting, he explained to his new comrade in arms. The Frenchman was eager to meet Greene; he told Washington that the "reputation of this General Officer made his arrival to be wished."

Greene left the children and Caty after about a week and set out first for Providence and then to the American camp in Tiverton. What had seemed like a mere sideshow was shaping up as a major confrontation. Washington, who had long favored an invasion of New York rather than an attack on Newport, now sensed the possibilities. A victory in Rhode Island, he said, would provide "the finishing blow to British pretentions of sovereignty over this country." The presence in Rhode Island of not only Greene but also the marquis de Lafayette signaled the new importance Washington placed on this hastily organized offensive.

Sullivan assigned Greene to the American right wing, with Lafayette on the left and Sullivan himself in the center. Greene's men were mostly Continental army regulars who had marched to Rhode Island with Lafayette. Many of the troops streaming into camp were New England militiamen, including a unit under the command of John Hancock, the former president of the Continental Congress. Nathanael Greene's cousin Christopher Greene marched into camp with his small unit of free blacks from Rhode Island. During the early months of 1778, while the army was huddled in Valley Forge, Christopher Greene and Nathanael's old friend Sammy Ward had begun recruiting an all-black regiment from their home state. Southern political leaders were aghast, but Rhode Island, true to its tolerant roots, persisted. The state's assembly and governor agreed to purchase the freedom of any slaves willing to fight—as long as they passed muster with Greene, Ward, and other officers. About a hundred and thirty men joined what would become the army's first all-black regiment, and they were assigned not to menial tasks but to the front lines in the planned Rhode Island offensive.

While Nathanael Greene played no direct role in this enterprise, it reflected well on him that the men who defied the prejudices of the times were friends or relatives of his. General James Varnum, his onetime commander in the Kentish Guards, formally approved the effort of cousin Christopher and friend Sammy Ward, as well as a lieutenant colonel named Jeremiah Olney.

The impending battle in Rhode Island brought these friends together again: Varnum, Ward, Christopher, and, of course, Nathanael Greene. Only four years had passed since Varnum and the two Greenes had so eagerly enlisted in the Kentish Guards, four years since they had drilled and trained in earnest on the green in East Greenwich, no doubt to the amusement of the town's elders and cynics. But their example inspired the likes of Sammy Ward, who followed his elders into the service when the war broke out and the Kentish Guards were transformed from play soldiers to the genuine article. Now they were officers and veterans who had seen the awful effects of war, who had persisted in the face of setback, defeat, and misery. Their Rhode Island upbringing and attitudes had inspired them to extend the cause of liberty to the young nation's outcasts.

And now, just miles from home, friends, and family, they were prepared to strike a blow for the freedom of Rhode Island.

The assault was to begin on August 10, when Sullivan's ten thousand troops were to cross a strait separating Tiverton from Aquidneck Island, north of Newport. At the same time, four thousand French marines would disembark from their ships and land on an island to the west of Newport. The allied forces would then squeeze the outnumbered British garrison from either side, with help from the French warships.

The day before the planned attack, however, Sullivan realized the British had abandoned their outer defenses on Aquidneck Island, so, without first informing the French, he ordered his men across the strait. The French were not pleased, and when a British fleet arrived off Rhode Island that very afternoon, d'Estaing and his thousands of troops weighed anchor and set sail to do battle on the sea. Sullivan, meanwhile, continued toward Newport while awaiting d'Estaing's return.

While the French chased the British and the Americans dug in outside Newport, the summer weather turned violent. Heavy winds and drenching rain on August 12 and 13 made life miserable and even fatal in the American camp. Several soldiers in exposed positions died during the storm. Greene spent these stormy days in a farmhouse behind the lines. There, he had more than the weather and the coming battle to worry about. Caty had sent word that she was feeling ill, which was bad enough. But the recent visit with his children, however short, had reminded Greene of the risk he was taking on behalf of his country. Thoughts of little George and Martha haunted Greene as he and the American assault force moved to within a couple of miles of Newport. He wrote to Caty on August 16:

> I am sorry to find you are getting unwell. I am afraid it is the effect of anxiety and fearful apprehension. . . . Would to God it was in my power to give peace to your bosom, which, I fear, is like the troubled ocean. I feel your distress. My bosom beats with compassion and kind concern for your welfare, and the more so at this time as your situation is criticial. I thank you kindly for your concern for my health and safety; the former is not very perfect, the latter is in the book of fate. I wish to live but for your sake and those little pledges of conjugal affection which Providence has blessed us with. Those dear little rogues have begun to command a large share of my affection and attention.

Greene's reference to a "troubled ocean" was not a coincidence. For even as he and the American troops suffered through the rain and gales, British and French sailors and marines in warships off Rhode Island were suffering, too. The storms brutalized ship and sailor alike, and both fleets were badly battered even though they never fired a shot at each other. The British eventually withdrew to New York, allowing the French to return to Rhode Island. Sullivan and Greene assumed that the offensive would resume, but d'Estaing decided he was not fit to fight. He told the Americans he had no choice but to leave Rhode Island and refit his ships in Boston. The joint offensive, which had offered much promise, would have to be scrapped.

Sullivan, a rough-hewn man not known for subtle language or delicate manners, was beside himself. "This movement has raised every voice against the French nation, revived all those ancient prejudices against the faith and sincerity of that people, and inclines them most heartily to curse the new alliance," Sullivan wrote. Greene, too, was furious, telling a friend that the British garrison "would be all our own in a few days if the fleet and French forces would only cooperate with us, but alas they will not." But Greene also understood that preserving the alliance with France was as important as preserving the Continental army. Sullivan's public criticism of the French threatened future cooperation. Greene, then, was thrust into the new and unfamiliar role of diplomat in the sudden crisis between America and France.

Sullivan sent Greene and Lafayette to d'Estaing's flagship, the *Languedoc,* to ask the French for more time. On the morning of August 21, as they boarded the small craft that was to take them to the *Languedoc,* Greene turned to Lafayette and said, presumably with a smile, "If we fail in our negotiations, we shall at least get a good dinner!" So he thought. Years later, Lafayette would recall that Greene became seasick once he was aboard the *Languedoc* and was in no mood to enjoy a fine French meal.

He persisted with his mission all the same. Using Lafayette as his translator, Greene pleaded with d'Estaing to remain in Narragansett Bay for forty-eight hours. They could still achieve their objective—the liberation of Newport—but success depended on the Americans and French operating together. The Frenchman told Greene that he agreed, but his captains wished to leave for Boston immediately. He asked Greene to summarize his arguments in a memorandum. Seasick and miserable though he was, Greene retired to a desk and spent the afternoon composing a formal and polite plea for cooperation. He promised the French that their warships could be repaired by his friends in Providence once the action in Newport was over. "The Garrison is important, the reduction almost certain," he argued. "The influence it would have upon the British Politicks will be very considerable. I think it therefore highly worth running some risque to accomplish."

Greene submitted his petition to d'Estaing that afternoon. Then, no doubt to his great relief, he and Lafayette left the pitching warship and returned to camp near Newport. The French answer arrived the next day, when they weighed anchor and sailed out of Narragansett Bay.

Thousands of militiamen saw the ships leaving that morning. Without the fleet's marines and firepower, they knew the expedition was doomed. So the militia companies left in droves. Sullivan's force of ten thousand quickly was reduced by half, further confirming Greene's low opinion of the militia's reliability.

Sullivan, his dreams of a glorious victory fading as the French warships disappeared from view, wrote a letter of protest to d'Estaing on August 22, accusing the French of treachery, cowardice, and any number of unmanly vices. The fleet's retreat, Sullivan's letter charged, was "derogatory to the honor of France . . . and highly injurious to the alliance formed between the two nations." Greene unwisely signed this indiscreet and inflammatory missive, avoiding a confrontation with his more experienced colleague. Before the Battle of Monmouth, he had joined Washington's other generals in signing a document containing advice with which he did not agree, and now he refused to confront the ill-tempered Sullivan over a letter he knew was bound to cause problems. The French action disappointed Greene as much as it did Sullivan, but Greene understood that a highly charged letter might cause permanent damage to America's vital alliance with France. But, rather than give voice to his objections, he meekly signed the letter, as he had at Monmouth.

As Greene suspected, the letter became an international incident. Lafayette sent a letter of his own to d'Estaing, assuring him that he had had nothing to do with it and, in fact, condemned it. But Sullivan was not finished: he issued an order to his remaining troops, confidently asserting that they didn't need the French after all. American arms, he wrote, would prevail despite France's "refusal to assist."

Sullivan might well have believed what he told his troops—that they needed no help from their ally—but Greene knew better. Sullivan's assertions, Greene realized, had implications beyond the alliance. To

Greene's chagrin, many delegates in Congress continued to insist that the war could be won with a small regular army reinforced with citizen soldiers in the militia service. The Rhode Island campaign, however, demonstrated the folly of such thinking. The militia melted away at the first sign of adversity. So the Americans needed the French, and needed them desperately.

Greene sent a private, conciliatory letter to Lafayette, which tempered the young Frenchman's anger. Greene was "sensible," Lafayette told Washington, and had offered views "very different from the expressions I have a right to complain of." Washington, who readily agreed that Sullivan's letter to d'Estaing was "impolitic," deputized Greene to resolve and contain the dispute that Sullivan had started. "I depend much upon your temper and influence to conciliate that animosity, which I plainly perceive . . . between the American officers and the French in our service," Washington wrote. The commander in chief clearly was worried that publication of the offensive documents would inflame public opinion against the French. So, Washington told Greene, it was imperative to make sure that Sullivan's words remained secret.

> I beg you will take every measure to keep the protest . . .
> from being made public. . . . [My] dear Sir, you can conceive
> my meaning better than I can express it, and I therefore fully
> depend upon your exerting yourself to heal all private
> animosities between our principal officers and the French,
> and to prevent all illiberal expressions and reflections that
> may fall from the Army at large.

Working with Lafayette, Greene soothed relations with d'Estaing, who actually offered to march the French marines from Boston to Newport if that would help the Americans. It was a fine gesture, but it was clear the expedition would not achieve its goal without a fleet in Narragansett Bay. Nevertheless, even with a depleted force, Greene urged Sullivan to attack. Choose three hundred experienced troops, Greene told Sullivan, put them aboard boats "with good Oars Men," and land them south of the British redoubts. The flanking maneuver would place the Newport garrison between Sullivan's main force and the detachment.

Greene later admitted that his plan was far too risky, and Sullivan wisely decided to withdraw to the northern part of Aquidneck Island under cover of darkness on August 28. If d'Estaing changed his mind and chose to return to Rhode Island—a vain hope—Sullivan believed he still might salvage something from this campaign. He deployed his troops along the two-mile width of the island and again assigned Greene command of the shrunken army's right wing. Sammy Ward, temporarily in command of the free black troops whom Christopher Greene had organized, was entrenched on a redoubt guarding Greene's right flank. Christopher Greene was deployed in the center of the American line, while Varnum's Rhode Islanders were arrayed on the left of Greene's line.

The British and Hessian forces from Newport attacked the American position not long after sunrise on August 29. The Americans fell back but then held as both sides began exchanging artillery fire. Greene favored more aggressive tactics, telling Sullivan he should move the entire force forward to crush the British. And once again, Sullivan chose to defend rather than attack, a prudent decision Greene later praised. As the battle continued into the afternoon, the British brought up four small warships to pound Greene's position, but he turned his artillery east toward the bay, firing on and eventually chasing away the warships.

At about two o'clock, Greene's position came under heavy assault as a Hessian unit tried to break through the American right. Greene counterattacked with a combination of Continental regulars, Massachusetts militia units, and a unit of light troops. Ward's black troops fought with conspicuous bravery, twice beating back a Hessian assault with bayonets and bare hands. The enemy soon retreated, to Greene's delight. "We . . . put the Enemy to the rout and I had the pleasure to see them run in worse disorder than they did at the battle of Monmouth," Greene later told Washington. He expressed his emotions more colorfully in a letter to one of his friends, the Unitarian minister John Murray.

To behold our fellows, chasing the British off the field of
battle, afforded a pleasure which you can better conceive
than I can describe. If, my dear Murray, I had before been an
unbeliever, I have had sufficient evidence of the intervention
of Divine Providence to reclaim me from infidelity.

The Americans suffered about two hundred casualties; the British and
Hessians, nearly three hundred. The battle was a draw, but once again,
the Americans had fought well and bravely, particularly those under
Greene's command. Greene soon learned, however, that the battle was
not quite over. Sullivan, bitter over what he considered a lost opportunity,
continued to criticize the French, adding to Greene's bulging diplomatic
portfolio. He wrote another discreet letter to d'Estaing, saying that he was
"Exceedingly hurt" and "astonished" by Sullivan's continued carping.
"We consider ourselves under great obligations to France for their generous . . . interposition, and I should be very sorry to be thought [ungrate-
ful] or to be wanting in respect to your Excellency, who came for the sole
purpose of befriending us." The Americans were relieved when d'Estaing
replied to Greene, saying that his letter "was of a nature to console me."
    The grand alliance survived.

After Sullivan's withdrawal from Newport, Greene returned home to
Coventry to be with his family again. Caty's child was due momentarily,
but Greene left for Boston before the birth. It is unlikely that he relished
the journey, for his agenda in Boston was a reminder that he once again
was quartermaster general and not a field commander. His tasks in
Boston included an accounting of new shoes, uniforms, shorts, and
blankets for the army, as well as meetings with Massachusetts politicians
during which he pleaded for price controls on such goods as hay and
corn. It was exhausting, detail-oriented work (he told Washington that
the "cloathing department" had purchased "7669 pairs of shoes"), a far
cry from his most recent service in Rhode Island.
    "My appointment is flattering to my fortune," Greene conceded, re-

ferring to the 1 percent commission he shared with his two deputies on all department orders. He added, however, that the post was "humiliating to my Military pride." He kept his business in Boston brief and was on his way home from John Hancock's house on September 24 when he came upon a family servant dispatched from Coventry to fetch him. Caty had given birth to a baby girl the day before, and neither was doing well. Greene rode through a wet, raw night and arrived home, soaked to the skin, at nine o'clock. Caty was ill and in bed; their baby was weak and seemingly destined for a tragically early grave.

They named the girl Cornelia Lott, a tribute to the daughter of their friend and host in New Jersey, Abraham Lott. With Nathanael at their bedside, Caty and little Cornelia grew stronger in the days after his arrival. This respite in his own home, now filled with laughter and hope, reminded Greene of the life he had given up for his country. It also brought to mind words he had written in the early months of the war, when he warned that militiamen would prove unreliable because, as part-time soldiers, they retained "all the tender feelings of domestic life" and so were not "sufficiently fortified" for the "shocking scenes of war." Now, Greene's own "tender feelings" softened his heart, or at least his resolve. But it was not the shock of war he sought to avoid, but the tedious paperwork and unheroic duties of the job he loathed. The Rhode Island campaign and the Battle of Monmouth had reminded him of why he had joined the army. But now it was time to return to Washington's side as the general in charge of making sure the soldiers had enough blankets and tents and hammers. Important work, to be sure. But not the work Nathanael Greene wished to perform.

Contributing to his melancholy mood was, as ever, the thought that somebody, somewhere, was criticizing him. "I am [persuaded] I have saved the public Millions of dollars," he told Rhode Island governor William Greene. "Yet I am told some [think] my merit less than my reward." When he heard complaints that some of his department's agents were corrupt, he replied that a "charge against a quarter-master general is most like the cry of a mad dog in England. Every one joins in the cry, and lends their assistance to pelt him to death."

"This is a [malevolent] age," he wrote in one of his last letters from Coventry before returning to Washington's headquarters in New York. "A season wherein envy, malice and detraction are very predominant."

He wished nothing more than to be relieved of this work, which sometimes kept him at his desk past midnight. Accounts from his deputy quartermasters and purchasing agents arrived regularly in his tent, detailing, to cite some examples, the numbers of riding bridles, barrels of tar, reams of writing paper, wooden bowls, canteens, shirts, tomahawks, and other items in various units. He confided to a friend that he hoped to be assigned a command in the South, where the British were preparing to launch an offensive that would lead to the fall of Savannah in late December 1778. A transfer to this newly active theater of the war, he told a friend, "will free me from the disagreeable department I am in."

But there would be no relief from the disagreeable department, at least not for some time. Greene dutifully reported to Washington in mid-October and soon was back to reading reports, hectoring politicians about the curse of runaway inflation, and issuing orders for forage, wagons, tools, and the like.

The war in the North was at a virtual standstill. The main British army was in New York City; the main American army guarded the Hudson River, waiting for the British to make a move. The status quo was more than just a moral victory for the Americans; it was a tangible sign of the army's resolve and leadership. The defeats of 1776, the disappointments of 1777, and the ordeal of Valley Forge had been terrible, but not fatal. The army had been preserved; it remained in the field, and the Revolution continued. Nathanael Greene understood the simple glory and utter necessity of mere survival.

By the time Greene returned to Washington, it was time to look for winter quarters again. Memories of his time at home were hard to shake, and he began to entertain hopes that Caty would make her annual visit to winter camp despite her difficult delivery of Cornelia and the infant's brush with death. Perhaps not surprisingly, Caty was not terribly enthusiastic about the trip. Little Cornelia was only a few months old, and Caty herself was not fully recovered from the baby's birth. Little George and

Martha were just getting familiar with her again after her yearlong absence—she had been home less than six months. And there was no denying the obvious: if she spent another winter and spring in camp, she most likely would return home pregnant again. Her last two deliveries had been difficult and nearly tragic, in that order. She had three children now, the oldest of whom, George, would soon turn three. Hardly a wonder, then, that she seemed less than eager to join Nathanael in camp.

Greene sensed her reluctance, and he tried his best to sympathize. He desperately wanted her to come—"I am impatient to see you," he wrote on November 13—but he made a gallant effort to understand why she might choose to stay home with her children. He said he would willingly sacrifice "this pleasure . . . rather than expose you too much in coming to camp." But it was clear he hoped she would decide otherwise. He urged her to bring little George along to keep both of them company through the winter. And then there was the opinion of little George's namesake. In a transparent ploy to get Caty on the road from Rhode Island, Greene noted that Washington had been asking about her. "I [dined] yesterday with His Excellency, who enquired very particularly after you and renewed his charge to have you at Camp very soon," Greene wrote.

He dispatched the letter by messenger, hoping that if his appeals didn't work, well, perhaps His Excellency's just might.

After a few weeks of scouting central New Jersey, Greene settled on Middlebrook—where he had been quartered briefly the previous year—as the main army's camp. From there, the army could keep its watch on New York while maintaining reliable supply lines. Greene established his headquarters in a two-story stone house, whose halls were soon filled with the effervescent presence of Caty and the laughter of young George Washington Greene.

She couldn't resist. She left Martha and Cornelia with relatives and then set out for New Jersey in early December. The journey was hardly auspicious. The weather turned wet and cold, and the roads were rutted and miserable. Second thoughts about her decision and anxiety about what the next few months might bring must have crossed Caty's mind, but she could not give voice to her doubts, not with George at her side. She arrived in New Jersey worse for the wear, but George was in good health, as his father was happy to note. "He is a fine, hardy fellow, full of play and merriment," Nathanael said.

Play and merriment were the orders of the day at Middlebrook. Unlike the dreadful winter at Valley Forge, Camp Middlebrook was a genuine respite from the war. The general officers and their wives treated themselves to balls and dinners—the contrast with Valley Forge could not have been stronger. One of the most memorable (and certainly most discussed) images from the winter of 1778–79 unfolded during an officers' dance at Greene's headquarters, when Washington took Caty Greene's hand and the two of them swept across the floor. "His Excellency and Mrs. Greene danced upwards of three hours without once sitting down," Mrs. Greene's husband noted, apparently without jealousy. "Upon the whole we had a pretty good frisk."

At times, however, Greene wondered if Caty should be resting more and dancing less. She was only months removed from Cornelia's difficult delivery, and her health was delicate in any case. He did his own dance around the subject, but Caty would hear none of it. She had come to camp to dance, and dance she did. Greene bit his lip and dropped the subject. It hurt him, he would later write, to see his wife's health "bartered away for a few Moments of fleeting pleasure."

Caty's health was not the end of his anxieties. Even as the officers danced with their wives, Greene's deputies barraged him with letters lamenting the lack of forage for the army's horses. Other supplies were scarce enough that Washington chose not to concentrate too many soldiers in Middlebrook; they were dispersed in other camps from Connecticut through the Hudson Valley and south through New Jersey. And now, with inflation taking a terrible toll on Continental currency, officers were complaining bitterly about their pay, and citizens were reluctant to sell their produce to Greene's agents. Greene blamed politicians for some of the distress. For example, Congress banned the use of wheat for forage, arguing that it should be used to feed soldiers and civilians, not horses. Congress also insisted on sending all supplies by land, rather than by river, which Greene preferred because it was cheaper and more reliable. All of this made Greene's already difficult job even more burdensome. He told John Hancock, "[The] scarcity of Provisions and Forage is not a little alarming. Whether the scarcity is real or artificial I cannot pretend to say; but I believe the Peoples dislike to the currency is one great obstacle to our purchases."

It was time for the war's military leaders to confer with its political leaders. Washington and Greene both went to Philadelphia in late December, thinking they would remain there for a few days. Instead, they remained in the capital and away from Middlebrook for six weeks, conferring with members of Congress on everything from military strategy to officers' pay to the rapid depreciation of the Continental dollar, which had lost 90 percent of its value in recent months.

Greene had little patience and even less appreciation for the deliberations of the war's civilian leaders. "They are [always] beginning but never finishing business," he complained. Accustomed to the austerity of his Quaker childhood and the rigors of camp life, Greene found the capital's parties and lavish entertainments offensive and distinctly nonrepublican—although it appears that he didn't turn down his invitations with a haughty scowl. Besides, Caty was with him, and she entertained no republican prejudice against a fancy-dress party or a bit of socializing. He said of his stay in Philadelphia:

> We had the most splendid entertainments immaginable.
> Large Assemblies and Evening Balls. It was hard service to
> go through the duties of the day. I was obliged to rise early
> and go to bed late to complete them. In the Morning a round
> of Visiting came on. Then you had to prepare for dinner
> after which the Evening Balls would engage your Time until
> one or two in the morning.

Displays of plenty offended him. He told his old friend James Varnum that he "dined at one table where there was [a] hundred and Sixty dishes: and at several others not far behind." A year ago, he and the soldiers were in Valley Forge, where men died because they lacked clothes and food. Now, he was invited to gluttony every night, and that worried him far beyond concerns about waste or equity. "The Growing avarice, and a declining currency, are poor materials to build our Independence on," he told Varnum.

Even from afar, Greene continued to run his department, attending to paperwork after his round of parties or, on some days, rising before dawn to write letters and issue orders. And he continued to confer with Washington on strategy: they talked about a possible attack on New York City, an increasingly favorite topic of Washington's, once the 1779 campaign season began, along with an expedition against Indian tribes who were aligned with the British or Tories in upstate New York and northern Pennsylvania. Greene offered this cold-blooded bit of advice to Washington: "To scourge the Indians properly there should be considerable bodies of men [marching] into their Country by different routes and at a season when their Corn is about half grown." He added, however, that the "only object" of such an assault "should be that of driving off the Indians and destroying their Grain." Later that year, Greene would provide the logistical support for such a scourging. Led by General Sullivan, an American expedition attacked and burned forty Iroquois villages and destroyed thousands of bushels of grain.

Before leaving Philadelphia in early February 1779, Greene brought up the delicate topic of his commissions. He had predicted weeks before that his department's "amazing expenditures"—made all the more amazing by the currency's relentless depreciation—would "give rise to many suspicions." To allay fears of corruption, he proposed that he and his top two deputies, Charles Pettit and John Cox, be paid on a straight salary instead of splitting a 1 percent commission. The annual salary Greene recommended, three thousand pounds sterling for each of them, was so high Congress chose to ignore the proposal.

Little had been accomplished during the weeks Washington and Greene spent in Philadelphia. The remaining weeks of winter passed in a whirl of less grandiose socializing and dancing in camp. From Greene's perspective, Congress continued to ignore his requests for more money and more support for the quartermaster's office. On a return visit to Philadelphia in April, during which he dined with the French minister, Greene once again heard complaints about the money he was making from his commissions. Predictably, this inspired a long letter to Washington.

> I have desired Congress to give me leave to resign as I apprehended a loss of Reputation if I continued in the business. They are not disposed to grant my request at all. But unless they change the system . . . I shall not remain long in this business. I will not sacrifice my Reputation for any consideration whatever.

He reminded Washington why he took over the quartermaster's office: "out of compasion to your Excellency. . . . Money was not my motive."

Greene needn't have been so defensive with Washington, a man who respected Greene's honor as much as he valued his advice and treasured his competency. In sadness, Washington replied:

> I am sorry for the difficulties you have to encounter in the department of Quarter Master, especially as I have been in some degree responsible in bringing you to it. Under these circumstances I [cannot] undertake to give advice, or even to hazard an opinion on the measures best for you to adopt. Your own judgement must direct.

If Greene resigned, Washington said he would recommend him as commander of the American army in the South. The British were on the march there, following up their victory in Savannah by capturing Augusta, Georgia. The American commander in the South, General Benjamin Lincoln, was rumored to be suffering from an old leg wound sustained during the Battle of Saratoga.

Lincoln, however, required no replacement. And even if he did, Congress, not Washington, made such appointments. And Congress was not particularly fond of Nathanael Greene at the moment.

Not long after Greene left Philadelphia for a second time and returned to Middlebrook, a large British and Hessian detachment moved north out of New York City and captured the posts of Stony Point and Verplanck's Point along the Hudson River. Fearing a long-expected British move up the river, Washington announced in late May that the army would move from Middlebrook to a more active position in northern New Jersey and the Hudson Valley. Greene was sent north to find a suitable site for a new camp. In a letter to Caty from New York, Greene gently suggested that the time had come for Caty and George to return to Rhode Island. "[It] would be for your advantage to set out soon; as the Roads would be growing worse every day," he wrote. "I don't wish by any means to hasten your [journey]; but only to state facts and leave you to consult your pleasure."

She had been reluctant to come to camp, and now she seemed reluctant to leave. She was pregnant again, which meant she would soon have four children aged four and younger. Her state of mind can only be guessed at, but her husband offered a hint in a letter to his cousin Griffin Greene. "Mrs. Greene is on her way Home," he wrote on June 18, 1779. "I . . . recommend her to your particular Notice, care and attention. Her situation will be rather disagreeable, which will render a little soothing necessary. Her mind is delicate and she feels sorrow with severity."

She left without saying good-bye, at least in person. Nathanael Greene remained in the Hudson Valley as Caty gathered little George and began the journey back to Rhode Island, apparently filled with sorrow. But what could have made her so sad? Camp had been a joy, but perhaps that was the problem. The whirl of parties was over; the long dances with George Washington, attracting the envious stares of the other wives, were just a memory. Now she was returning to domestic reality, with the annual ordeal of childbirth awaiting her—although she might not have realized it, since she was only several weeks into her pregnancy.

The march to a new camp in New Windsor, New York, was carried out with great efficiency, even though Greene complained that the "Teams are failing and the Waggons breaking hourly. . . . The Waggons [are] loaded with women and lazy Soldiers." Still, Greene had the army in place and prepared to defend the Hudson River by mid-June. Once again, Greene had carried out his prosaic and tiresome duties with great efficiency and competence.

Washington expected nothing less of his reluctant quartermaster general.

10 | "O, This War!"

Though Nathanael Greene pined for military glory and the fame that came with it, there was little to be had in the North. The war between Clinton's main army and Washington's had been reduced to a series of skirmishes and sideshows, of marches and countermarches, and of abandoned plans to break the stalemate. The British held New York and Newport; the Americans, Boston and Philadelphia. Clinton had entertained designs on Boston, Washington continued to plan an attack on New York, but in the end, neither could summon the required resources, communications, and coordination.

The French and British navies fought engagements in the West Indies, members of a British peace commission (which included the two Howe brothers) tried in vain to broker a settlement, and partisan militias roamed the swamps and forests of the South. But for the main American army in the North in 1779, there was little to do but watch and wait and march when it was told to march.

The lull allowed Greene to attend to his personal and business affairs, which were not unrelated to his duties as quartermaster general. As he had already indicated quite openly, his commissions were "flattering" to his "fortune." Greene's biographer Theodore Thayer estimated that he received about one hundred and seventy thousand dollars in commissions during his tenure as quartermaster. But with the Continental dollar in free fall, Greene quite naturally looked for opportunities to invest those commissions before they became worthless.

In April 1779, Greene formed another business association, becoming a partner with the army's commissary general, Jeremiah Wadsworth, and Barnabas Deane, who hailed from a prominent merchant family. To shield himself from accusations that he was using his military service to build a private fortune, Greene kept his involvement with Barnabas Deane secret—as did Wadsworth. "[It] is my wish that no Mortal should be acquainted with the persons forming the Company except us three," Greene told Wadsworth. "I think it is prudent to appear as little in trade as possible. For however just and upright our conduct may be, the World will have suspicions to our disadvantage." Greene used codes when he wrote to Wadsworth and Deane about company business.

Greene and Wadsworth both invested ten thousand pounds in the firm, which was called Barnabas Deane & Company. Like Jacob Greene & Company, the Deane partnership invested extensively in privateers. But unlike Jacob Greene & Company, it did not receive contracts from the quartermaster's department.

This was not, however, the extent of Greene's investments. He bought land in Rhode Island, New Jersey, and in the Hudson Valley. He and his deputy Charles Pettit made several investments in privateers and other ships and were part owners of an iron foundry, Batsto Iron Works, on the New Jersey shore. In the end, many of these investments would prove disastrous. The firm of Barnabas Deane & Company was worth only about five thousand pounds within two years of its formation, despite several initial successes.

Greene's correspondence from 1779 and 1780 reveals that he was in frequent touch with his business associates and was immersed in the details of his investments. In late 1779, for example, he closely followed the progress of Griffin Greene, his cousin, who was attempting to sell a shipment of wine in Hartford, Connecticut. And he was ever vigilant in looking for new opportunities to invest his commissions. He formed a partnership with Samuel Otis, a Boston patriot and merchant, to buy yet another privateer despite a clear conflict of interest: Otis's firm received large contracts from the quartermaster's office to supply tents and other equipment.

Nathanael Greene was one of many American officers who spent the war years attending to both military and financial strategies. Most of the top deputies in the quartermaster general and commissary general departments were businessmen and merchants who simply would not forfeit the right to earn and invest money privately while serving the struggling new nation. They saw nothing wrong with such behavior. The patriot-merchant Robert Morris, a member of Congress, said, "[I will] discharge my duty faithfully to the Public and pursue my Private Fortune by all such honorable means as the times will admit." Patriots like Morris and others emerged from the war richer than they were before, thanks to shrewd investments.

Greene's stewardship over the quartermaster's office came under growing criticism from Congress not because he was in business with some of his department's contractors or because his own company, Jacob Greene & Company, did business with the department, but because of his lack of accountability. The quartermaster's department was spending colossal amounts of money—its monthly payroll was nearly five hundred thousand (highly depreciated) dollars for about three thousand employees—and some of its agents unquestionably were corrupt, inefficient, or both. Yet when Congress asked for an accounting of the department's spending, Greene bristled, as if by merely raising the issue Congress somehow was questioning his virtue.

In mid-1779, Congress sought to reign in the department's spending, authorizing individual states to dismiss agents who were suspected of either corruption or incompetence. Familiar by now with Greene's sensitivity, Congress made a point of expressing its confidence in the quartermaster general's honor and integrity. But Greene understood that

Congress was undermining his authority, and he protested vigorously but to no avail.

These bureaucratic and political tangles reminded Greene, as if he needed such reminders, how much he hated his job. His limited engagement on the front lines in Rhode Island allowed him to forget about politics and logistics for a few weeks, and he yearned for a return to the seeming simplicity of strategy and tactics. He launched a concerted campaign to prepare Washington, and himself, for the day when he would be a line officer once again.

Greene joined Washington and more than a dozen major generals and brigadiers for a council of war at West Point on July 2, 1779. The topic of the meeting was Washington's request for advice about a new offensive campaign. But as Greene greeted old friends like Steuben, McDougall, Wayne, and Knox, he was forming an agenda of his own. If they agreed with him that he was entitled to a field command even while serving as quartermaster general, he might begin to cut the shackles that chained him to his desk. After the meeting, Greene wrote letters to a dozen colleagues, asking them a simple question: did he not have "the same right to command in a time of action . . . as if [he] did not hold the Quarter Master General's Office"? There was an implied threat in his letter, for he stated, "[If holding the quartermaster's job would] exclude me from the honors of the line, I shall know how to take my measures." He asked the other generals to respond quickly; he would take their answers to His Excellency, the commander in chief.

The replies he received, however, surprised and saddened him. While half of the generals agreed with his assertion that he had a "right" to command, they were either his friends or generals with more seniority than he had; in other words, they would not lose their command if Greene were to assert his "right" to a position in the line. But others disagreed profoundly, chief among them Lord Stirling. Greene brought his case to Washington anyway, and, worse yet, Washington agreed with Stirling and the other dissenters. Firmly but gingerly, the commander in chief told Greene that while he retained his title of major general, he did not have a right to a field command.

The military reason which prevents a Quarter Master
General from exercising command in ordinary cases I take to
be this: that whatever may be the fact, the presumption is,
that both in action and out of action, he has, generally
speaking, sufficient employment in the duties of his office,
and circumstances alone can decide when these are
compatible with actual command.

To soften the blow, Washington deftly praised Greene for having "executed" his duties with "ability and fidelity."

Nathanael Greene's shackles grew tighter still.

Adding to his burdens were new concerns about the health of Caty and the children. George had a sore on his chest, Martha still was suffering from rickets, and eleven-month-old Cornelia remained small and frail. Caty herself, now four months pregnant, was suffering from stomach pains and, alarmingly, bleeding from her mouth. Nathanael Greene had achieved some measure of the glory he had dreamed of in his childhood, when he first imagined himself a soldier, but now he was powerless to help his ailing family far away in Rhode Island. He had left hearth and home willingly, even eagerly, to heed his country's call, but with his family in need, calling out to him for help, he could not come to their aid.

Frustrated, angry, and frightened, he blamed himself for Caty's illness. She had been reluctant to come to camp the previous winter, and he had used every method of persuasion he dared—even citing George Washington's wishes—to put her on the road to Middlebrook. Now they both were paying a price for that visit. He should not have allowed her to dance so soon after Cornelia's traumatic birth; he should have insisted that she rest. "Many times I was almost ready to say Caty you shall not dance again," he told her in a letter dated August 16, "but my resolution as often failed me." He feared Caty would regard him "more the tyrant than the husband" and would "lessen her affection" for him. And so he allowed her to dance. If nothing else, Greene's attitude reveals an uncommonly open-minded view of marriage. Other husbands surely would have played the tyrant's role and expected their wives to obey.

He wished desperately to shove aside his paperwork and chores and ride to Rhode Island. "How tenderly would I nurse you," he told Caty. "How attentively would I watch my sweet Angel."

By the end of August, he was in a deep depression. He tried to write Caty again on the night of August 29, but his anxieties overcame him. "I therefore laid down my pen and went to bed," he told her when he finally summoned the energy to write the following day.

It was beginning to occur to him that Caty's ill health might be related to a familiar condition: pregnancy. As if the thought might not have occurred to Caty, by now a pregnancy veteran, Greene noted: "Methinks you can [determine your condition] from a number of female circumstances." Indeed, those "circumstances" had already told Caty all she needed to know. Greene was not without a helpful suggestion if her symptons continued and she was not pregnant. "I strongly recommend your going into salt Water, not once or twice, but every day or two for a month to come," he wrote. He was vague about how this would relieve her distress, although he added that a doctor friend of his was by his side as he wrote, and the doctor himself recommended this cure.

> I wish to hear from you every hour, but while your health is on
> the decline, [I] don't wish you to write long Epistles. . . . How
> is the sore on Washington's breast? Does it increase or
> decline? . . . Has Cornelia got better? How is Patty [i.e.,
> Martha]? I suppose a great chatter box. Is she frequently put
> into the cold bath? Nothing will perfect her shapes but the
> continuation of that practice. I beg you therefore not to omit it.

Caty apparently did not respond to her husband, at least not quickly enough for Greene. He wrote another letter accusing her of neglect, which inspired Caty to write a long letter (alas, lost to history) in which she poured out her heart. She must have felt overwhelmed: not only was she pregnant for the fourth time since 1775, she was not getting along with her in-laws. Complicating matters, she knew that the timing of her pregnancy might preclude her annual visit to winter quarters—her baby was due in midwinter. After her pleasant stay in Middlebrook, filled with dances and the company of Martha Washington, Caty would have been distressed to contemplate winter in Rhode Island with a newborn and three other small children. Besides, this time there would be little chance of getting pregnant, not so soon after her January delivery.

Caty's letter chastened her husband. "I am exceeding unhappy to have added to your distress by complaining of your [neglecting] me," Greene wrote. And as much as he would miss her company over the winter, he strongly advised Caty to stay home this year.

Caty ignored her husband's pleas. She was determined to join him once he decided where the army would spent the winter. She soon had an answer. After months of little activity during the campaign season of 1779, the army would return to the New Jersey village the soldiers remembered from a previous winter's camp: Morristown.

The months before the Americans returned to Morristown offered some cheerful news: the British evacuated Newport to reinforce their garrison in Savannah, Georgia; American surprise raids on Stony Point in New York and Paulus Hook in New Jersey (present-day Jersey City) had routed British defenders; John Paul Jones and the *Bon Homme Richard* had brought the naval war to the British coast, and the Spanish entered the conflict, mostly in an attempt to recover Gibraltar.

These developments inspired Washington to dream, once again, of conquering Clinton's garrison in New York City, and Greene spent several weeks in the fall of 1779 working on the logistics of such an assault. Those preparations, however, were in vain. Washington's fantasy of a smashing victory in New York evaporated when the British captured Savannah in October, leading d'Estaing—whose fleet was an integral part of Washington's plan—to return to France.

The British assault in Georgia was a significant development. Like Washington, Clinton was weary of the stalemate in the North. Unlike the

American commander, however, Clinton had the resources to move the war to the South, which he saw as his enemy's soft underbelly. If the British could conquer the South and return Georgia and the Carolinas to the king's rule, they could continue marching north through Virginia until Washington realized that all was lost.

There was no secret about the British strategy. Clinton himself, along with the inevitable Cornwallis, set sail from New York in late December 1779, after the fall of Savannah. The British generals planned to continue the campaign in the South through the winter months. Clinton left about eleven thousand Hessians and loyalist militia in New York, believing, correctly, that the Americans were far too weak to challenge even this depleted garrison.

Washington and Greene, their strategy centered on the Hudson River, were not sure of Clinton's final destination. So they could risk no movement that might weaken their position near that broad and vital waterway. Morristown, or more specifically an area three miles southwest of the town called Jockey Hollow, would keep the Americans close enough to the Hudson Valley while moving nearer to supply lines and forage for the winter.

In mid-December, ten to twelve thousand American soldiers settled into the now familiar routine of clearing land (about six hundred acres) and building huts (nearly a thousand, twelve men to a hut) that would serve as their quarters for as long as six months. With huts laid out in neat rows, areas set aside for parade grounds, and roads providing access to regimental villages, winter camp at Morristown resembled a small city.

Once again, it was Nathanael Greene's job to keep this city supplied with food, clothing, tools, wagons, and other necessities. But even as the first trees were felled in Jockey Hollow, it was becoming clear to Greene that this winter promised none of the music and frivolity that made Middlebrook, just a dozen or so miles to the south, such a welcome delight. The Continental dollar continued its spectacular slide toward worthlessness; its value was about three cents. Farmers and merchants were unwilling to sell their goods to the army in return for useless scraps of paper, a foreboding development. But the army could, if Washington said so, simply take what it needed. Washington despised such measures, but they at least were within his control.

Neither he nor Greene, however, had any power over winter itself. And as American soldiers labored over their tiny huts, bitter winds shook the bare branches of Jockey Hollow. Snow and hail fell during the first two weeks of December, as the army built its temporary city. Indeed, the weather was so severe that some work stopped or was postponed, delaying the process of getting the men into their huts, which measured fourteen by fifteen feet. Greene, as a major general and the quartermaster general, of course was entitled to more comfortable quarters, and that entitlement was all the more important because his pregnant wife had shown up for her annual winter holiday in late November. Nothing, neither her own doubts nor the imminent birth of her fourth child nor the serious illness of her brother, Simon, could keep Caty Greene away from winter camp. She had turned over her children to the care of relatives and set out on a journey whose landmarks she knew so well by now. Greene was astonished to find her, in the full bloom of her pregnancy, standing before him in the gathering gloom of late autumn. He had told friends that Caty very likely would not be in camp this year. The baby, after all, was due soon.

Finding decent housing was not easy, even for a major general. An aide, James Abeel, had chosen the home of a local patriot and merchant, Jacob Arnold, as Greene's headquarters. Arnold owned a fine home on the village green in Morristown, and Abeel installed a separate kitchen for the general and his wife, but it was not long before Arnold's patriotism gave way to impatience. He soon told Greene he would have to find other quarters. With the weather already bitter, with a wife due to give birth in a month, Nathanael Greene was not about to be thrown into the street. He wrote to Arnold on December 16:

> Some people in this neighbourhood are polite and obliging,
> others are the reverse. It was and is my wish to live upon good
> terms with the people of the House and I have [endeavored]
> to accomodate my family so as to render it as little inconvenient
> as possible. . . . On you alone the manner of our living

together will depend. If you are friendly and obliging you
shall not find me wanting in justice and generosity.

Greene and Caty remained in Arnold's house, although it is not
known whether their reluctant host ever became friendly and obliging.

There was little money to be had, and so the army's supplies were dangerously low as 1779 drew to a close. The army's express riders, whose courage and horsemanship kept the lines of communications open, were threatening to ride away from their duties unless Greene found a way to increase their pay. In a petition addressed to Greene, fourteen riders maintained it was "impossible to ride for the present pay"; therefore "[we will refuse to do so] until your Honor thinks [it] proper to raise the pay. . . . Our present pay is but a small pittance and no ways equivalent to the many things We stand in need of which We are Obliged to Purchase." They had their answer shortly, and it came not from Greene but from Congress; the delegates, in a cost-cutting move, discharged the army's express riders.

Greene sensed that yet another crisis was unfolding, telling his friend and business partner Jeremiah Wadsworth: "We have had the most alarming accounts from all quarters of the approaching . . . famine and want. Flour and Forage are [exceedingly] scarce." After heroic service as the army's commissary general—the officer in charge of food supplies—Wadsworth resigned in early December and was awaiting the appointment of a successor even as the supply line to Jockey Hollow and Morristown was beginning to break down. Greene, perhaps envious of Wadsworth's impending freedom, submitted his own resignation to Congress on December 12. Congress pretended not to notice.

A few days before Christmas, Greene wrote: "We are at this time in the greatest distress for want of cash, being out of forage, having extended our Credit as far as possible, and the people are ready to pull us to pieces on account of the losses they sustain from a delay of payment [and] by the depreciation of the money."

Civilians near camp were unhappy with Greene's housing arrange-
ments. Like Greene himself, officers were not expected to live in huts
with the rank and file, but owners of private residences were behaving
much like Greene's own temporary landlord. Greene wasted precious
time and energy examining New Jersey's laws on the touchy subject of
quartering soldiers in civilian homes. He concluded that the law was
against him, and told Washington that "the Inhabitants cannot be pre-
vailed upon to receive the Officers." Among the officers without proper
quarters was General Benedict Arnold, who was in camp to attend his
court-martial on charges that he misused his powers as the military governor of Philadelphia.

Greene's report about Morristown's petulant homeowners bitterly
disappointed Washington. "I regret that the Inhabitants should be unwilling to give shelter to men who have made and are still making every
[sacrifice] in the service of their Country," he told Greene. Washington
already feared that the army, and possibly the Revolution itself, suddenly was on the verge of collapse. After hectoring Congress in vain
about the faltering supply line and the possibility of starvation in camp,
he turned his attention to the quartermaster's department and found it
wanting. Surprisingly, Greene did not take his mentor's implied criticisms to heart, perhaps because he understood that the army was on
the verge of catastrophe, and Washington felt powerless to prevent it.
The commander in chief could only lash out, criticize, condemn, and
otherwise lament imminent disaster. On December 19, Greene told
Wadsworth that Washington was in "a state [of] distress" and was blam-
ing "every body, both innocent and guilty." The quartermaster's department, he noted, was "not altogether exempt" from Washington's
complaints.

Greene asked Wadsworth to remain at his post as commissary general
while "the storm rages." Nevertheless, Wadsworth was determined to retire by the end of 1779.

On Christmas Day, a cold and dreary day in camp, an anguished
Greene wrote of the army's increasingly bleak prospects and of the bitter

reception Morristown's citizens offered the hungry and tired men who were fighting and sacrificing for their liberty.

> They receive us with coldness, and provide for us with
> reluctance. The Army is in great distress for want of
> Provision and forage. . . . Our affairs are in a disagreeable
> train from the wretched state of our business of finance. . . .
> [A] thick cloud hangs over our heads at this hour threatening
> us with destruction.

Within a few days, snow was falling from a number of thick, dark clouds. It fell, and fell, and fell some more. It fell on the soldiers as never before; it was nothing like the Christmas snowstorm of 1776, nothing like the snows of Valley Forge two years earlier. It began falling on January 2, a bitterly cold day with gusting winds from the west and northwest, and it continued for the better part of four days. The scanty supplies of food, clothing, and equipment that were being shipped to camp were now out of reach, unable to make it through the snow and drifts. "Our Army is without Meat or Bread; and have been for two or three days past," Greene wrote on January 4. "Poor Fellows! they exhibit a picture truly distressing. More than half naked, and about two third starved."

By January 6, eighteen inches of snow had fallen, making the roads to Jockey Hollow and Morristown impassable. The soldiers' suffering was, by nearly all accounts, worse than at Valley Forge. Greene told a friend:

> The Army is upon the eve of disbanding for want of
> Provisions, the poor soldiers having been several days
> without. . . . Provision is scarce at best; but the late terrible
> storm and the depth of the Snow and the drifts in the
> Roads prevent the little stock coming foward which is in
> readiness at the distant Magazines. . . . The Roads must be
> kept open by the Inhabitants or the Army cannot be

subsisted. And unless the good people immediately lend
their assistance to [forward] supplies the Army must
disband.

So desperate was the army's plight that Greene decided the snow actually was a blessing. If the roads were not clogged, he said, "I believe the
Soldiers would take up their packs and march" out of camp. He told
Wadsworth that hundreds were "without shirts and many other necessary articles of clothing." A few cattle were driven into camp on January
5, but that was hardly enough to relieve the army's hunger. The following day, troops left camp and grabbed what they could from local citizens, with Washington's reluctant approval.

The ice, the snow, and the cold were relentless, and not just in Jockey
Hollow. The waters around New York City froze, as did portions of
Chesapeake Bay. This, the fifth winter of the Revolution, was like no
other. Desperate soldiers ate the bark off sticks, ate their shoes, and, on
at least one occasion, ate a pet dog. In an unaddressed letter, Greene, a
veteran of every winter camp thus far, offered a terrible word picture of
conditions in early January.

> Such weather as we have had, never did I feel. . . . In the
> midst of snow and surrounded on every side by its banks,
> the army has been cut off from its magazines, and been
> obliged to fast for several days together. We have been
> alternately out of meat and bread for eight or nine days past,
> and without either for three or four. . . . Provisions are
> scarce indeed, not from any scarcity in the country, but from
> want of money to purchase it.

A welcome break in the weather after nearly two weeks of storms
eased the crisis temporarily, allowing Washington to turn his attention
from food and supplies to offensive operations. The narrow strip of water separating New Jersey from the British stronghold of Staten Island
was frozen solid, allowing the possibility of a winter raid without the

need for boats. Washington turned to Greene for advice, and, with characteristic energy, the quartermaster general put aside his clerical burdens for a moment and reverted to his role as the army's chief strategist. He sketched out for Washington a plan calling for a surprise assault by a detachment of twenty-five hundred men that would cross the ice and raid several British outposts on the island. He proposed *Clinton* as the operation's password. (Clinton was, of course, the commander of the British garrison, although he was at that moment in the South.) This choice of a password, Greene told Washington, "may deceive the Enemy."

Using sleds that Greene had rounded up from the New Jersey countryside, Lord Stirling led the raiding party across the ice and into Staten Island on January 15. This accomplished little, save to astonish observers in the decades and centuries to come, who saw a starving army on the verge of ruin transformed, in a matter of days, into a force capable of a small but bold action.

The starvation was over, but winter was not, and it continued to heap suffering upon the army's sagging shoulders. More than two dozen snowstorms buried the camp in six-foot snowdrifts, making supply a never-ending nightmare. The absolute misery, along with the continued breakdown in supplies, reminded Greene that he wished for nothing more than to be relieved of his duties as quartermaster general. Congress, unable to levy taxes, had divested itself of the supply business. Instead, states were charged with the responsibility of supplying troops raised within their individual borders. The new system was an ineffective patchwork and made Greene's job that much more difficult. He had become a vigorous advocate of strong, centralized government, at least on broad issues affecting the nation as a whole. His business career and his firsthand experience as a soldier emphasized organization and coordination above all else, and the new system of supply was anything but well organized. He sent a letter to the president of Congress, Samuel Huntington, in mid-January, noting that he had submitted his resignation a month earlier but had heard nothing.

Congress continued to ignore his request, but it put together a committee to reorganize the quartermaster's department. To Greene's disgust, among the committee members was Thomas Mifflin, in Greene's eyes one of the instigators of the defunct Conway Cabal and an undoubted critic of both Greene and Washington. Not surprisingly, Greene's friend and aide Charles Pettit saw Mifflin's appointment as evidence of a "plot" to embarrass Greene.

In the midst of these bleak proceedings, the Greene family grew by one. Caty Greene gave birth to a baby boy on January 31, and they named him Nathanael Ray Greene. He was the center of attention among the women in camp, a welcome distraction from the snow and the cold. Whatever Greene's unhappiness with Congress, with the uncooperative citizens of Morristown, with Mother Nature herself, he was delighted with his new son. He sent a teasing letter to his business partner Barnabas Deane, who was unmarried, to tell him of the arrival of his "fine son." Greene wondered why Deane would go through life "without ever tasting some of the sweetest pleasures that falls to the lot of Mortals."

But even the sweetest pleasures had to be swept aside for drudge work. "The business of my Department is growing more and more desperate every day," Greene told Wadsworth. Food supplies were low again. After sending yet another letter to Philadelphia asking why his resignation had not been accepted, Greene decided to go to the capital to raise the issue personally with members of Congress. There would be no happy parties and balls during this visit with Congress; Greene was prepared to tell the politicians precisely what he thought of them. "Their conduct," he wrote to Wadsworth, "is intolerable." He told Washington that he expected little good to come of his negotiations—"unless it is dismissing my self from the Department, which I most devoutly wish." Washington wished him well, and almost as an aside, he confided to Greene that he was concerned about British advances in the South. Thousands of British troops under Clinton's personal command had begun a siege outside Charleston, and Washington feared for the American garrison and his commander in the South, Benjamin Lincoln. He mentioned to Greene that he was worried about "the effect which the loss of [Charleston] may produce on the minds of People" in the South.

Greene conveyed Washington's concerns to the nation's political leaders, but he did not achieve what he so "devoutly" wished—his dismissal from the cares and burdens of the quartermaster general's department. He was convinced that his archenemy, Mifflin, once again was plotting against him under the guise of cutting the quartermaster's expenses. It was becoming clear to him that Congress would not authorize the money he believed the army needed to fight a new campaign. After less than a week of talks with Congress, Greene was depressed, pessimistic, and ill. With a nod to his friend Thomas Paine, he told Wadsworth, "These are the times that will try men's Souls." He wrote yet another letter to Samuel Huntington, the president of Congress, reminding him that Congress had yet to act on his letter of resignation as quartermaster. He told Huntington that he was tired of meetings, tired of waiting for Congress to pass a resolution declaring its confidence in the quartermaster's integrity. (Some lawmakers thought there should be an investigation of the department before members offered their support for the quartermaster.) His presence in the capital, Greene declared, "is no longer necessary," so he announced that he would leave Philadelphia immediately.

Greene's curt language and lack of diplomacy did nothing to win new friends in Congress, as became evident after his allies quickly drew up a new resolution of support. During a private debate one of his supporters—he was never identified—asserted that Greene was entitled to congressional support because he was the "properest person" to become commander in chief should anything happen to Washington. According to Philip Schuyler, the former general who was now a member of Congress, the speaker added that Washington himself believed that Greene was his natural heir.

The resolution failed.

It was clear that Greene had alienated too many people in Philadelphia. "I feel my self . . . soured, and hurt, at the ungenerous . . . treatment of

Congress," he told Joseph Reed, the president of the Pennsylvania legis-lature. "[I believe] it will be impossible for me to do business with them, with proper temper; and besides I have lost all confidence in the justice and rectitude of their intentions." Angry and disgusted, he left the capi-tal on April 10 and returned to the snow and cold of Morristown. He summed up his dark thoughts in a letter on April 15.

> I have been among the great at Philadelphia and have a worse
> opinion of the issue of our cause than ever. Never was there
> a people that employed themselves so much about trifles.
> Their whole policy is a chapter of new expedients, and long
> debated upon little matters of form. . . . Our treasury is
> empty. The business of finance is in a doubtful way. Public
> credit is lost, and National confidence expiring. Our Army
> [is] small and still upon the decline and little or no prospect
> of having it recruited this Spring.

In a letter written in code to his friend Wadsworth, Greene offered his opinion of the Revolution's political leaders: "Truth and righteousness is of no account with these [people]."

More than ever, politics, criticism, and paperwork dampened his fer-vor for the cause. Truth and righteousness could not be found in politi-cal debates, in spreadsheets, or in budgets. They could be found only on the battlefield, where Nathanael Greene belonged.

At Valley Forge two years before, springtime had brought both relief from the weather and pride in the army's astonishing transformation thanks to Baron von Steuben's winter-long training. Spring at Morris-town, however, brought only continued misery, and not all of it was re-lated to the snow that remained on the ground into early April. The Greenes suffered a personal blow when Caty's brother, Simon, died at age twenty-nine on Block Island. Caty remained in camp after receiving the bad news.

Meanwhile, the Continental dollar's inexorable decline meant that as never before, merchants, farmers, and citizens refused to sell their goods to the quartermaster's department or to the commissary general. Food and other daily supplies continued to dwindle; long-term provisions for the coming campaign were nonexistent. Some soldiers had not been paid in months. Not that it mattered, for their meager pay could buy precious little at a time when a pair of shoes in Philadelphia cost twenty-five dollars, and a hat and a simple suit of men's clothes cost two thousand dollars in Boston. "Our distress," Greene wrote, "is [beyond] description."

There was no escaping the tension and anxiety in camp, even when officers and their wives gathered for modest social outings. At one such party in one of the officer's quarters, an earnest Rhode Islander, George Olney, apparently objected to the drinking of his colleagues, including Greene. To show his disapproval of this frivolity, Olney turned on his heel and retreated to the more sober company of the officers' wives in another room. Fueled by drink, the officers dispatched an expeditionary force with orders to return Olney to his rightful place with the men. The women put up a stubborn resistance, and reinforcements—in the form of none other than the commander in chief himself—were called in. Washington grabbed hold of a wrist belonging to Deborah Olney, the fugitive officer's wife. Mrs. Olney was as stern a soul as her husband. Rather than go along with the joke, she let loose with a verbal cannonade that left everyone in the room speechless. To the commander in chief, she said, "Let go of my hand or I'll pull every hair out of your head!" Jaws dropped. The words hung in the hair. The joking, the horseplay, the welcome respite from the winter's privations—all came to a sudden end. The officers and their wives quietly went their separate ways.

The deprivation continued, even after the snow and ice were long gone. On May 25, two regiments from Connecticut decided to take matters into their own hands. Starving and poorly clothed, they marched out of camp and made it known that they planned either to seize what they could from the locals or to simply return home. The army was on the verge of mutiny, but, to the credit of the troops, it was halfhearted at best. Officers reasoned with the soldiers, and they returned to camp, with little harm done. Still, it was an ominous development. Greene confided to the governor of Rhode Island, William Greene, that he feared discontent would "run through the whole line like wild fire."

Even worse news, if that could be imagined, arrived in camp a few days later: the American garrison in Charleston under Benjamin Lincoln, a force of nearly three thousand Continentals and two thousand militia, had surrendered. It was by far the most devastating defeat of the war, surpassing even the loss of Fort Washington in 1776. American hopes had just been revived with reports that the French were sending a large fleet and more than six thousand troops to help their erstwhile ally. But now this—a terrible, devastating surrender of the southern army, even as the main army continued to suffer in Morristown.

The Hessian commander who was left to watch over New York in Clinton's absence, General Wilhelm von Knyphausen, now had his eye on a victory of his own. Even as Clinton was preparing to return to New York, leaving Cornwallis to continue to prosecute the southern strategy, Knyphausen was planning an attack on New Jersey, reckoning that the demoralized, poorly supplied main American army could be smashed or badly damaged after its horrendous winter camp. The Hessian was no stranger to Greene, for he had led the successful assault on Fort Washington and had been arrayed across from Greene's division at the Battle of Brandywine. The son of a Prussian colonel, Knyphausen, like Greene's antagonist Lord Cornwallis, was a symbol of Old World militarism and privilege, a representative of a way of life the American rebels wished to banish from their continent.

Five thousand British and Hessian troops crossed from Staten Island into Elizabeth Town, New Jersey, on June 6 and advanced inland toward the town of Connecticut Farms. There they met surprisingly stiff resistance from New Jersey militia. (Knyphausen had been told that the state's militia were on the verge of mutiny and would likely switch sides if attacked.) The patriot show of force was not in Knyphausen's battle plan. Frustrated, the British and Hessians burned farms and civilian homes and killed Hannah Caldwell, the wife of a prominent Presbyterian clergyman named James Caldwell, who also served as one of Nathanael

Greene's deputy quartermasters. Reports of British atrocities spread through nearby villages, and men who might have been inclined to stay at home instead grabbed their firearms and turned out to join local militia units.

Knyphausen's unexpected movement attracted the attention of Washington and Greene, still in their winter camp in Morristown. They assumed Knyphausen's assault was a distraction, and that Clinton would soon arrive back in New York and launch a new offensive up the Hudson River.

Whatever Clinton's intentions, Washington decided he must confront Knyphausen, and he chose his quartermaster general to lead an assault on the Hessian general on the night of June 8. Though Greene's reaction is not recorded, he must have been delighted. Not so many months ago, he had argued that he was automatically entitled to battlefield command despite his job as quartermaster. Washington, to his chagrin, disagreed. But now, as Washington prepared the first assault of the new campaign season, Nathanael Greene had a command.

And then it began to rain. The assault was called off—although it didn't matter. Knyphausen, puzzled and frustrated, began withdrawing back to Elizabeth Town that night.

The Hessians would bear watching, and Greene was deployed to a position in the Watchung Mountains overlooking Springfield to keep an eye on the enemy. As he left Morristown to travel south on an aging saddle horse, Caty and baby Nathanael departed camp for their northerly journey to Rhode Island. Greene bought a secondhand carriage to accommodate the little family and their luggage, but even then, it was a brave man who purchased a used vehicle. Warned that the carriage required a close inspection, Greene ordered some repairs before he dared put Caty and their son aboard. They were on their way home by mid-June, with Caty bearing instructions from her husband to pay a social call on the wife of his friend (and her future admirer) Colonel Jeremiah Wadsworth. Greene believed Caty's visit would strengthen his friendship and business relationship with the prosperous Wadsworth. "Society," he explained to Caty, is "bound together by many ligaments, tho affection is the great [tie]." Wadsworth, he added, "loves you as much as he respects me."

The fleet bearing General Clinton and his thousands of troops was spotted sailing past Sandy Hook and into New York Harbor on June 17. Knyphausen and his Hessians remained in Elizabeth Town, near Newark. Washington summoned Greene back to Morristown to discuss how the Americans might counter the anticipated British offensive, likely to consist of a thrust into New Jersey and a large movement up the Hudson toward West Point.

The map of the New York–New Jersey region had become much more complicated, indeed. And the Americans were correct in believing that Clinton was intent on following up his victory in the South with a move against Washington in the North. Although Clinton was not pleased to learn that Knyphausen had crossed into New Jersey on his own accord, he decided to make the best of it. Reinforced with British troops, Knyphausen was ordered to advance toward Springfield. Clinton then made preparations to move north, as the Americans anticipated, to see how Washington responded.

This was more than routine maneuvering. If Knyphausen could lure Washington into battle in New Jersey, Clinton would be free to make a dash for West Point, overwhelm the garrison there, and—finally—assert British control over the Hudson. It was hard to imagine how the Americans could survive such a blow so soon after their southern army had surrendered in Charleston.

Greene never doubted what the British strategy must be. Still, there was a chance Clinton might yet bluff an assault on West Point, draw the Americans toward the river, and then countermarch south, cross into New Jersey, and attack Washington from the rear. These marches involved thousands of men, hundreds of wagons, and tons of supplies, yet, given the stakes, they were sublimely delicate. Indeed, Washington's response was subtle. He and the bulk of the army moved north on June 22, headed for Pompton, New Jersey, and a position close enough to

West Point that he could respond to a threat, but not so commited that he exposed his rear to a surprise assault. He left Greene behind in Springfield to counter Knyphausen's threat.

Hours after Washington's departure, a nervous American spy who had been monitoring the British force in Elizabeth Town arrived at Greene's headquarters. The spy, Greene observed, was "in great trepedation." He reported that General Clinton was putting his army in motion to move north. "Their object," Greene told Washington, "is to . . . prevent your getting into West Point." Greene put his troops on alert, telling them that they should be prepared to move "at a moment's warning." But when there was no further word of troop movement—Greene didn't know it, but the British were slow in moving out—he wondered if the spy actually was a British agent intent on confusing him.

Just after dawn on the morning of June 23, Greene received word from his scouts that Knyphausen was marching in his direction. The Hessian commander had six thousand troops, vastly outnumbering Greene's collection of a thousand regulars and perhaps two thousand or so militia. From his headquarters in Bryant's Tavern just west of Springfield, Greene quickly scrawled a message to Washington—"The Enemy are out and on their march towards this place in full force"—and then hastily organized his defenses. He placed General John Stark, a veteran who was one of the heroes of Bunker Hill, and several militia units in the high ground of the Watchung Mountains to guard his flanks. Then he took up his position behind the line in Springfield.

The British attacked in two columns, one led by Knyphausen marching along Galloping Hill Road toward the American right, the other under General Edward Mathew on Vauxhall Road on Greene's left. Knyphausen's group would assault Greene's main force, and Mathew's would try to turn Greene's left flank. By eleven o'clock, Knyphausen's men had advanced through Greene's front line of defenses in Connecticut Farms and Vauxhall Road and were approaching a bridge that crossed the Rahway River and led into Springfield. Greene had barely placed his men in position to guard the roads and bridge when Knyphausen's men appeared. The town erupted in fire and smoke as both forces opened up with artillery. A Rhode Island regiment under Colonel Israel Angell fiercely contested the bridge before retreating in good order.

Greene sent another urgent message to Washington, who was about fifteen miles away and could hear the sounds of Knyphausen's artillery: "The Militia to our aid are few and that few are so divided as to render little or no support."

Greene realized that Mathew was trying to turn his flank and gain access to the Hobart Gap, where Galloping Hill Road led to Chatham and Morristown. To counter this threat, Greene delayed and retreated, and then delayed and retreated some more, until he had fallen back past Springfield and onto the high ground of Short Hills. Washington, in the meantime, reversed course when he heard of Greene's retreat, ordering the main army to march toward Morristown. Clinton, who had, in fact, sent troops upriver toward the Hudson Valley, made no move to support Knyphausen and soon called off the operation and returned to New York City.

After Greene fell back to the hills, the British-Hessian assault stalled and then halted completely. "Being thus advantageously posted, I was in hopes the Enemy would have attempt[ed] to gain the [heights]," Greene wrote. They did not. Instead, they put Springfield to the torch and then retreated to Elizabeth Town. The Americans had suffered more dead, fifteen to fourteen for the British, but the number of British wounded was higher, seventy-four to fifty-nine Americans.

Greene's strategy and tactics had been superb, and although Springfield was not a major battle, it was an important victory: Knyphausen's retreat did not stop until he was back in New York. New Jersey was cleared of British forces for good. And Greene had been given a chance to display his flair for the battlefield, a talent he believed was wasted on the chores of the quartermaster's department. In his general orders, he bragged to his troops that "old Knyp" had been beaten so badly he took out his frustrations by burning Springfield "savage like."

Had Mr. Knyphausen's temerity prompted him to advance to the Short-Hills, we query if he would have led on another division of German boors to accomplish his satanic designs again.

Clinton had bungled his opportunity to seize the moment—and the Hudson. But he had another move to make, one Greene could not have anticipated. He was corresponding with the American commander of West Point, General Benedict Arnold.

Greene rejoined Washington in northern New Jersey, thrilled by his triumph over Knyphausen and resolved to reclaim his position as a military strategist and battlefield commander. He had been quartermaster for more than two years, and the service had been miserable. Furthermore, it was getting worse. With the states now responsible for supplies, the department was more chaotic and coming under more criticism than ever before.

Washington shared Greene's frustration. He warned Congress that the army "can no longer drudge on in the old way."

And Nathanael Greene had had enough of drudge work. In late July, Congress announced a reorganization of the quartermaster's department, which decreased its staff and salaries and nearly eliminated departments that oversaw forage and the supply of wagons. Greene immediately resubmitted his resignation, this time in language that Congress could not ignore. In a letter dated July 26, he said that the reorganization plan was so flawed that overseeing it would be a "physical impossibility," in part because Congress had fired his best assistants. He referred more than once to Congress as the *administration*, a loaded term that most Americans associated with the British ministry and its hated ways. He continued:

> It is unnecessary for me to go into the general objections I
> have to the plan. It is sufficient to say that my feelings are
> injured. . . . My rank is high in the line of the Army; and
> sacrifices on this account I have made, together with the

fatigue and anxiety I have undergone, far overbalance all the emoluments I have derived.

Delegates in Congress rose to condemn the insolent quartermaster general. Joseph Jones, a member of Congress from Virginia, complained bitterly that Greene's letter "lessened" him "not only in the opinion of Congress but . . . of the public." Henry Laurens asked Richard Henry Lee, "What can have tempted him to treat Congress with sneer and sarcasm?"

There was talk in Congress of not simply accepting Greene's resignation as quartermaster but ousting him from the army entirely. Congress retained such powers over army personnel and would exercise them shortly by naming Horatio Gates as the new commander of the shattered southern army, with no input from the commander in chief.

At headquarters, Washington thus far was but an anguished bystander to this awful spectacle. At this vital hour, with the South in disarray and the northern army locked in a bitter stalemate, he hardly needed delegates in Congress denouncing the man who had so ably served him for so long. Then again, Greene had not shown Washington proper deference in choosing this moment to lash out at Congress. Greene and Congress were acting as though they were engaged in a personal feud, not a war upon which their lives, fortunes, and sacred honor depended.

Wearily, the commander in chief finally sent a message through Jones, asking Congress to reconsider any plans to "suspend" Greene "from his command." Several days later, Congress named Colonel Timothy Pickering, a critic of Washington's, as the new quartermaster general. There was no further movement against Greene, and he agreed to serve—without commissions—in his hated job until the new man learned the system.

On August 16, 1780, the new commander of the southern army, Horatio Gates, was annihilated near Camden, South Carolina. It was the second catastrophe in four months in the South. Gates suffered two thousand casualties—his entire force numbered about fifteen hundred Continentals and two thousand militia—and once he retreated, he did not stop until he was two hundred miles from the battlefield.

Gates had spent the years since Saratoga basking in the glow of that famous victory, but he was, in fact, an ineffectual general who had gotten lucky once, but only once. His leadership in the South was dreadful, for he stumbled into a general action—the very sort of battle both Washington and Greene had learned to avoid in the North—without careful preparation. His army was starving and ill-prepared for another major battle; indeed, his own staff was stunned to learn that Gates was intent on attacking Cornwallis only a month after his arrival in the South. When Gates estimated his strength at about seven thousand, a horrified colonel pointed out that the correct figure was more like three thousand. Gates replied, in essence, that the precise number really didn't matter. It is one of the war's ironies that Washington's two worst major generals were the two British-trained professionals, Charles Lee and Horatio Gates.

The disaster at Camden made Lord Cornwallis master of the Deep South. And it was clear he had no intention of stopping there. Morale thoughout the country plummeted, and so did discipline. During a foraging expedition in northern New Jersey, several soldiers under Greene's command rampaged through civilian homes and farms with shocking violence. Two soldiers fired at local citizens. Greene's distress was obvious in a report he sent to Washington: "The . . . plunder and violence is equal to anything committed by the Hessians. . . . I think it would have good effect to hang one of these fellows in the face of the troops without the form of a [trial]." With Washington's approval, Greene ordered the hanging to proceed.

The incident shook him profoundly. He believed that such outrages were the province of the enemy, not of patriotic soldiers fighting for their liberty. He could not understand how troops fighting for such a cause would degrade their uniform and that cause. He began to question his optimism. "There is so much wickedness and viliany in the World and so little regard paid to truth, honor and justice that I am almost sick of life," he told Caty. On September 7, 1780, he confesssed further anxieties to his friend Benedict Arnold. "We are starving here for want of provisions," he wrote from his camp in New Jersey. "Our Troops don't get one days meat in four. This can't hold long, what is to become of us?"

Perhaps the French could help. On September 17, Washington set out from headquarters in Bergen County for a conference in Hartford, Connecticut, with French general Jean Rochambeau and Admiral Charles Ternay. "In my absence," Washington told Greene, "the command of the army devolves upon you. . . . I leave the conduct of it to your discretion."

Greene was temporary commander in chief for no more than twenty-four hours when he heard news that a British fleet of ten ships had been spotted off Sandy Hook, sailing for New York. He dispatched a message to Washington, still en route to Connecticut. Washington told Greene to put the army in motion toward Tappen, New York, to help fortify Arnold and West Point in case the British made a move up the Hudson.

The army broke camp at ten o'clock on the foul, chilly morning of September 20 and marched through Bergen County and the lower Hudson Valley, its vast forests turning from green to orange, red, and gold. The army arrived in Tappen after a slogging march of three days, and Greene settled into what he assumed would be a quiet few days filling in for George Washington. A package containing new shirts and a poem from Caty arrived on September 22, and it provided a welcome distraction from the war's declining fortunes and the miserable weather. "I will venture to say there is no mortal person more happy in a wife than myself," he told Caty. He then broke the news that he was nothing less than the temporary commander of the American army. "This makes me a great man for a few days," he wrote.

His mood darkened, though, even as he wrote. The frustrations of the summer, his quarrels with Congress, the disasters in the South, the lack of discipline among the troops—these were burdens he could no longer shoulder. "What puppies and pygmies men are. . . . Many of us are the dupes of knaves and the tools of folly. O this war! I wish to God it was over!"

At nine o'clock on the morning of September 25, Greene issued orders for a series of complicated drills involving the whole army except for "the sick and camp guards." Regiments from New Jersey, New York, and Pennsylvania gathered on a makeshift parade ground as Greene watched from an observation point. The troops wheeled left and right, right and left, responding to signals from a fieldpiece mounted on a nearby hill.

Greene was pleased. The men moved smartly and with pride. Not for the first time in the war, the troops had lifted Greene's spirits and allowed him to forget the politicians, the Tories, and the critics.

Hours later, after night fell, an exhausted express rider bolted into camp with an urgent message for General Greene. It was a letter from Alexander Hamilton, a member of Washington's traveling party. "Arnold has fled to the Enemy," the message read.

Arnold? The hero of Saratoga? The man to whom Greene had confided his anxieties, who seemed so sympathetic? Benedict Arnold?

West Point clearly was in danger, and perhaps it was too late. Greene ordered the Pennsylvania regiments to march south in anticipation of a surprise assault. He ordered the rest of the army to be prepared to move on the "shortest notice."

After a sleepless, anxious night, Greene prepared his morning orders for September 26. The news about Arnold's treachery was shocking, but Greene was far from dispirited. Indeed, he seemed almost exhilarated by the close call, by the capure of Arnold's middleman, Captain John André, and by the quick work of his troops in responding to the threat. He would soon tell his wife that far from being demoralized, he was renewed with fighting spirit. The discovery of Arnold's treason before it could be brought to fruition, he told Caty, "appears to have been providential, and convinces me that the liberties of America are the object of divine protection."

He broke the news to his troops. "Treason of the Blackest dye was yesterday discovered," he told them. "General Arnold, who commanded West Point . . . was about to deliver up that Important Post into the hands of the Enemy. Such an event must have given the American cause a deadly wound if not a fatal stab." On this dark day, Nathanael Greene saw light: this was a sign of the enemy's desperation, he said, because they had been forced to try with "Bribery and Corruption what they cannot accomplish in a manly way."

Nathanael Greene was Washington's choice to preside over John André's court-martial, which took place in a church in the village of Tappen. On October 1, the tribunal found that André had acted "in a private and secret manner" behind the lines—in other words, he was a spy and therefore was condemned to death.

But what kind of death would it be? André asked to be shot as a soldier rather than be hanged like a common criminal. Many of the American officers were inclined to grant André's request, for he carried himself with courage and eloquence. Greene, however, insisted that the court had no choice. André, he said, was "either a spy or an innocent man. If the latter, to execute him in any way will be murder; if the former, the mode of his death is prescribed by law."

André was hanged in Tappen, New York, on October 2.

Less than two weeks later, on October 14—an hour of mortal peril for the country and the Revolution—Nathanael Greene was appointed commander of the Southern Department of the Continental army after Gates's monumental failure in South Carolina. Washington notified John Mathews, a young member of Congress from South Carolina, about Greene's promotion.

"I think I am giving you a general," wrote Washington. The thought must have cheered Mathews, who was an ally of Greene's. Then, however, the young politician read Washington's caveat: "[But] what can a General do, without men, without arms, without clothing, without stores, without provisions?"

That was Nathanael Greene's assignment: stop the British, save the Revolution, and do it without men, arms, clothing, stores, and provisions.

11 | "The Prospect Is Dismal"

The war in the South would be like nothing Nathanael Greene experienced in the North, where the campaign season traditionally came to a close as the days shortened and temperatures fell. In the South there would be no winter's respite from the ambitions of Lord Cornwallis and his eight thousand troops. Greene would not have the luxury of methodically rebuilding his pitifully small force of a thousand Continentals and slightly more militia. He would have to be prepared to fight through the winter, with the beaten, ill-equipped remnant of an army.

Very few of the rules Greene had learned on the battlefields of New Jersey and Pennsylvania would apply to his new command. The southern war would, by necesssity, emphasize improvisation and mobility, for traditional set-piece battles had led to the American disasters in Savannah, Charleston, and Camden. Greene already was formulating an unconventional campaign employing guerrilla tactics of hit and run, never risking the all-or-nothing battle that might end the war. He had learned under Washington the importance of keeping soldiers in the field, for in that way, this army of rebels might win by losing, slowly and methodically draining the enemy until he tired of bloody sacrifice. Greene outlined his unconventional strategy to Washington, saying that he planned to equip a force of about a thousand infantry and eight hundred cavalry, supplemented by local militia. "I see but little prospect of getting a force to contend with the enemy upon equal grounds," Greene wrote, "and therefore must make the most of a kind of partizan war." Washington recognized the genius of the plan—and its necessity. "I [entirely] approve of your plan for forming a flying army," he wrote Greene on November 8.

Supplying such a force, however, presented another set of problems. Greene's supply line, when it functioned at all, stretched hundreds of miles, to Virginia and even farther north. When Greene asked for additional arms and perhaps a detachment of French soldiers based in Newport, a pained Washington explained that such help would not be coming.

Strategically, too, the South was unlike the North. There was no single vital river such as the Hudson to defend at all costs; instead there were dozens of smaller rivers, streams, and tributaries, not to mention disease-infested lowland swamps and rugged backcountry mountains, to consider when moving the army and supplies. Greene studied maps that bore place-names and features unknown to him: the Yadkin River, the Pee Dee, the High Hills of Santee. In the South, he would be a stranger in a foreign land.

Indeed, the South was unfamiliar in more than geography. Britain's southern strategy not only had broken two Continental armies but had demolished civil authority in Georgia and South Carolina. While Greene certainly did not enjoy his dealings with politicians in the North, at least states like New Jersey and Pennsylvania had functioning legislatures that could assist the army with supplies and recruits. But that was no longer true in the lower South. South Carolina's governor, John Rutledge, had fled with Gates's army into North Carolina after the rout at Camden. Both South Carolina and Georgia were virtually restored to British rule, resisted only by bands of partisan guerrillas under the command of men like Francis Marion, Andrew Pickens, and Thomas Sumter. In the North, Greene developed a healthy distrust of militiamen. But in the South, these mobile, effective, and often ruthless citizen soldiers were the bulwark of the faltering American cause. They were all that was left after the reckless Gates destroyed the main southern army at Camden.

The patriot irregulars were not the only well-armed bands roaming the southern countryside. Tory militia—more numerous, more fervent, and more deadly than those Greene enountered in the North—took heart from Britain's victories in the region, and recruits were pouring into the ranks, eager to join the winning side. Tory units manned some of the forts the British were building in South Carolina, and they were an integral part of Cornwallis's ambitious plans for pacifying the lower South and bringing the war into North Carolina and Virginia.

Greene, then, would be facing not only Cornwallis and his increasingly notorious cavalry commander, Banastre Tarleton, but also thousands of his fellow Americans. The war in the South truly was a civil war and so would be more vicious than anything Greene had encountered.

It is impossible to exaggerate the gravity of Nathanael Greene's position in the fall of 1780. His new command promised to be a military, political, and logistical nightmare. After the devastating American defeats in Charleston and Camden, after Arnold's betrayal, an American victory still seemed as implausible as it did during the retreat through New Jersey in 1776 or during the winters at Valley Forge and Morristown. As he made his way south from state to state, begging for supplies, for money, for support beyond encouraging words, Nathanael Greene seemed to be riding toward oblivion, with death and destruction his only companions.

Greene's cavalry commander, Henry Lee, understood how close the cause was to failure. If the British defeated Greene, he wrote, "the Carolinas and Georgia inevitably become members of the British empire." The enemy would then move into Virginia, and soon "[all] the country south of the James River . . . would be ground to dust and ashes. Such misery, without hope, could not be long endured." It would be just a matter of time, Lee wrote, before the cause was abandoned and "reannexation to the mother country . . . would be solicited and obtained."

Everything, then, depended on Nathanael Greene.

From his days in Rhode Island, where politics was so interwined with individual leaders—Hopkins versus Ward—Greene understood the importance of personal leadership, of the ability of charismatic leaders to inspire, encourage, and organize. He saw personal leadership exercised most dramatically in the person of George Washington, who by force of character alone kept alive the Revolution in its earlier, darkest hours. Now, at this new critical moment, surrounded by the shattered remnants of a broken cause, Greene knew that his own leadership ability would be put to the test. "I believe the views and wishes of the great body of the people are entirely with us," he wrote. "But remove the personal influence of a few and they are a lifeless, inanimate mass, without direction or spirit."

It was not the most sanguine expression of republican confidence in the people. One can hardly imagine Thomas Jefferson writing such a sentence. But then again, Thomas Jefferson had not marched through New Jersey during the lonely depths of 1776, had not begged his fellow citizens for forage and supplies in the fields of Pennsylvania, and had not tried to fight a war in the name of countrymen who so often seemed apathetic at best, or hostile at worst.

Greene and his second in command, the capable Baron von Steuben, arrived in Philadelphia on October 27 to request the money and matériel they would need to rebuild the southern army. They spent more than a week in the capital—which was about a week longer than Greene wished to stay—meeting with committees, discussing logistics, and generally pleading for more of everything. His meetings did not go well. "Congress can furnish no money, and the Board of War neither clothing or other necessities," he wrote to Washington. "Indeed the prospect is dismal, and truly distressing."

Hoping to do better with patriots of more means, Greene appealed to merchants in Philadelphia to supply his troops with five thousand uniforms. The merchants told him that they were too busy. Actually, they believed they would never get paid, a consideration Greene regarded with contempt. "[If] there is not public spirit enough in the people to defend their liberties, they will well deserve to be slaves," he told Washington. Eventually, grudging patriotism had its day; local merchants sold fifteen hundred uniforms to the Board of War for Greene's troops.

Before leaving Philadelphia for additional begging sessions in other states, Greene received unexpected good news from the South. Several weeks earlier, on October 7, American guerrillas had routed an enemy detachment of a thousand loyalists and about a hundred British regulars at a place called Kings Mountain in South Carolina. British and Tory casualties were enormous, some 60 percent, and among those killed was a young and promising British officer, Patrick Ferguson. The American militiamen mutilated his corpse, an extra act of savagery designed to send a message to other Americans who sympathized with the British. If they acted on their sympathies, they, too, might meet Ferguson's fate or the fate of Tory militiamen who were killed even after they attempted to surrender.

The defeat at Kings Mountain forced the seemingly unstoppable Cornwallis to postpone his planned advance into North Carolina. And the American message to the local Tories apparently was well understood. Cornwallis told his superiors in London that the pro-British civilian population was "totally disheartened." Suddenly, Greene's burdens seemed slightly lighter as he left Philadelphia and continued his journey to the South.

Greene rode through Delaware, Maryland, and Virginia, stopping to ask political leaders for help with supplies and recruitment. He was met with sympathetic nods, expressions of support, and not much else. He told Washington, "They promise me all the assistance in their power, but are candid enough to tell me, that I must place little [dependence] on them, as they have neither money nor credit, and from the temper of the people are afraid to push matters to extremities."

He wrote that depressing letter in the early morning light of a bedroom at Mount Vernon, where he was a guest of Martha Washington's. The southern autumn had descended on the fields of northern Virginia, leaving trees bare and adding a bite to sunset. The northern army, he knew, would welcome the change of seasons, just as his wife did, for cold weather meant winter quarters, and winter quarters meant a respite from battle, if not always from suffering. The only respite he would receive now was this short stay at the home of his commander in chief.

His travels already had taken him more than two hundred miles and nearly eight weeks, with much more riding to come before reaching North Carolina. But Greene remained in Mount Vernon barely twenty-four hours, just enough time to socialize with Mrs. Washington and take a short ride around the plantation before setting off for Richmond and a meeting with Governor Thomas Jefferson.

Though he presided over the nation's richest state, Jefferson was in no better position to offer help than his less celebrated colleagues in Maryland and Delaware. Virginia had been expected to recruit thirty-five hundred men for Continental service, but only fifteen hundred had turned out. And those few who did enlist were hardly in fighting form. Some quickly deserted; others were so unhealthy that Greene believed they would be of little use on the battlefield. Jefferson promised Greene a hundred wagons to transport his meager supplies, but even with the power to seize private property, the governor's agents could round up only eighteen. "Our prospects with respect to supplies are very discouraging," Greene glumly reported to Washington.

Greene's discussions with Jefferson left him uninspired and pessimistic. The governor could summon no inspiring phrases or poetic tributes to send Greene on his way to battle. Instead, there was only grim accounting and gloomy statistics. Greene wondered, not for the first time, how and why such burdens had fallen on his shoulders. He had given so much to the cause, and now, in this critical hour, all he asked for was the tools to do his job. But his fellow patriots said they could only do so much. Greene found himself longing for the relative comforts of the North, for the company of Washington, of Caty, of his friends like Henry Knox and Jeremiah Wadsworth. Melancholy and dread overcame him as he considered the enormity of what lay ahead. He wrote to Washington:

> I cannot contemplate my own situation without the greatest
> degree of anxiety. I am far removed from almost all my friends
> and connections, and have to prosecute a war . . . with almost
> insurmountable difficulties. . . . How I shall be able to support
> myself under all these embarrassments God only knows.

These were not the sentiments George Washington wanted to read
from his ebullient and loyal subordinate, the man he had entrusted with
nothing less than the cause itself. He knew his friend was capable of self-
pity, but surely now was not the time for Greene's flights of woe-is-me.
Woe was the cause itself, as Greene surely knew.

But Greene could not help but reflect on what the looming catastrophe would mean for his reputation, so carefully guarded and fiercely defended.

> My only consolation is, that if I fail I hope it will not be
> accompanied with any peculiar marks of personal disgrace.
> Censure and reproach ever follow the unfortunate. This I
> expect if I don't succeed. . . . The ruin of my family is what
> hangs most heavy upon my mind. My fortune is small; and
> misfortune or disgrace to me must be ruin to them.

After putting these dark thoughts on paper, he left Steuben in Richmond to defend the army's barren depots and set out for North Carolina.

Grim as Greene's prospects were, he could take some solace in the quality of his new subordinates. The partisan commanders, particularly Marion, Sumter, and Pickens, were fighters who knew the terrain as neither
Greene nor Cornwallis knew it. Greene also came to rely on another talented foreign officer, Thaddeus Kosciuszko of Poland, who had served
as the southern army's chief engineer under Gates. It would be the Pole's
assignment to ford the region's rivers as Greene moved his army through
alien territory.

As he studied the terrain of this hostile region, Greene the organizer, Greene the supplier, Greene the quartermaster immediately understood that the logistical challenges of the South could be summed up in a word: *boats*. He would need them, plenty of them, for the roads that supplied him would be rivers, and his lines of retreat invariably would involve crossings great and small. The Roanoke, the Yadkin, the Dan, the Pee Dee, and hundreds of small streams coursed though the southern landscape like so many veins and arteries. Greene dispatched men to survey the rivers, to note "the Depth of the Water, the Current & the Rocks & every other Obstruction that will impede the Business of Transportation."

Greene then turned his attention to horseflesh and brainpower. In the mobile war he was planning, cavalry would play a significant role in monitoring the enemy's movements, harassing his flanks, and seemingly appearing from nowhere on the battlefield. The commander of these quick-striking troops would have to be daring and shrewd—and he was. In Lighthorse Harry Lee, Greene added to the impressive cast of supporting characters he was assembling for the new campaign. Assisting Lee was William Washington, a cousin of the commander in chief. And then there was a tough, hulking backwoodsman named Daniel Morgan, a veteran of the French and Indian War. Morgan had quit the army in 1779, claiming he was too ill to continue but privately nursing a grievance over promotions. He returned to duty, however, after Gates's disaster at Camden, and he now offered his services to Greene.

The new southern commander did not hesitate to seek the counsel of strangers who could instruct him not only in the terrain but in the particular bitterness of the southern war. Years ago, long before he joined the army, the young Nathanael Greene eagerly collected friends who were better educated and better read than he was, and he learned from them. Now, in his first independent command of the war, Greene was secure enough to surround himself with able, talented people—some of them professional soldiers with far more experience than he had.

He arrived at the American camp in Charlotte on December 2 and took over command from Gates the following day with surprisingly little tension. The cordiality between the two no doubt was a sign of the desperate moment; though they had clashed before, Gates and Greene knew that their differences meant nothing now. Washington had given Greene authority to conduct an inquiry into Gates's retreat from Camden, but Greene decided against such a proceeding. In fact, in the coming months, he would defend Gates, a magnanimous gesture at a time when Congress was looking for scapegoats.

Greene immediately sent a message to Francis Marion, whom he had never met: "Your Services in the lower Part of South Carolina . . . have been very important and it is my earnest Desire that you continue. I like your Plan of frequently shifting your Ground. It frequently prevents a Surprize and perhaps a total Loss of your Party." He confided to Marion that he wished to immediately recruit spies—"the Eyes of an Army"—to keep tabs on Cornwallis. Marion was not used to such gracious treatment from Continental generals, and it left a strong impression: here was a general who respected the work of the militia. Ironically, of course, Greene had been a strong critic of the militia. But now he had no choice but to ingratiate himself with men who had continued to resist the British offensive even after the regular Continental army fled.

The troops in Charlotte offered their new commander little to inspire confidence. In describing the "condition of this army, if it deserves the name of one," Greene told Washington: "Nothing can be more wretched and distressing than the condition of the troops, starving with cold and hunger, without tents and camp equipage. Those of the Virginia line are literally naked, and a great part totally unfit for any kind of duty." He was furious with Jefferson for Virginia's neglect of its soldiers. (Each state was responsible for supplying its regiments.) He sent the governor a blistering letter, telling him that "it is impracticable to preserve Discipline when Troops are in Want of every Thing. . . . [Be] assured that you raise men in vain unless you clothe, arm and equip them properly for the field."

Meanwhile, Continental troops from Maryland had complaints of another sort. Not long after Greene took over from Gates, Maryland's officers presented him with a petition charging that the state's political leaders were offering bonuses and promotions to men who joined the state regiments—as opposed to Maryland's regular Continental regiments. As a result, the officers said, their most experienced colleagues and troops were leaving Continental service and joining the state militia, leaving the Maryland line dangerously undermanned. The Marylanders' complaints, though valid, only added to Greene's logistical, strategic, and political headaches. He did his best to mollify the officers, whose men made up the heart of Greene's little army, telling them, "[While the] subject you write upon is delicate . . . [as] an officer I feel for you." He promised he would put in a word for them with Maryland's governor. Within a few months, Greene himself would be complaining about the "want of officers in the Maryland line."

Even more horrifying than the state of the army was the war's special brutality in the southern backwoods: neighbors were pitted against neighbors, Americans fighting Americans, civilians slaughtered, homes and farms burned. Greene told Samuel Huntington, president of the Continental Congress, that the "whole country is in danger of being laid waste by the [patriots] and [Tories], who pursue each other with as much relentless fury as beasts of prey. People . . . are frequently murdered as they ride along the road."

He continued to harangue local officials for supplies and men, and asked Washington to act on his behalf with governors and other civilian leaders. His years as quartermaster general were not in vain, because they taught him a vital lesson that he was now acting upon: he knew he needed supplies before he could fight. It took him only a few days to realize that the southern army's deputy quartermaster, Captain Joseph Marbury, was not cut out for the job. "The Gentleman . . . is a very honest young man but his views have been confined to mere Camp issues." Greene would need somebody like himself, who knew how to feed and supply an army on the move. He found that person in a young colonel named Edward Carrington. And he appointed the equally competent William Davie as commissary general. Both men were experienced battlefield officers who were new to the rigors of supply. But Greene was not a man who necessarily placed a premium on experience—how could he? He valued talent and competence, and got both in his two main supply officers.

Part of a commander's job, as he had learned under Washington, was diplomacy. Although Greene had not earned a reputation for that particular art form, as any member of Congress might testify, he was conciliatory and patient with his officers and troops. He smoothed over jealousies based on promotions, he continued to reach out to militia commanders, and he looked after the health and welfare of his soldiers. With such tactics, he slowly rebuilt the morale and the discipline the army would need in the test that lay ahead.

But morale and discipline fed nobody. And neither did the countryside around Charlotte. To eat, and to survive, meant moving the army.

On December 16, 1780, Nathanael Greene made one of the most audacious decisions of the war. On his own, without consulting a council of war or local commanders, he decided to divide his army in the face of Cornwallis's stronger force. Greene and the bulk of his army would march southeast, into South Carolina, to a camp near Cheraw Hill along the Pee Dee River. A detachment of about six hundred men under Daniel Morgan would march from Charlotte to the southwest, along the Pacolet River in South Carolina.

The tactic defied all the laws of warfare. Military manuals insisted that a weaker general should never divide his troops when confronted by a stronger opponent capable of smashing the whole, never mind two weakened units. Even more extraordinary was Greene's disposition of his troops: one hundred and twenty miles would separate his camp from Morgan's, with Cornwallis between them.

He justified the maneuver as follows: If the British attacked him, they would leave their forts in South Carolina vulnerable to Morgan. If they attacked Morgan, Greene would be free to move against Charleston or other British strongholds. Dividing the army also reduced the pressure on logistics, for it would be easier to supply two small, widely dispersed forces than a single army concentrated in one camp.

He ordered Morgan to keep Cornwallis's left flank busy and to buoy the morale of patriots in the western backcountry of South Carolina, who would be heartened to see an American show of force in a state under virtual British occupation. But he did not expect much more of Morgan's men. They were too weak, he said, to make any "opposition of consequence."

He underestimated Daniel Morgan.

There would be no winter camp for Caty Greene this year, not with her husband on the march in the South, so she relieved her boredom and anxiety with frequent trips to Newport, now populated with thousands of French soldiers since the British departed. She delighted in their company, and they in hers, for Caty was vivacious and didn't particularly care if her behavior raised a judgmental eyebrow. Several of the French officers she befriended in Newport took her up on an invitation to visit her in Coventry. One, a soldier named Claude Blanchard, must have taken Caty by surprise, for he noted that there was no bread in the house when he arrived. Blanchard was equally surprised to note just how desolate the Greene homsestead and its surrounding property were. "There is not a single fruit-tree, not even a cabbage" on the property, he wrote. "Another countryhouse is pretty near, inhabited by two ladies who compose all the society Mrs. Greene has."

Sensitive to Caty's anxiety, Washington himself wrote to her, offering his headquarters as a conduit for letters between the Greenes: "If you will entrust your letters to my care, they shall have the same attention paid to them as my own." Gestures like this one help explain the fierce loyalty and affection both Greenes held for Washington.

Though her admirers saw only her soft side, Caty could be just as ferocious an antagonist as her husband. In early 1781, she received a letter from Deborah Olney, the officer's wife who had confronted Washington so memorably at Morristown, accusing her of fabricating the story and spreading it around. Caty replied in a fashion that no doubt made her husband proud. "I will not be so impolite as to charge you with telling fals[e]hoods but your memory must be very perfidious," she told Mrs. Olney. "As to your tearing out the [General's] Eyes I heard nor said nothing . . . but you did say you would tear out his [hair]—and I can bring sworn evidence to the truth of it." This is one of the very few extant letters of Caty's, and while it is, in fact, filled with the spelling mistakes that mortified her husband (such as *vertues* rather than *virtues* and *parciallity* instead of *partiality*), it isn't much worse than her husband's.

As for Nathanael, he, too, was taking pains to make sure that Caty would not become overanxious as word filtered north about the plight of the southern army. "I am posted in the Wilderness, on a great river, endeavoring to reform the army and improve its [discipline]," Greene wrote to Caty from his new camp on the Pee Dee. He described an almost idyllic life: "[The] weather is mild and the climate moderate, so much so that we all live in [tents] without the least inconvenience." He said that he and his brother officers were spending their days "recapitulating the pleasures and diversions of Morristown." If the men were indeed reveling in the memories of the previous winter's camp, they certainly were choosing their stories carefully. Memories of the constant snow, the near starvation, the suffering and privation certainly would not have made for pleasant discussion over a campfire.

Greene was trying to assure his worried wife, for his words bore little relation to reality. The march from Charlotte to Cheraw on the Pee Dee took place in anything but "mild" weather. It rained for days, turning the roads to mud and the journey into an ordeal. Inevitably, food supplies were low, and the troops fanned out into the countryside to find something, anything, to eat. When they finally arrived in Cheraw, the troops were only somewhat better off. Falling back on his youthful study of the Old Testament, Greene wrote to Morgan, "Our prospects with regard to provisions are mended, but this is no Egypt."

In other letters, his descriptions of his situation were even more pointed. The very same day he wrote his lighthearted letter to Caty, December 29, Greene sent a very different message to General Robert Howe, one of the several former commanders of the Southern Department: "When I left the Northern Army I expected to find in this Department a Thousand Difficulties to which I was a Stranger in the Northern Service, but the Embarrassments far exceed my utmost [apprehension], nor can I find a Clue to guide me through the Complicated Scene of Difficulties. I have but a Shadow of an Army."

Lord Cornwallis soon decided to be rid of this shadow. He told one of his field commanders, Lord Rawdon—the man who had so cheerfully described British rape on Staten Island in 1776—that he believed Greene was too weak to "attempt any thing." Cornwallis, on the other hand, was about to be reinforced with fifteen hundred troops under the command of General Alexander Leslie, and a British invasion force under the turncoat Benedict Arnold was on its way from New York to bring the war to Virginia. The time was right to take the offensive in the Carolinas. If he destroyed his divided enemy, Cornwallis could march north to link up with Arnold and complete the British reconquest of the South. Still, he was wary of his frequent antagonist. He would later write: "[Greene is] as dangerous as Washington. He is vigilant, enterprising, and full of resources—there is but little hope of gaining an advantage over him. I never feel secure when encamped in his neighbourhood." With that in mind, Cornwallis asked Rawdon to keep a close watch on the American's movements. Rawdon didn't see the need for such caution. He assured Cornwallis in a letter dated January 11: "I have so many persons watching Greene, that I think he cannot make any movement without my receiving early notice of it."

To further restrict Greene's movements, Benedict Arnold and his fifteen hundred troops moved against the southern army's supply depots in Virginia in early January. Arnold carried out his orders with relish and soon sent Governor Thomas Jefferson and the state's legislature fleeing from Richmond. Greene now had to keep a wary eye on events in Virginia, for Arnold's army posed a potentially deadly threat to the southern army's scanty supplies and vital land lines of communication with Washington. Steuben tried to reorganize the shaken Virginia militia and Continentals until reinforcements from the North arrived—that is, if Washington could find any to spare. The increasingly anxious commander in chief knew he could hardly stand by while Greene faced the prospect of being caught between Arnold (to the north of Greene's position) and Cornwallis (to the south). He eventually rounded up some

Continentals and sent them, with Lafayette at their head, southward. But Greene would need a good deal more help as the British moved in for the kill. Washington focused his attention on the French fleet, anchored in Newport, Rhode Island. If the French could be persuaded to sail to the South . . .

For the moment, though, he could offer Greene only an expression of confidence. "Amidst the complicated dangers with which you are surrounded," Washington wrote, "a confidence in your abilities is my only consolation. I am convinced you will do everything that is practicable." Given Greene's worship of his commander in chief and his hunger for recognition, such words must have brightened his outlook, even as Washington reminded him that the cause itself depended on Greene's little army.

In the backcountry of western South Carolina, a poorly supplied Daniel Morgan believed his position was becoming untenable. He asked Greene's permission to move into Georgia, but Greene, fearing any change in the brittle status quo, urged him to remain in South Carolina. He also advised Morgan to fight only when necessary.

Cornwallis offered no such advice to his aggressive cavalry commander, Banastre Tarleton, who was eager to find and crush Morgan. In fact, Cornwallis encouraged his subordinate, sending him reinforcements and telling him, "If Morgan is . . . any where within your reach, I wish you to push him to the utmost." Cornwallis decided not to wait for Arnold to build up his forces in Virginia, consolidate his gains, and then turn south to squeeze Greene in a pincer movement. He believed he could crush the weak and divided southern army now. And so, in mid-January, Tarleton set out with some eleven hundred of Britain's best troops in search of Daniel Morgan's ragged band of six hundred Continentals and a few hundred militia. Meanwhile, Cornwallis would be free to attack Greene; in the face of his divided enemy, Cornwallis divided his own force.

On January 13, Greene dispatched a jaunty message to Morgan: "Col.

Tarlton is said to be on his way to pay you a visit. I doubt not but he will have a decent reception and a proper dismission."

Three days later, with Tarleton at his doorstep and a river to his rear, Morgan decided to make a stand near the North Carolina border in a place called Cowpens, so called because it had been used as quarters for cattle. It was an odd choice for the American commander—the area was wide-open, practically inviting Tarleton's cavalry to gallop through the American position with swords flailing. But Morgan decided he would rather stand and fight, even in such a position, than be attacked on the march.

On the morning of January 17, Morgan deployed his men in three lines and gave them very specific instructions, crafted to take advantage of his strengths and, at the same time, to concede his weaknesses. His forward line consisted of about a hundred and fifty sharpshooters. They were militiamen, prone to run away at the first sign of trouble. Morgan brilliantly incorporated this inevitablility into his order of battle: the sharpshooters were to fire twice—from fifty yards—and then retreat. A second line, made up of militia under the command of Andrew Pickens, would do likewise. Morgan told them to aim for Tarleton's officers.

After the men on the second line did their damage, they would fall back and re-form as a third American line of defense, positioned on high ground, prepared for the final British push. In reserve, ready to counterattack as the British moved forward, were American cavalrymen under William Washington. "Just hold up your heads, boys," Morgan told his troops, "and then when you return to your homes, how the old folks will bless you, and the girls kiss you for your gallant conduct."

It was a brilliant plan, and its influence on Greene would prove to be profound.

After a four-mile predawn march, the most feared British commander of the war, Tarleton, and his crack troops assailed the American position just before seven o'clock on the morning of January 17. What followed was nothing short of a military miracle. Morgan's sharpshooters fired a deadly volley at Tarleton's overconfident cavalry, forcing them to fall back. The sharpshooters then filed out of the forward position, as Morgan had planned.

As the British cavalry re-formed, Tarleton's infantry marched toward the second line, manned by Pickens and his troops. The Americans waited until the British were nearly at point-blank range, fired two devastating volleys, and then retreated. Washington's cavalry charged the British right and then circled around the British rear. Tarleton assailed the right flank of Morgan's third and final line of defense, but his men were driven back.

After an hour of intense fighting, hundreds of British troops put down their weapons and surrendered—their discipline utterly broken. A stunned Tarleton retreated.

The British casualties were appalling: of their eleven hundred troops, they lost one hundred killed, more than two hundred wounded, and six hundred captured. By contrast, only a dozen Americans were killed and about sixty wounded.

Cowpens was a spectacular American victory and an unmitigated disaster for the British. A minute before Tarleton sent his troops toward Morgan, the American cause in the South seemed as hopeless as it had ever been. An hour later, all had changed. Cowpens transcended mere casualty figures; it gave heart to the region's patriots, and it stunned loyalists. Greene was extremely conscious of public opinion and perception, understanding that patriot civilians would be more inclined to join local militia or the Continental army if the cause did not seem lost. Cowpens showed that it was not.

Several days passed before Greene received a message from Morgan, dated January 19: "The Troops I had the Honor to command have been so fortunate as to obtain a compleat Victory over a Deatchment from the British Army commanded by Lt. Colonel Tarlton." Greene was delighted but also relieved; Morgan had taken a huge gamble and, in fact, had ignored Greene's plea to avoid combat. But, as Greene indicated in a letter to Washington, the brilliant victory at Cowpens could not mask the huge difficulties the American army still faced. Greene was worried, too, that the politicians who controlled money and supplies—however scarce and few—might be inclined to relax after hearing about Cowpens. Greene told his friend James Varnum that the "Army is in a deplorable condition; and not withstanding this little success, must inevitably fall [prey] to the enemy if not better supported. . . . Don't imagine that Lord Cornwallis is ruined: for depend upon it, the Southern States must fall, unless there is established a well appointed Army for their support."

Greene was right about Cornwallis—he was far from finished. Enraged by the British defeat at Cowpens, he was newly determined to crush his enemy. The Americans still were divided, but he was reinforced. Along with twenty-five hundred troops, Cornwallis set out in search of Morgan, who was retreating toward North Carolina. After finishing off Morgan, he would turn his attention to Greene. To speed his pursuit, he ordered his troops to burn all their excess baggage, wagons, and provisions. Even the army's rum was thrown aside, the unkindest sacrifice of all. The British would now move faster, but they would have to live off the land—a circumstance Greene surely would have advised against. Legend has it that when Greene heard that his formerly well-supplied nemesis had so rashly put a torch to his precious cargo, he smiled, perhaps for the first time since assuming his command. "Then he is ours!" he said.

Greene decided he must reunite his army or face disaster. After giving orders for his wing to march toward Salisbury, North Carolina, he set out to meet with Morgan on his own, with only a handful of men to protect him. He was alarmed when Morgan sent a dire message, describing himself as "emaciated" and saying that he was growing "worse every hour." Plagued by painful back ailments and rheumatism, Morgan hinted in his message that he could no longer function in the field—and this, with Cornwallis gaining ground on him.

Greene and Morgan linked up on January 30 after a perilous, soggy ride of more than a hundred miles through loyalist country. Greene had hoped that Cowpens would inspire local militia units to turn out as a confrontation with Cornwallis neared. But during his ride through the countryside, Greene discovered that there had been no such outpouring. "The people have been so harassed for eight months past and their domestick matters are in such distress," he wrote to Congress, "that they will not leave home; and if they do it is for so short a time that they are of no use." He deplored the lack of patriotism, but he had neither time nor energy to expend on regrets. Cornwallis was nearby, and Greene knew his enemy would attack as soon as he could. The Americans had to move quickly or be crushed.

Greene understood that he had one very important advantage. Although he was being chased, he at least would be moving north, toward his supply centers in Virginia. Cornwallis, on the other hand, was moving farther away from his supply base in South Carolina—and he was marching with light troops newly stripped of their tents, their baggage, and their provisions. The more Greene marched, the wearier Cornwallis would become. His rum-less troops could be forced to wander through the winter landscape of North Carolina, made to ford the region's rambling rivers, made to climb up and down slippery hills. Greene's strategy soon became evident: he would bait Cornwallis into a chase. Morgan was skeptical of Greene's plan, preferring his own idea of retreating into the countryside of South Carolina. He said he would not be responsible for the disasters he foresaw. "Neither will you," a testy Greene replied. "For I shall take the matter upon myself."

Greene sent Morgan on his way north, staying behind by the Catawba River in hopes of recruiting new militia forces. The mission was in vain, however, and when Greene heard that Cornwallis was across the river, he rode hard to Salisbury to catch up with Morgan. According to legend, as he arrived at Steele's Tavern in Salisbury, an exhausted Greene met an army acquaintance who was stunned to find the commander of the Southern Department traveling by himself.

"What! Alone, general?" the acquaintance supposedly said. "Yes," Greene replied, "tired, hungry, alone and penniless." As Greene's biographer Theodore Thayer pointed out, it's hard to believe that Greene actually rode without even a small guard. But the glum summary of his condition sounds entirely true. The wife of the tavern's proprietor was moved by the sight and words of this downcast general. She disappeared from her guest's sight for a moment, then reappeared bearing two bags of coins. "You need them more than I do," she told Greene. Damp-eyed, Greene accepted the offering of a patriot.

Rather than wait for the the the other wing of his army to arrive in Salisbury, Greene changed the location of the planned linkup to the town of
Guilford Court House, farther north in North Carolina. The British continued to match Greene step for step, and at one point, Cornwallis believed he had Greene trapped with his back to the Yadkin River. But the
command of detail that had marked Greene's service as a quartermaster
served him well in the field; he had boats ready to take him across the
river—literally in the nick of time. When Cornwallis reached the Yadkin,
now stripped of boats, the Americans were camped on the other side. To
vent his fury, Cornwallis ordered his artillery to fire on the American
camp, with little effect. According to eyewitnesses, Greene was writing
letters when a ball landed near his headquarters. "His pen never rested,"
the eyewitness reported.

The linkup at Guilford Court House, hampered by steady winter
rains, was complete on February 9, when Greene held a rare council of
war with three subordinates: Morgan, Brigadier General Isaac Huger,
and Colonel Otho Williams. It must have pained Greene even to look at
Morgan, for the hero of Cowpens was ailing again: he was thin after his
march through the backcountry, and his rheumatism was flaring up once
more. Shortly after the council, Morgan retired from the army, depriving
Greene of one of his best field commanders.

Greene told his subordinates that the recombined army had fewer
than fifteen hundred Continentals and about six hundred militia, many
of whom, he said, were "badly armed and distressed for the Want of
Clothing." Chasing them, Greene reckoned, were as many as three thousand troops under Cornwallis. A dreadful choice presented itself: this
weak army could turn and fight against overwhelming odds, or it could
continue to retreat through North Carolina and into Virginia, a distance
of some seventy miles, then it would cross the Dan River, near the main
American supply depots, and see whether Cornwallis continued his pursuit or turned away. Rejecting the first option, Greene knew that the
alternative—continued retreat—would mean the concession of North
Carolina to Cornwallis. It was a mortifying scenario, particularly after
Cowpens, but it was the only real choice Greene believed he had. Still, he

was loath to decide the issue on his own. Ever conscious of his reputation, of rumors and slanders casually whispered in the parlors of Philadelphia, he wanted consensus so that no enemy—Thomas Mifflin and his ilk—could say that Nathanael Greene lacked the will to stand and fight. He put the question to the other three officers (Morgan, Hugar, and Williams): should they fight Cornwallis now and so risk the army itself, or should they retreat into Virginia? The other officers agreed with Greene's gloomy assessment. "[It] was determined that we ought to avoid a general Action at all events," they wrote.

After the council of war broke up, Greene sadly informed Washington that he would abandon North Carolina. It was yet another blow in a bleak season for the Continental army. Greene explained: "We have no provisions but what we receive from our daily collections. Under these circumstances I called a council who unanimously advised to avoid an action and to retire beyond the Roanoke [in Virginia]." Greene made sure to include a copy of the council's proceedings, so that Washington could see that the retreat was not just his idea.

But now Greene had to beat Cornwallis, only thirty-five miles away, to the Dan River. At several points during the chase so far, Cornwallis had covered as much as twenty miles in a day. If Cornwallis caught up with Greene before they reached the river, the Americans would be crushed.

The race for the Dan began on February 10, when Greene once again divided his force, sending some seven hundred under Colonel Williams to stay between the main American force and Cornwallis, whose line of march was roughly parallel with Greene's. The British commander was about to be outfoxed again, for he believed that Greene would have to cross one of the Dan's upper fords, and the British were deployed accordingly. But Greene already had arranged for boats to be waiting for him downriver at Irwin's Ferry.

Williams's screening force confused Cornwallis long enough for Greene to make good his escape toward the river. He and his men were exhausted; Greene told Williams that he had slept only about four hours in four days of marching. But the frantic pace of the march paid off on February 14, when Greene's army safely crossed the Dan to conclude one of the most brilliant strategic retreats of the war. Greene sent a welcome message to Williams, who had carried out his assignment with great success: "All our troops are over and the stage is clear. I am ready to receive you and give you a hearty welcome."

The Americans had crossed four rivers and marched two hundred miles since Cowpens, all the while drawing Cornwallis farther from his supplies, all the while avoiding the general action that might have ended in defeat not just of the army but of the Revolution itself. Alexander Hamilton, an admirer of Greene, said of the march to the Dan:

> To have effected a retreat in the face of so ardent a pursuit, through so great an extent of the country, through a country offering every obstacle, affording scarcely any resources; with troops destitute of every thing . . . to have done all this, I say, without loss of any kind, may, without exaggeration, be denominated a masterpiece of military skill and exertion.

Even the British were impressed: Tarleton would later write that every move Greene made "from the Catawba to Virginia, was judiciously designed and vigorously executed."

Cornwallis, on the other side of the Dan and wary of the roving patriot partisans in his rear and on his flanks, waited several days and then ordered his men to march back to North Carolina. In a letter to London, he explained that his army was "ill-suited to enter . . . so powerful a province as Virginia." He was ill-suited because he was ill-supplied and hardly better off than his ragged enemy. He had been outgeneraled by the self-taught soldier from Rhode Island, but at least Greene was in Virginia now. North Carolina was cleared of the Continental army, though not the stubborn bands of patriot guerrillas. Cornwallis ordered his men to march sixty miles south to Hillsborough, North Carolina, where he issued a proclamation declaring victory and laying the groundwork for a restoration of Crown rule in the province.

The British didn't know it, but Nathanael Greene—resupplied and rested—had no intention of remaining safely over the Dan while his enemies celebrated his retreat. On February 22, just a few days after Cornwallis began his march to Hillsborough, Greene recrossed the Dan and then returned to North Carolina. He knew that he and Cornwallis were destined to meet again, and very soon.

The southern campaign was fought not only in the backcountry forests and the lowland swamps but also in the minds of the region's civilians. Both Greene and Cornwallis understood the importance of public opinion and public perception. They both depended on the citizen soldiers of the militia, and the fervor with which men joined these bands often depended upon the tide of the war. Cornwallis explained to London just how fickle his support was, telling Lord George Germain, secretary of state for the American colonies, that the militia were reluctant to turn out "whilst a doubt remained on their minds of the superiority of our Arms." To illustrate the point, the British commander found hundreds willing to join the loyalist militia corps when he triumphantly marched into Hillsborough to commemorate Greene's departure from the state. Greene, on the other hand, wished—needed—to give hope and heart to North Carolina's patriots while serving notice to its Tories that the Continental army in the South still was in the field, beaten but unvanquished. In late February, he told Washington that "most of the prisoners we take are inhabitants of America," a situation he found mortifying.

Greene's force remained pathetically small, about sixteen hundred, when he returned to North Carolina. But he put out a call for state militia, and the men were responding. Meanwhile, Washington sent him the good news that regular Continentals from Pennsylvania would soon be marching to his assistance. (They never made it, for they were delayed in the North and then were needed in Virginia.)

Through late February and early March, the two armies shadowed each other. Cornwallis was fully aware that Greene had returned to the state, although he was never sure precisely where he might be. Greene was based between Troublesome Creek and Reedy Fork Creek to the north of Guilford Court House and the British. But, Henry Lee later recalled, he changed "his position every day" and so "held Cornwallis in perfect ignorance of his position." They were about twenty miles apart, and there was frequent skirmishing, particularly between Lee's and Tarleton's mobile cavalry forces. At times in early March, the main camps were three miles from each other, though separated by rivers. The constant movement and incessant maneuvering wore down the ill-supplied British and tested Cornwallis's patience.

Still, the British force was strong and formidable, and Greene was not yet prepared to fight. But his very presence in North Carolina rallied the patriot cause and disheartened the loyalists who were so vital to the British southern strategy. "I have been obliged to practice . . . by finesse which I dare not attempt by force," he told Jefferson. He kept Washington informed of the life-or-death maneuvering under way in North Carolina, telling him that he was "within ten or twelve miles of the Enemy for several days," but was unwilling to risk a battle just yet. Instead, he sent detachments under Lee, Williams, and Pickens to harass and annoy Cornwallis, assignments they carried out so well that the British withdrew several miles south to Bell's Mill on the Deep River for a respite.

Greene confided in nobody. As a member of Washington's many councils of war in the northern campaigns, he had seen plans argued to death and bad advice offered as wisdom. As he prepared for Cornwallis, Greene called no council of war. He kept to himself, rising early, moving among the troops, and attending not only to strategy but to logistics.

One morning he passed by the tent of a colonel from Virginia who was sound asleep. Greene woke him up, exclaiming, "Good heavens, Colonel, how can you sleep with the enemy so near?" The sleepy but shrewd soldier replied, "Why, General, I knew that you were awake." Greene would later say that he never received so high a compliment as the colonel's.

The tension took a toll on his health. On March 5, from his camp in Boyd's Mill on Reedy Fork Creek, he told Lee that he was suffering from a "violent inflamation" in his eyes. To relieve his distress, he submitted to the usual medical practice of the day: he was bled. Not surprisingly, he told Lee, "The inflamation is still troublesome and my eyes weak and painful." Those sore eyes, however, soon beheld a wondrous sight: reinforcements of more than two thousand militia and Continental regulars. With these new troops from Virginia and North Carolina, Greene had more than four thousand men, enough, he determined, to offer Cornwallis the battle he so eagerly sought. For once, Greene's forces were numerically stronger than Cornwallis's army of about two thousand. But how long would he hold that advantage? As Greene told Jefferson, "[Militiamen] soon get tired out with difficulties, and go and come in such irregular Bodies that I can make no calculations on the strength of my Army." Apparently, Cornwallis had the same trouble keeping track of Greene's army. His spies had told him that the Americans now had up to ten thousand men.

The stakes in the coming fight were outlined in a candid letter Morgan sent Greene from his retirement in Virginia: "I expect Lord Cornwallis will push you till you are obliged to fight him, on which much will depend. You'll have from what I see, a great number of militia—if they fight, you'll beat Cornwallis, if not, he will beat you and perhaps cut your regulars to pieces, which will be losing all our hopes." Morgan offered some blunt advice: when the time came for Greene to stand and fight, he should position some of his veterans behind lines manned by the militia. The veterans, he wrote, should be given "orders to shoot down the first man that runs."

Just after dawn and breakfast on March 14, Greene and his men moved out of camp at Speedwell Iron Works and marched a dozen miles south to the battlefield of Greene's choosing: the tiny town of Guilford Court House, where he had gathered his men together in early February for the last leg of the race to the Dan. Cornwallis and the British were a little more than ten miles to the southwest, encamped near a Quaker meetinghouse.

Greene had no doubt that Cornwallis would attack him the following day, probably early in the morning. He immediately put his order of battle into place. It was a replica of Daniel Morgan's at Cowpens.

In the center of the battlefield was the New Garden Road, which

Cornwallis's men would follow from their camp to meet the Americans. The road was narrow, but it led to a wide clearing where Greene would position the first of three defensive lines. Manning the first line, behind a rail fence and on both sides of the New Garden Road, would be a thousand members of the North Carolina militia, among Greene's least experienced troops. They would have a superb view as the British marched out of the woods, through a muddy, plowed field, and toward the rail fence. Greene, again following Morgan's precedent, would ask his front line to deliver two or three well-executed volleys and then retire to the second line. William Washington's cavalry protected the right flank, while Henry Lee was positioned on the left.

The Virginia militia were to be deployed in the second line, some three hundred to four hundred yards behind the North Carolina militia and protected by a screen of woods. Greene would form his third line about seven hundred yards behind the second and facing another wide, open field that bent to the left after the second line. On the third line would be his fourteen hundred Continental regulars, two regiments from Virginia and two from Maryland—the heart of his army. They would be drawn up on the brow of a gently rising hill, a superb defensive position. The British not only would be exposed to American fire but would have to stumble across a small stream to reach the position, which was near the courthouse from which the village got its name. To the rear was the Ready Fork Road, which would serve as Greene's line of retreat.

It was late winter in North Carolina, and nightfall brought a chill to camp. Both armies lit campfires and prepared themselves for the ordeal that would begin at daybreak, if not before. From his position on the courthouse hilltop, Greene no doubt reflected on what lay ahead. His fortune, he knew, rested with the performance of the North Carolina and Virginia militia. Would they run away at the first sight of the disciplined British? Would they drop their weapons at the approach of Tarleton's fearsome cavalry? And, if they did, would Cornwallis finally crush this nettlesome, troublesome American army?

The coming of dawn would provide the answers.

Henry Lee's cavalry and a unit of Virginia riflemen were Greene's eyes and ears through the busy, tense night. At about four o'clock in the morning, Greene learned that the British indeed were on the march. Without the benefit of breakfast, the British had begun their twelve-mile trudge through the predawn chill toward Guilford Court House. Cornwallis was eager to strike, and his supplies were low, so his soldiers would march and fight on an empty stomach.

Greene moved his men into position, riding among them to offer small words of encouragement and mopping his brow at the sun burned away the morning chill. To his scared, inexperienced North Carolina militia, he gave no hint of his doubts. "Three rounds, my boys," he reminded them, "and then you may fall back."

The first shots were fired a little after seven o'clock, when Tarleton's cavalry, arriving in advance of the British infantry, skirmished with a portion of Lee's cavalry a few miles south of the American position. But Cornwallis and his infantry didn't arrive until well after noon, later than Greene might have expected. Though hungry and slightly demoralized—Cornwallis had lost about four hundred men in recent weeks to desertion—they were an intimidating sight. They formed precise, disciplined lines as they moved into position on both sides of the New Garden Road. General Alexander Leslie commanded the British right with the 71st Regiment of Highlanders and a regiment of Hessians; Lieutenant Colonel James Webster was on the left with the 33rd and 23rd regiments. Tarleton's dragoons were deployed on the road itself. Their swords and their dreaded bayonets picked up the late-winter sun; their flags and drums made the spectacle altogether magnificent.

American artillery opened fire, inspiring the same from the British. After twenty minutes of ineffective display, the British moved forward. Greene could not see the action, for the woods of the second line and the angle of his position blocked his view. He relied on his ears.

The North Carolina militia fired too early, when the British were more than a hundred yards away. The men in the center of the American line then fled, well before they could do any significant damage. Those on the flanks, however, stayed at their position as the British came within forty yards. Both sides paused, as if to contemplate, for a moment, the hell they were about to unleash on each other. And then the British charged. The militia fired again and then fled, although, like those who ran before them, they did not join the Virginians behind them. Most simply left the battlefield entirely.

The main British force moved forward, toward the woods that screened the Virginians, while smaller units moved against the American covering parties under Washington and Lee. The Virginia men stood their ground as their right flank came under heavy attack from Webster's men. After half an hour of fierce fighting, the Virginians began to give way, but not entirely. Cornwallis himself rode forward to take command of the action.

The Virginians delayed the British and threw off Cornwallis's carefully coordinated plan for the assault on the final American position. Without pausing to re-form his line, the British general pressed Webster's men forward, toward the hill, toward the infernal Greene.

Webster's men, who had beaten back the right flank of the second American line, now moved against Greene's hilltop defenses without support. Awaiting Webster near the center of the American line were some of Greene's best soldiers, the men of the 1st Maryland Regiment. They unleashed a powerful, murderous volley, stunning troops who believed they could turn the battle into a quick rout. Greene rode up and down the American line, exposing himself as he shouted encouragement to his men. Webster's zeal presented Greene with a bold opportunity: with the rest of the British force still trying to untangle themselves from the second line and the woods, he could send his third line forward in a surprise counterattack.

He had no clear view of the fighting still under way in the second line, no real intelligence about Cornwallis's position. To risk the army was to risk the Revolution—how many times had he said as much during the northern campaigns? And so he let the opportunity pass.

Webster retreated to re-form, and the remainder of the British army soon appeared in the clearing that faced the last American line. Cornwallis moved his reserves under General Charles O'Hara toward the inexperienced 5th Maryland Regiment on the American left. Many Marylanders turned and fled without firing a shot at O'Hara's men. The British were moving forward, threatening to outflank the American position, when William Washington's cavalry swooped down from their right. The result, Tarleton later wrote, was great slaughter. The 1st Maryland, which had devastated Webster, now turned to attack O'Hara's men.

Once again, the battle hung in the balance as the American counterattack cut down the advancing British. Cornwallis, watching the tide turn against him, ordered his artillery to open fire with grapeshot on the American left. It was a cold-blooded decision, for it meant the British cannons would take their toll indiscriminately—His Majesty's troops would be killed and maimed along with the Americans. O'Hara, wounded and behind the lines with Cornwallis, protested to no avail. The British guns began blowing gaps on the American left, slaughtering friend and foe alike.

The 1st Maryland buckled and then began to fall back. Greene, who had nearly been overtaken by a British advance, saw that his left was about to collapse. The outcome of the battle was not a given, but he could not and would not risk his army. He ordered a retreat.

The Battle of Guilford Court House was over after two hours of fierce fighting. Greene left the field in defeat; Cornwallis was triumphant.

The cost of Britain's victory, however, was horrific. Cornwallis lost more than five hundred men—25 percent of his army—either dead or wounded. Greene suffered about eighty dead and one hundred eighty-five wounded. He retreated ten miles to Speedwell Iron Works, where he dutifully filed a report to Congress. "From the best information I can get the Enemy's loss is very great," he wrote, with little exaggeration. His natural optimism reasserted itself, despite his having suffered a tactical defeat. His letters to Washington no longer bemoaned his fate or spoke of the seeming inevitability of misfortune and defeat. Greene was experienced enough to understand that he had been defeated in only the narrowest sense; that he had, in fact, sold the British another hill—just like

Bunker Hill—at a price almost too dear to bear. "Our Men are in good spirits and in perfect readiness for another field Day," he reported. He knew Cornwallis was in no position to follow up on his "victory."

Indeed, he was not. He lingered on his hard-won field for two days but then fell back, leaving his wounded to the care of the Americans. Greene's young aide Lewis Morris Jr. wrote to his father, a distinguished New York patriot and signer of the Declaration of Independence: "Like Peter the Great we shall profit by defeat, and in time learn to beat our Enemy—one more such action, and they are ruined." Morris was not alone in his assessment of the wound Greene had inflicted on the British. When word reached London of Cornwallis's triumph at Guilford Court House, an antiwar member of Parliament, Charles James Fox, observed, "Another such victory would ruin the British Army."

Greene wrote home to Caty on March 18, as the dead were being counted and buried. By chance, he had received a letter from her the day after the battle, and her pleasant, chatty news of life at home in Rhode Island offered him "some consolation" after living through the fire and hell of combat. In his reply, he spared her the gruesome details of the late action, reassuring her that none of her friends was among the dead. "I had not the honor of being wounded," he wrote, which was a roundabout way of telling her he was healthy and well.

So many of his men, however, were wounded, and it is not likely they considered their suffering an honor. They were left to the care of local residents with uncertain and perhaps dubious medical skills. With their tribulations on his mind, Greene wrote a moving letter to Quakers living in New Garden near Guilford Court House, asking for their help in tending to his wounded. He took the occasion to cite his own Quaker background and to hint, gently, that some patriots were skeptical of Quaker claims to absolute neutrality.

> I was born and educated in the professions and principles of
> your Society; and am perfectly acquainted with your
> religious sentiments and general good conduct as citizens.
> I am also sensible from . . . the misconduct of a few of your

own, that you are generally considered as enemies to the independence of America. I entertain other sentiments. . . . I
respect you as a people, and shall always be ready to protect
you from every violence and oppression.

These were noble sentiments, and Greene no doubt meant every
word. But he had himself expressed a few choice words about Quakers
during the Pennsylvania campaigns, and *respect* was not one of them.

After both armies rested briefly, Greene and Cornwallis exchanged roles.
The British general was now retreating toward Wilmington, North Carolina, a port city where his broken army could be resupplied. Greene was
in cautious pursuit, looking for a chance to strike. "It is my intention to
attack the enemy the moment we can get up with them," he told Lee on
March 22, even though his men were short on bread and ammunition.

But soon he was short on men. The bulk of his militia were eligible to
go home in late March, and they made it clear that they intended to do
exactly that. Camped at Ramsey's Mill along the Deep River, Greene
paused and decided he could not "attack the enemy" without the militia.

He gave up the chase but not his aggression. With his smaller force of
about twelve hundred Continentals and only about two hundred and fifty
militia, he decided to leave North Carolina and march south, toward
Camden, South Carolina. "In this critical and distressing situation I am
determined to carry the War immediately into South Carolina," he informed Washington. "The Manoeuvre will be critical and dangerous;
and our troops exposed to every hardship. But as I share it with them I
hope they will bear up under it with that magnanimity which has already
supported them." Greene was proud of his troops and appreciated their
sacrifice and their suffering. He did not command them from lofty
heights. He shared their hardships and lived with the consequences of
his decisions.

Greene thought that Cornwallis would pursue him. But the British
general was too exhausted to contemplate another campaign through the

Carolinas, too battered to reprise the role of Greene's strategic foil. "I am quite tired of marching about the country in quest of adventures," Cornwallis wrote. Virginia, he decided, should be the center of British operations in the South.

Cornwallis left Wilmington on April 24. His march would take him to another port city: Yorktown.

ad seen the last of Lord

hase of the southern cam-

it turned out—that Corn-

unter, and so might once

making. With Cornwallis

a, and with Lord Rawdon

ritish forces in the South

t the patriot militia would

aw an immediate threat in

ating in three parts of the

t a more powerful but dis-

th Carolina and Georgia,

ut still formidible Corn-

ar. This was still another

to an officer from North

Carolina: "Don't be surprised if my m

your Ideas of military propriety. War is

are often [saved] by ways and means th

Greene admitted that his strategy w

playing with Cornwallis: he wanted his

head, and wonder what, exactly, Natha

told Baron von Steuben, still in Virgin

assault against Arnold, "[The] bold n

British] think I have secret reasons wh

He had no "secret reasons." Ther

obvious choice: if he could not pursue

hundreds of militiamen meant that h

against Rawdon and a string of forts th

loyalist defenses in South Carolina a

and secure a retreat," he told Steuben

By now, though, Greene was exp

first part of that equation was boun

Supplies remained the bane of his

Congress: "I have been anxiously wa

appears to me to be remote."

Perhaps, he thought, one of the

Greene dispatched a message to Gen

join the march into South Carolina

sions he might lay his hands on. "[O

pend," he noted. Greene would so

obliged to heed the orders, never

mander of the Southern Department

"[I will] promote & facilitate your L

in the march to Camden nor compli

supplies. Greene began to realize th

sans like Marion and Pickens, Tho

danced to his own melodies.

Greene needed help from the li

would receive precious little from h

1 2 | Victory

Nathanael Greene did not believe he had seen the last of Lord Cornwallis. His strategy for the next phase of the southern campaign was based on his hunch—mistaken, as it turned out—that Cornwallis would resume his former role as the hunter, and so might once again be lured into a strategic trap of Greene's making. With Cornwallis pursuing him, with Benedict Arnold in Virginia, and with Lord Rawdon trying to hold South Carolina and Georgia, British forces in the South would be widely scattered. Greene believed that the patriot militia would be more likely to turn out to assist him if they saw an immediate threat in their state or locality. Three British forces operating in three parts of the region figured to inspire the militia in a way that a more powerful but distant threat would not.

In moving his army in the direction of South Carolina and Georgia, Greene was turning his back on the battered but still formidible Cornwallis, exposing himself to an attack from his rear. This was still another violation of the military textbook. He explained to an officer from North

Carolina: "Don't be surprised if my movements don't correspond with your Ideas of military propriety. War is an intricate business, and people are often [saved] by ways and means they least look for or expect."

Greene admitted that his strategy was based in part on a game he was playing with Cornwallis: he wanted his foe to furrow his brow, shake his head, and wonder what, exactly, Nathanael Greene was thinking. Greene told Baron von Steuben, still in Virginia and waiting in vain for an allied assault against Arnold, "[The] boldness [of my plan] will make [the British] think I have secret reasons which they cannot comprehend."

He had no "secret reasons." There was only what struck him as the obvious choice: if he could not pursue Cornwallis—and the departure of hundreds of militiamen meant that he could not—then he would move against Rawdon and a string of forts that were the bulwark of British and loyalist defenses in South Carolina and Georgia. "If I can get supplies and secure a retreat," he told Steuben, "I fear no bad consequences."

By now, though, Greene was experienced enough to know that the first part of that equation was bound to prove the most troublesome. Supplies remained the bane of his army, as he impatiently reminded Congress: "I have been anxiously waiting for succour, but the prospect appears to me to be remote."

Perhaps, he thought, one of the militia commanders would help. Greene dispatched a message to General Thomas Sumter, asking him to join the march into South Carolina and to bring along whatever provisions he might lay his hands on. "[On] this our whole operation will depend," he noted. Greene would soon learn that Sumter did not feel obliged to heed the orders, never mind the suggestions, of the commander of the Southern Department. Although Sumter assured Greene, "[I will] promote & facilitate your Designs," he neither joined the army in the march to Camden nor complied with Greene's polite requests for supplies. Greene began to realize that while he could depend on partisans like Marion and Pickens, Thomas Sumter, the famous gamecock, danced to his own melodies.

Greene needed help from the likes of Sumter because he knew he would receive precious little from his commander in chief, more than a own, that you are generally considered as enemies to the independence of America. I entertain other sentiments. . . . I respect you as a people, and shall always be ready to protect you from every violence and oppression.

These were noble sentiments, and Greene no doubt meant every word. But he had himself expressed a few choice words about Quakers during the Pennsylvania campaigns, and *respect* was not one of them.

After both armies rested briefly, Greene and Cornwallis exchanged roles. The British general was now retreating toward Wilmington, North Carolina, a port city where his broken army could be resupplied. Greene was in cautious pursuit, looking for a chance to strike. "It is my intention to attack the enemy the moment we can get up with them," he told Lee on March 22, even though his men were short on bread and ammunition.

But soon he was short on men. The bulk of his militia were eligible to go home in late March, and they made it clear that they intended to do exactly that. Camped at Ramsey's Mill along the Deep River, Greene paused and decided he could not "attack the enemy" without the militia.

He gave up the chase but not his aggression. With his smaller force of about twelve hundred Continentals and only about two hundred and fifty militia, he decided to leave North Carolina and march south, toward Camden, South Carolina. "In this critical and distressing situation I am determined to carry the War immediately into South Carolina," he informed Washington. "The Manoeuvre will be critical and dangerous; and our troops exposed to every hardship. But as I share it with them I hope they will bear up under it with that magnanimity which has already supported them." Greene was proud of his troops and appreciated their sacrifice and their suffering. He did not command them from lofty heights. He shared their hardships and lived with the consequences of his decisions.

Greene thought that Cornwallis would pursue him. But the British general was too exhausted to contemplate another campaign through the

Carolinas, too battered to reprise the role of Greene's strategic foil. "I am quite tired of marching about the country in quest of adventures," Cornwallis wrote. Virginia, he decided, should be the center of British operations in the South.

Cornwallis left Wilmington on April 24. His march would take him to another port city: Yorktown.

thousand miles away. Washington was delighted to learn that Cornwallis had been so badly mauled at Guilford Court House; still, he reminded Greene, the war remained very much in the balance. General Clinton commanded a large force in New York City and was capable and bold enough to move his army south by ship if an opportunity to crush Greene presented itself. "I . . . regard your affairs as critically situated," Washington told Greene in mid-April, a month after Guilford Court House. "[The] enemy are accumulating a large force in the Southern States; we have several concurring accounts that a further detachment is preparing at New York to be commanded by Clinton himself." Those reports turned out to be untrue, but even if they were accurate, Greene could expect little in the way of assistance. "You may be assured that we give you all the support in our power," Washington wrote. "I wish our means were more adequate."

Washington was more candid in a letter to Congress in April. "We are at the end of our tether," he wrote.

Greene appealed to the region's politicians to come to the aid of their embattled country. Once again, he was dissatisfied with their responses, particularly those of the Virginia politicians. At issue was horseflesh, and the lack of it among Greene's cavalry, the most important units of his command. Although Greene had the power to seize the horses he needed, a power he always used sparingly, the Virginia legislature passed a bill limiting such seizures to horses valued at less than five thousand pounds in highly inflated currency. (The true value was less than forty pounds.) This effectively eliminated most horses worth seizing. Greene told a sympathetic Jefferson that he "would not trust a dragoon upon" the scrawny, weak mounts he was collecting, and later wondered if "Horses are dearer to the Inhabitants" of Virginia than "the liberties of the People." Greene never ceased to be disappointed with the responses of civilians as well as politicians to the needs of his suffering army.

Greene and his fifteen hundred men began their march south toward Camden, South Carolina, on April 7. When Cornwallis realized that his antagonist had outfoxed him yet again, he told London that he feared Lord Rawdon and the British posts in South Carolina and Georgia were doomed. The Crown's men in the lower South, he wrote, were "so scattered" that they were in "the greatest danger of being beat in detail."

It was springtime in the Carolinas, and the trees were in full blossom, the rivers swollen and fast. Two of Greene's most capable subordinates, Light Horse Harry Lee and Francis Marion, the legendary Swamp Fox, already were in action, laying siege to a small British garrison in Fort Watson, South Carolina. Sumter, however, was nowhere near Camden, despite Greene's requests that he cooperate in the planned assault. Greene sent a plaintive dispatch to the insubordinate militia commander: "My greatest dependence is on you for supplies of Corn and Meal. Both of these Articles are immediately wanted, and unless you can furnish me with them it will be impossible for me to keep my position." Almost as important as the corn and meal was the physical presence of Sumter and his men, but they, like the supplies, were conspicuous by their absence. Greene worried that his messages to Sumter had fallen into the hands of loyalist militia.

Greene brought his march to a halt on April 20 on Hobkirk's Hill outside Camden. Defending the town were nine hundred British and loyalist troops under the command of Lord Rawdon himself, the man who would now shoulder the burden of Britain's deteriorating southern strategy.

Greene inspected Rawdon's defenses and was surprised to see that they were, as he admitted in a letter to Sumter, "much stronger than I expected." While he was intent on destroying Rawdon's force, he decided he dared not risk his army against such a well-entrenched opponent. So he would, in the manner of Pickens and Lee at Fort Watson, lay siege to the post, daring Rawdon to venture out from behind his defenses. His army was stronger than Rawdon's, and Greene had hopes that it would grow stronger still, if only Sumter would arrive.

As they prepared for the siege, Greene's men set up camp on Hobkirk's Hill according to their order of battle. The militia were on the front lines, with the cream of the southern army—two Continental regiments from Virginia and two from Maryland—behind them, along with the artillery. To the left of the American position ran Pine Tree Creek, screened, appropriately enough, by thick forest.

On the night of April 24, as Greene's men prepared their siege, a solitary American soldier fled Greene's camp and turned himself over to Rawdon's men in Camden. He told the British that Greene still was awaiting reinforcements, had no artillery (which was false), and was vulnerable to a surprise attack. Rawdon acted quickly: the following morning, he ordered his men to move out of Camden and toward Hobkirk's Hill, where Greene's men were eating breakfast.

The British filed out of Camden and marched behind the trees on the American left. The movement was not detected until Greene's forward pickets came under attack at ten o'clock, only three hundred yards from the main American position. Rawdon had achieved complete surprise, but thanks to the pickets' quick work, the main American force had time to form a defensive line before the British and loyalists were upon them.

Greene, with a good view of the field, saw that Rawdon's assault line was narrow and therefore susceptible to a counterattack on its flanks. In other battles, Greene had been reluctant to gamble with bold moves and counterattacks, but this time, he was determined to be more aggressive. It was he, after all, who sought out this battle. Greene ordered the 2nd Maryland Regiment to counterattack the British right flank, while the 1st Virginia Regiment counterattacked Rawdon on his left. The remainder of his army, the 1st Maryland under Colonel John Gunby, which had fought so well at Guilford Court House, and the 2nd Virginia, moved down the hill toward the enemy's center. To complement the counterattack, Greene brought up newly arrived artillery and fired a short-range volley of grapeshot at the center of the British line. He sent William Washington and his cavalry flying down the American left to attack the British rear and cut off their lines of retreat. However, thanks to the damnable shortage of horses, about thirty of Washington's eighty-seven men did not have mounts.

Rather than fight his usual defensive battle, Greene aggressively sought to trap Rawdon with a classic double envelopment, that is, attacking him on both flanks. Timing and ferocity were vital: he wanted a simultaneous attack, and with fixed bayonets.

Rawdon countered Greene's movement by bringing up troops from his rear and lengthening his line, making it harder to turn his flanks. Fighting was fierce, and Greene was in the middle of it, shouting orders, trying to make sense of the sound of musket fire, peering through the smoke, and waiting on reports from his officers. One of Greene's aides, Colonel William Davie, said, "General Greene exposed himself greatly in this action . . . so much so, that one of the officers observed to me that his conduct during the action resembled more that of a captain of grenadiers, than that of a major general." The battle seemed to be going his way when the 1st Maryland, perhaps Greene's best unit, began to fall apart on the American left after at least one of its officers was killed. The shortage of officers in the Maryland line, which Greene had complained about months earlier, may have contributed to the sudden breakdown in discipline: there was nobody to step forward to replace the man (or men) cut down. Gunby, the regiment's commander, was momentarily confused and ordered his troops to halt their advance. The British seized the chance and pushed forward with fixed bayonets of their own, threatening the entire American position.

At any moment, Colonel Washington and his cavalry were expected to swoop down on the British rear and turn the tide of battle. But the depleted Washington had taken a circuitous route to get behind the British—so circuitous, in fact, that most of his men were too far behind the line to be of any use.

Just minutes after victory seemed within his grasp, Greene suddenly was on the defensive, fighting desperately to hold off the British onslaught. With much of his army falling back, he had little choice but to order a general retreat to save his army from destruction. As he left the field, Greene spotted a group of artillerymen struggling to pull their cannons out of the brush and away from the British. He got off his horse and helped pull the pieces to safety.

The Americans fell back six miles. As at Guilford Court House, the British victory was dearly bought: the British suffered about two hundred and fifty casualties, about a quarter of Rawdon's force. American casualties were about the same.

This time, however, Greene took no comfort in the carnage he had inflicted. This time, he believed victory could have and should have been his. Where had Sumter been? And what about Gunby, whose men had been so heroic at Guilford Court House? Bitterly, Greene lashed out at the commander of the 1st Maryland, telling his friend Joseph Reed, the president of the Pennsylvania legislature, "We should have had Lord [Rawdon] and his whole command . . . in three Minutes, if Col. Gunby had not ordered his regiment to retire." This was Greene at his worst: petulent, filled with self-pity, and desperately trying to protect his reputation from those confounded critics who were ever so willing to find fault with him. He chose Gunby as a scapegoat when, in fact, his own decisions to counterattack on Rawdon's flanks and send Washington's cavalry into the fray may have tipped the battle in Rawdon's favor.

This defeat could not be promoted as a strategic victory, and Greene knew it. He confessed to Reed that the battle's outcome left him "almost [frantic] with vexation. Fortune has not much been our friend." Two days after the battle, Greene's troops came upon some two dozen American deserters. They were brought before a court-martial, which found them guilty of desertion. Greene did not hesitate. He ordered five of them hanged.

His mood was testy and bleak, as evidenced in his reply to a letter from his friend Henry Lee, who had asked for reinforcements: "You write as if you thought I had an army of fifty Thousand Men. Surely you cannot be unacquainted with our [actual] situation." To Washington, Greene confessed, "I am much afraid these States must fall, never to rise again."

Tensions were high and emotions raw throughout the American ranks. When Greene criticized Francis Marion over complaints that his men were taking horses from local Tories—a common-enough practice but one that Greene believed to be both unjust and impolitic—the offended Swamp Fox fired back with a threat to resign his command. A clearly exasperated Greene replied, with more than a little self-pity:

> It is true your task has been disagreeable; but not more so
> than others. It is now [going] on seven years since the

> commencement of this war. I have never had leave of
> [absence] an hour nor paid the least attention to my own
> private affairs. Your state is invaded, your all is at stake. . . . I
> left a family in distress and every thing dear and valuable to
> come & afford you all the assistance in my power, and if you
> leave us in the midst of our difficulties . . . it must throw a
> damp upon the spirits of the Army.

Greene, of course, had spent more than a little attention to his private business affairs. But now was not the time. He surely was astonished that he had to remind Marion—not Sumter, but Marion—of his duty.

Years later, Colonel Davie remembered a depressing conversation with Greene at about this time. In Davie's recollection, Greene told him:

> Congress [seems] to have lost sight of the Southern States,
> and to have abandoned them to their fate, so much so that we
> are even as much distressed for ammunition as men. . . .
> [We] will dispute every inch of ground in the best manner
> we can—but Rawdon will push me back to the mountains,
> Lord Cornwallis will establish a chain of posts along the
> James River and the Southern States, thus cut off, will die
> like the Tail of a Snake.

Greene's bitterness and despair led him to toy with the idea of leaving the Carolinas—not with the army but by himself—to take over American forces in Virginia. He already had ordered Baron von Steuben to leave Virginia and join the main southern army in South Carolina (Steuben never made it); perhaps he and the baron should simply switch places. Feeling very sorry for himself, Greene told Lee that the baron would certainly "arrange matters very well," and that he had little doubt the army would be better off without him.

Before he had a chance to act on this unlikely plan, astonishing news arrived in camp. On May 10, Lord Rawdon evacuated Camden, marching his beaten-up army toward the seaport of Charleston. For the moment anyway, Rawdon was conceding the interior of South Carolina to Greene in order to ensure the safety of Charleston and its access to supplies. Marching alongside Rawdon's men were dozens of South Carolina Tories and their families, fearful of the fate that might await them in the countryside with the main British army gone.

Word of Rawdon's retreat banished Greene's darkest thoughts and mooted any ridiculous idea that he would leave the army in Steuben's charge. Greene's aide Colonel Dudley was summoned to the general's tent for breakfast on May 11, the day after Rawdon began his march to the coast. The general greeted Dudley with a "pleasing" expression and a handshake, asking him if he had heard the good news.

"No sir," Dudley replied. "What news?"

"Rawdon evacuated Camden yesterday afternoon."

It truly was a breathtaking turn of events. His spirits lifted, Greene returned to the simple strategy he had outlined in a letter to a French ally, the chevalier de La Luzerne: "We fight, get beat, rise and fight again."

Greene now turned his attention to a string of British forts in South Carolina built roughly along the line of the Santee, Congaree, and Saluda rivers, from Fort Watson in the east to Ninety Six in the west. Fort Watson, some sixty miles northwest of Charleston, already had fallen to the Americans. Greene believed the others could be picked off one at a time.

Even before Rawdon abandoned Camden, Greene had sent Lighthorse Harry Lee and Francis Marion to assault Fort Motte, a supply depot and home to more than one hundred and fifty troops on the Congaree River. In the meantime, Sumter assailed a garrison of loyalist militia in Orangeburg, west of Charleston and south of Greene's position at Ancrum's Plantation on the Congaree. The forts, isolated once Rawdon retreated, fell quickly; Sumter took Orangeburg on May 11, while Lee and Marion captured Fort Motte on May 12. With exquisite timing, Greene arrived at Fort Motte right after the British surrendered—just in time to celebrate the victory by dining with Marion, whom he had never met before, Lee, and the British officers who were now Greene's prisoners.

Making full use of his mobility, Greene then sent Lee on a dash for Fort Granby, near present-day Columbia, South Carolina. "I depend upon your pushing matters [vigorously]," Greene told Lee. Lee did exactly that, forcing the fort's surrender on May 15.

The "war of the posts," as this phase of the campaign was called, involved small numbers of troops and low-intensity operations heavily dependent on partisan militia. There was none of the drama of the large-scale battles of the North, like Monmouth or Long Island. The stakes were not as high as they were at Guilford Court House. The American victories, however, were vital all the same, and they caught the attention of Washington and other military and political leaders in the North. "The brilliant repeated successes which reflect so much glory on the Southern Army will be attended with the most important Consequences," wrote Washington. The fall of each fort represented another blow to British control of the Deep South, and with each blow, the spirits of the region's Tories fell. By contrast, patriots in South Carolina sensed that the tide of battle was turning. Greene believed it was time to restore the state's patriot government, which had collapsed after Gates's defeat at Camden. He told John Rutledge, the governor of South Carolina, that "Civil Government" ought "to be set up immediately" because the public should be ruled by "Civil rather than Military authority." He would soon offer the same advice to patriot leaders in Georgia, urging them to form a legislative council to reestablish order.

Greene had a very pragmatic reason for urging patriot leaders to reassert their political authority in the South. As the war dragged on through another summer, there was talk of a new peace initiative from Europe. Greene feared that Britain might claim undisputed civil authority over the southern states and so could be entitled to continued rule over the region as part of a peace compromise. If, however, a patriot government were functioning in the South, Britain's claims would be hard to justify.

There was, too, another, more idealistic side to Greene's emphasis on civil authority. Like other American commanders during the Revolution, Greene understood that America's liberty depended upon civilian government, not military control. Though he certainly had the power to impose himself on civilian leaders in the South, he had no intention of playing the role of governor-general in the Carolinas or in Georgia. His place was on the battlefield, not in the statehouse.

There was no question that civil authority was desperately needed. In the backwoods of the Carolinas and Georgia, Americans were committing atrocities on other Americans: patriots casually slaughtered Tories, and vice versa. Grievances between the two groups often predated the war or were justified by citing the other group's atrocities. Greene soon learned that an American militia officer, LeRoy Hammond, was rampaging through Tory territory near the Saluda River in central South Carolina. He was horrified, as he made clear in a letter to one of the militia leaders he had grown to trust, General Andrew Pickens. He asked Pickens for help in putting an end to American outrages and explained why tit-for-tat reprisals were not only inhuman but bad public relations: "The Idea of exterminating the Tories is not less barbarous than impolitick; and if persisted in, will keep this Country in the greatest confusion and distress. The eyes of the people are much upon you, the disaffected cry for Mercy, and I hope you will exert your self to bring over the Tories to our interest."

This generous attitude was in sharp contrast with patriot demands for vengeance in the South. But Greene was determined to offer the Tories a chance to reconsider their loyalties. In an open letter addressed to "the Inhabitants Upon the Saluda," he assured the Tory population of his "abhorence and detestation" with regard to Hammond's crimes. He said he would welcome them to the American cause if they offered "a [sincere] repentence for what is past."

After victories at Orangeburg and Forts Watson and Motte, Greene decided the time had come to commit the main army to battle. He marched his one thousand–plus Continentals sixty miles to the west, to the British post known as Ninety Six, manned by about five hundred Tory militia. While Greene was on the march, he sent Lee and Pickens to assail another British post, this one in Augusta, Georgia. Marion was dispatched to do likewise in Georgetown, South Carolina.

Ninety Six, a village surrounded by an impressive stockade, owed its name to its location, believed to be ninety-six miles from the British frontier posts to the west. By Greene's reckoning, Tories outnumbered patriots by five to one in the area, and they considered the fort a visible sign of Britain's commitment to their defense.

The fortress was designed to impress: ditches, bunkers, and a fearsome set of sharpened tree trunks—called an abatis—protected the stockade from sudden assault. Greene arrived outside Ninety Six on May 22 with thoughts of assaulting the fort. One look at the defenses convinced him and his chief engineer, Thaddeus Kosciuszko, otherwise. Instead of attacking, he decided to lay siege to Ninety Six, despite the absence of proper siege equipment. He was not optimistic. "[The] fortifications are so strong and the garrison so large and so well furnished that our success is very doubtful," Greene told Lafayette.

Greene's pessimism was well-founded. From the beginning of the siege, the fortress and its defenders proved too strong and too wily for the American attackers. After more than a month of digging approaches to the stockade's main fort, and paying a price for each inch in blood and exhaustion, Greene learned that his nemesis, Lord Rawdon, had been reinforced with two thousand troops in Charleston and was marching to relieve Ninety Six.

Greene decided to attack the fort in hopes he could bring the siege to a quick end before Rawdon arrived. On Monday, June 18, Greene's men opened fire on the post from two sides. But the Tory defenders shrewdly counterattacked with fixed bayonets, fighting Greene's men hand to hand in the ditches outside the fort, with the Continentals getting the worst of it. Greene saw that the assault was hopeless, and ordered a retreat. The following day, Greene and his men called a halt to their siege and marched away from Ninety Six, ever watchful for the approach of Rawdon and his reinforcements.

Once again, Nathanael Greene was retreating in the face of the enemy, deprived yet again of that victory he so desperately desired. He vented his frustrations in a letter to Congress: "It is mortifying to be obliged to leave a Garrison so near reduced, and I have nothing to console me but a consciousness that nothing was left unattempted that could facilitate its reduction." Still, he was able to tell Congress his effort was not in vain: "Had we not moved this way this Country would have been inevitably lost, and all further exertions would have failed." In fact, while Greene was overseeing the failed siege of Ninety Six, Marion captured the British post at Georgetown on May 29, and Lee and Pickens forced the surrender of Augusta on June 5. And, in a pattern that was becoming all too familiar to the British in the South, even Greene's setback at Ninety Six advanced the American cause. Rawdon's men suffered terribly in the South Carolina heat and humidity during their two-hundred-mile march from Charleston. And when they arrived, finally, at Ninety Six, they did not stay long. Rawdon decided the post could not be held, and so it was evacuated and burned. The Tory defenders along with their families and friends were ordered to march back to Charleston with the main British army.

July was no time to be marching through South Carolina. The summer weather was cruel and sickening, exempting nobody. The young and promising Rawdon became so ill he was forced to retire when he reached Charleston. Greene briefly considered attacking Rawdon's numerically superior force but wisely chose to let circumstances be his best ally. While the British and Tories suffered on their way back to Charleston, Greene marched to the shade and repose of a region south of Camden called the High Hills of the Santee, near the confluence of the Santee, Congaree, and Wateree rivers. The name alone suggests the comforts Greene's men enjoyed while their enemies battled heat, humidity, and deprivation. The American camp was on high, cooler ground above the rivers, away from the mosquito-infested swamps in the Carolina lowlands—just the place for a camp that would, for six weeks, serve as a summer equivalent of winter quarters.

The respite offered Greene an opportunity not only to rest his exhausted troops but to reflect on the astonishing turn of events in the South since the Battle of Guilford Court House just four months earlier. Since then, the seemingly unbeatable British had been more than simply stopped; they had been forced, in a series of small-scale actions, to retreat from the interior, holding only a small band of territory extending from Charleston, South Carolina, to Savannah, Georgia. Their posts in the backcountry were gone. Their allies, the Tories, were demoralized and in disarray. The Continentals and the militia had captured three thousand enemy troops since March. Cornwallis had been forced to move his operations to Virginia, while his successor, Rawdon, was broken in health and spirit, destined to be captured at sea while en route to England.

This reversal of American misfortunes in the South had been achieved with minimal resources, which Washington himself acknowledged in a letter to Greene dated June 1. "The difficulties which you daily encounter and surmount with your small force add not a little to your reputation," Washington wrote. Those words brightened Greene's day.

The victory at Cowpens, the race to the Dan, the strategic victory of Guilford Court House, the invasion of the lower South, the brilliant successes of the southern militia—all achieved with a ragamuffin army—won for Nathanael Greene the reputation he had dreamed of as a rebellious Quaker schoolboy. He had won nothing, and yet, he had defeated everything that the British and fortune had thrown at him. He was realistic enough to know that he had been beaten time and again; he was shrewd enough to know that the defeats didn't matter. He told his old friend Jeremiah Wadsworth:

> Our army has been frequently beaten and like a Stock Fish
> grows the better for it. Lord Cornwallis, who is the modern
> Hannibal, has rambled through [a] great part of the
> Southern States, and his Tour has [sacrificed] a great
> number of Men without reaping any solid Advantages from
> it, except that of distressing the poor Inhabitants.

With his legendary ability to hear with astonishing clarity the most muffled criticism, Greene noted that the painter and patriot John Trumbull had criticized him for being unable to conduct a "timely retreat." But what would people like Trumbull say now? Greene told Wadsworth:

> I hope I have convinced the World to the contrary; for there
> are few Generals that [have] run oftener, or more lustilly, than
> I have done. But I have taken care not to run too far; and
> commonly have run as fast forward as backward, to convince
> our Enemy that we were like a Crab that could run either way.

Greene hardly needed to defend himself, even with at least a hint of humor. His campaign had few critics; indeed, Lafayette told him: "Your popularity is now to the Highest pitch. You are the general every Body [speaks] of, and every one prides in your Maneuvres."

Caty Greene, restless in Rhode Island, was eager to join her husband in the South. Her husband was determined to keep her away.

Even in his new camp in the High Hills of the Santee, where the Americans enjoyed water, shade, and a respite from fighting, Greene knew that the South was no place for a civilian who didn't have to be there. Caty Greene had been at his side during the bitter winter camps in Valley Forge and Morristown; she, along with Martha Washington, Lucy Knox, and others had seen firsthand the suffering and deprivation of war. But the South in the summer of 1781 was very different from the North of winter camp. Tories and patriots continued to assail each other with the special ferocity of a civil war. Even though Greene's army had forced the surrender of enemy forts and had persuaded Rawdon to withdraw to Charleston, the roads, swamps, and forests of the Carolinas and Georgia held dangers Caty could not imagine.

In a letter to his wife, Greene told her what to expect on the long journey from Rhode Island to South Carolina, which "would require a guard to secure you from the insults and villiany of the Tories." He continued:

South Carolina and Georgia have been the seat, and are still, of a hot and bloody war. Therefore you would have had no resting place in this country. . . . Besides, the hot season of the year would have made sad havock with your slender constitution. It is true our separation has been long and my wishes are equally strong with yours for a happy meeting. . . .

I wish I was there with you, free from the bustle of the World and the miseries of war. My nature recoils at the horrid scenes which this Country affords, and longs for a peaceful retirement where love and softer pleasures are to be found. Here, turn which way you will, you hear nothing but the mournful widow, and the plaints of the fatherless Child; and behold nothing but houses desolated, and plantations laid waste. Ruin is in every form, and misery in every shape.

Caty remained in Rhode Island.

In Virginia, the marquis de Lafayette was in the midst of a campaign that was as bloody and dangerous as Greene's camp in South Carolina was peaceful and safe. Even as the British in the Deep South were retreating from the interior, Cornwallis and Tarleton were on the loose in George Washington's home state. Civil administration collapsed, and it seemed possible that after Greene's successes in the lower South, Virginia might well fall under British occupation.

The embattled state was technically part of Greene's Southern Department, but he was nearly powerless over these events hundreds of miles away. He desperately wished to help Lafayette, who had become a friend despite their difference in age—and despite Greene's public criticism of foreign-born Continental officers. The Frenchman won Greene's affection in much the same way young Sammy Ward had years earlier: he eagerly sought out Greene's advice and deferred to him as a wise and experienced mentor. That surely was the best way to Greene's often insecure heart. Lafayette made it clear he was not a threat to his elder's seniority, referring to himself as "Your Lieutenant" and taking care to note that under Greene's command he was becoming "So wise a Man."

In the summer of 1781, the British were on the verge of smashing the Frenchman and foiling Greene's strategic victories in the Carolinas and Georgia. If Cornwallis, Arnold, and more British reinforcements under General William Phillips crushed resistance in Virginia, they could march their combined force into North Carolina and possibly restore, yet again, the lower South to British rule. Greene knew how much was at stake in Virginia and again contemplated leaving the Carolinas to take personal command in that state. In the end, however, he helped his friend Lafayette in the only way he could: Though he desperately needed reinforcements for his own troops, he chose not to move Continentals from Virginia to the Carolinas. And he stayed in constant touch with Lafayette, advising him to avoid, "if possible, a general action."

Lafayette followed Greene's advice—and made sure Greene knew it—but in early July, he found himself perilously close to the general action Greene had told him to avoid. Cornwallis and his seven thousand troops had lured the Americans into battle near Green Spring by offering as bait what appeared to be only the British rear guard. In fact, the entire British army lay in wait. Lafayette was able to withdraw in good order, but it was a close call.

A month later, Cornwallis marched to Yorktown. With its access to the sea, he thought it would make a fine new base from which to continue the war in Virginia.

On August 21, Washington and Rochambeau left New York and marched their troops south, toward Yorktown.

Nathanael Greene's men had rested and fortified themselves for six weeks in the High Hills of the Santee. Now, Greene believed, they were ready to resume the war. Reinforcements in the form of a few hundred Continentals and local militiamen increased Greene's little army to a little more than two thousand. The British had continued to suffer in the lowlands after venturing out of Charleston following Rawdon's departure. Greene received reports indicating that the British regulars, equal in number to the Americans and now under the command of Rawdon's successor, Alexander Stewart, were ill and demoralized. If Greene attacked, he could force Stewart back into Charleston, leaving Greene ready to face Cornwallis—never far from Greene's strategic calculations—if His Lordship somehow slipped out of Virginia and marched south.

Although the two opposing camps were separated by less than twenty miles, Greene could not march directly toward Stewart, for summer rains made river crossings difficult. So Greene marched north toward Camden and then south toward Stewart's camp, near the village of Eutaw Springs along the Santee River, northwest of Charleston. The British were camped nearby in an open area.

The American march was leisurely and undetected. As it was under way, Lafayette sent a letter to Greene with unbelievable news from Virginia: The French fleet, he reported, had sailed safely into Chesapeake Bay, isolating Cornwallis from the sea. And Washington and Rochambeau were on their way!

Greene ordered his troops to cook one day's provisions and allowed them a gill of rum on September 7. They were seven miles from the British position near Eutaw Springs. At four o'clock the following morning, the men roused themselves from sleep, lined up in one of four columns, and marched toward the enemy.

Greene placed his militiamen, troops from North and South Carolina, in the front, along with Lighthorse Harry Lee's legion. Francis Marion and Andrew Pickens were with the militia up front. Behind the militia were Greene's Continentals, including some men in the Maryland and Virginia regiments who had been marching with him since the winter. The order of battle by now was familiar: militia up front, with orders to fire and fall back, with the more reliable Continentals behind them.

The British didn't realize that Greene was so close, a tribute to the American general's careful planning. Stewart later noted that Greene's troops patrolled the "by-paths and passes through the different swamps," making intelligence work difficult. Civilians in the area kept quiet, too, although they must have seen Greene and his men marching toward the British camp.

On the morning of September 8, Stewart dispatched more than a hundred British troops under the command of Major John Coffin to investigate a rumor, spread by two deserters, that American troops were nearby. They soon discovered that the rumor was true—Greene's entire army was only some four miles away. Stewart scrambled to get a skirmish line forward to hold off the advancing Americans closing in from the east.

Greene's troops moved through a thick forest, which at least offered the comfort of shade as the day grew hotter. British skirmishers put up mild resistance before retreating, and Greene pressed forward. Both sides saluted each other with artillery fire until Greene's men were ready to assail Stewart's line.

A "most tremendous fire began on both sides from right to left," Greene later wrote. But the "tremendous fire" did not inspire flight among the American militia. With Marion on the right and Pickens on the left, the Carolina militia stood fast and fired disciplined volleys. Ten, twelve, fifteen, as many as seventeen times the American militia loaded their weapons and fired, taking and absorbing casualties. Suddenly, the British left, made up of the 63rd and 64th regiments, moved forward to counterattack with fixed bayonets. The militia on the American right faltered, but Greene brought up Continentals from North Carolina to bolster the line. These troops, under the command of Jethro Sumner, were among Greene's most inexperienced Continentals. They had joined Greene during his summer respite in the High Hills of the Santee.

Facing British fire for the first time, the North Carolinians did not disappoint their commander. They stood, fired, and advanced, yielding nothing when the British regulars fired back. Lee's cavalry swung into position to turn the British left flank, prompting Stewart to reinforce his endangered line with Coffin's cavalry. As Greene monitored the fierce fighting on his right, he "could hardly tell which to admire most, the gallantry of [the] Officers or the bravery of the Troops. They kept up a heavy and well-directed fire, and the Enemy returned it with equal spirit, for they really fought worthy of a better cause."

Greene had saved his most experienced troops for the decisive moment, and now it was upon him. The British were showing signs of reforming in the center, and the North Carolina Continentals were on the verge of falling back. Waiting for such a moment were the Maryland and Virginia Continentals. Bloodshed and carnage were not new to these veterans; they had seen what steel and shell did to human flesh. Joined by some Delaware troops, they moved forward. As they did, the British left and center began to collapse. Redcoats and Tory militia turned and fled toward their encampment near the village of Eutaw Springs. Only the British right, led by Major John Majoribanks, stood its ground.

The Americans pursued the retreating British through their camp, but there Greene's men halted, for they could not help but notice that the camp was well stocked with rum, food, and other supplies. They had been fighting for hours on a brutally hot day, and victory seemed certain—and so the militia and even some of the more disciplined Continentals paused to rest and to celebrate. There were few officers to shame them back to their duties, for the loyalist militia had successfully adopted the patriot tactic of picking off officers to create even more chaos on the battlefield. Sixty out of a hundred American officers would become casualties on this day, and of Greene's top six commanders, only Lee and Otho Williams would emerge unscathed.

Greene was unaware of the terrible breakdown in discipline and could hardly have anticipated it. The militia had been superb, the Continentals efficient and brave. They had seen the backs of British soldiers, not a familiar sight. But, living amid the deprivation that was the lot of an American soldier, they could not resist temptation.

Greene still was engaged in battle. The American left was pushing hard against Major Marjoribanks's skillful resistance. Hoping to make the rout complete, Greene ordered William Washington's cavalry to circle around the American left and finish off Marjoribanks, whose men were gathered in a thicket of trees. But Washington's men met with disaster; they charged without waiting for infantry support, and a volley of deadly fire from the British right killed or wounded many officers. Washington himself was wounded and captured.

At the far end of the British camp was a sturdy brick mansion. Some of the fleeing loyalist militia took cover inside, outracing Greene's men who tried to occupy the house before it fell into British hands. The loyalists slammed the door just before the Americans got there, leaving behind several British officers who were immediately taken prisoner and used as shields as the Americans withdrew in the face of enemy guns pointing from the house's windows.

The Americans brought forward artillery, but the cannonballs did little damage. As the loyalists inside fired on the besieging Americans, Major Marjoribanks's men, having quietly fallen back toward their camp, launched a counteroffensive, overtaking the American guns, and then surprising the American troops who were drinking rum in the British camp.

Greene's men had been fighting for four hours, and they were now either exhausted and dehydrated or drunk and useless. In addition, their ammunition was running low. The British, on the other hand, were rallying around the stone house defenders. Greene considered and then rejected an all-out assault on the position, believing that he could ill afford more casualties. The day had been bloody enough.

Once again, Greene ordered his men to pull back from the British position. He was not conceding defeat, for he believed the British could not hold the stone house for very long and would be forced to withdraw. The Americans marched seven miles back to their own camp in a state of exhaustion and covered with sweat and grime. They left behind nearly a hundred and forty of their colleagues, dead and lying under the blazing sun. As for the wounded, some three hundred and seventy-five men, they gathered them up and transported them back on litters.

The British had suffered heavy losses: about eighty-five killed, three hundred and fifty-one wounded, and an amazingly high number of missing, some two hundred and fifty-seven, most of them taken as prisoners.

Given his sensitivity to criticism and his own sense of martial pride, Greene could not bear to admit that he once again had left the field in British hands. He stated that although the bulk of his army had retreated, he had "left on the field of action" a "strong" picket force to keep watch over Stewart, softening the impression that he had left the field entirely. He told Lafayette that he had "obtained a complete victory," and he claimed that despite being "greatly out numbered"—that certainly was not true—he had taken five hundred prisoners, which would have amounted to about a quarter of Stewart's army. More plausible was Greene's simple characterization of the Battle of Eutaw Springs. It was, he said to Lafayette, "a most bloody battle."

Bloody it was. And it was also the last full-scale battle of the Revolution.

As Greene suspected, Stewart and his men did not remain near Eutaw Springs very long. Having sustained enormous casualties—the number of British dead, wounded, and missing was close to seven hundred from a force of about two thousand—they began limping back to Charleston on September 9, even as the field still smoldered and some of the wounded still cried out for water. Greene and his army attempted to pursue them, but he called off the chase after hearing that they had been reinforced. The Americans returned to camp in the High Hills of the Santee.

The British rejected Greene's notion that he had won a tactical victory at Eutaw Springs. Stewart, in fact, said Greene lied about leaving a picket force on the battlefield. The Americans, however, eagerly accepted the general's version of events. In a sense, both the British and Americans were right—not surprising given the ambiguous character of the war in the South. It was true that Greene had withdrawn from the field, not the sort of tactic associated with victorious generals. But it was also true that Greene had inflicted intolerable punishment on the British, and that they themselves were forced to withdraw after holding the battlefield. A British officer named Lieutenant Frederick Mackenzie noted of Greene that "the more he is beaten, the farther he advances in the end." With just a whiff of contempt, Mackenzie said that Greene had been "indefatigable in collecting troops and leading them to be defeated."

Whether or not Greene won the Battle of Eutaw Springs, there is no disputing the toll he inflicted on Britain's southern strategy. The interior of the Deep South, while still plagued by hostilities between Tory and patriot, was no longer in British hands. Even before Eutaw Springs, Benjamin Rush, a member of Congress who had once been critical of Greene, told the general, "The South Carolina refugees in [Philadelphia] drink [to] your health every day" because "they view you as one of their deliverers from the tyranny of Britain."

Washington dispatched similar hosannas to his protégé. From his headquarters outside Yorktown, where Franco-American armies and the French fleet had Cornwallis trapped, the commander in chief wrote an elegant letter of congratulations.

> How happy I am dear Sir . . . to congratulate you upon a
> victory as splendid as I hope it will prove important. Fortune
> must have been coy indeed had she not yielded at last to so
> persevering a pursuer as you have been. I hope now she is
> yours [and] she will change her appellation of fickle to that
> of constant.

It hardly mattered to Greene what the British thought of his claims to victory. George Washington believed them.

Thanks to Greene's strategic victories, civil administration under American governors and legislators was being restored to a region that, only months before, had been under British occupation. Nathanael Greene had, in fact, fought, been beaten, risen, and fought again.

Nathanael Greene was the hero of the moment. Congress, a body Greene regularly infuriated and that would have welcomed his resignation a year earlier, awarded him a gold medal "emblematical of the battle and victory" at Eutaw Springs. The medal featured a heroic profile of Greene, looking quite a bit thinner than in most portraits. On the back, in Latin, was an inscription: "The Safety of the Southern

Department. The Foe conquered at Eutaw . . ." A congressional resolution continued the fiction that Greene had won a "decisive" victory
with a "force inferior in number to that of the enemy."

The recognition Greene so desperately wanted, and needed, finally
was his. His old friend and former aide Thomas Paine sent him a con-
gratulatory letter that spoke to Greene's standing as a hero and savior of
the Revolution. "How you have contrived without money to do what you
have done I have scarcely a conception of," Paine wrote.

> I am inclined to suppose you have acted like a judicious and
> honest Physician in desperate cases, that is, you have cut the
> matter short, and in order to save and serve the Country,
> have made people do what they otherwise would not have
> done tho' their own good was the object. . . . I think we are
> now in the fairest way we have ever yet been.

Like the generals whose stories he read by candlelight as a child,
Nathanael Greene wore the laurels of a famous victory. If the praise was
exaggerated and the achievement less than advertised, perhaps it made
up for all of his bad luck in previous battles, and all of his unappreciated
drudge work as quartermaster general. Henry Knox summed up
Greene's campaign in the South in language that was beyond debate:
"[Without] an army, without Means, without anything, [Greene] has
performed Wonders."

There were more wonders to come, and although they would take
place in the southern theater, the commander of the Southern Department, Major General Nathanael Greene, would have to watch them
from afar.

Communications between Greene and Washington had been spotty
through the summer of 1781, to Greene's surprise and annoyance. He
certainly knew about the astonishing developments under way in
Virginia—Lafayette was a constant correspondent—but Washington had

told him nothing. Or so Greene thought. In fact, Washington had been writing diligently, but his letters never reached Greene. (Letters between the two men took anywhere from a week to about a month to make their way back and forth.) "This failure," Washington told Greene on September 28, "gives me Reason to fear some foul Play on the Route." The messages must have been intercepted.

Not that it mattered. For at two o'clock on the afternoon of October 19, the British army of Lord Cornwallis—the man who had spent the spring trying to crush Nathanael Greene and his ill-supplied band of rebels—filed out of its camp in Yorktown, stacked its arms, and surrendered.

Greene learned of the great victory on the evening of October 27, and he and his men celebrated with a daylong feast beginning the following morning. Greene received letters of congratulations from friends, politicians, and army colleagues, and he dispatched letters of his own to his brilliant subordinates in the South, like Francis Marion. His friend James Varnum, who had commanded the Kentish Guards so long ago when they were playing at war, wrote to express his "peculiar Pleasure . . . that the Brows of my worthy Friend were encircled with unfading Laurels."

On November 2, Nathanael Greene sent a short letter to the man who had sent him to the South when all seemed lost. "I beg leave to congratulate your Excellency upon the glorious and important success of your Arms," he wrote. "Nothing can equal the joy that it gives to this country, and I contemplate the consequences with infinite pleasure."

A few days later, a letter arrived from Henry Knox, who was with Washington in Yorktown. Greene and Knox had known each other since the days when British troops patrolled the common in Boston and revolution was far from the minds of most Americans. They were young men, and they shared an amateur soldier's fascination with war and a radical American's belief in liberty. When war came, they both impressed their commander in chief with their passion for the cause, their competency, and their loyalty. Through the difficult winter camps, through candlelit councils of war in Washington's headquarters, and through hard and often disappointing campaigns, they became not just colleagues but friends.

And now, in places like Yorktown and Eutaw Springs, these two New Englanders were among the most improbable victors in military history. "It was a happy fight for America," Knox wrote Greene. Soon, he promised, reinforcements would be sent to the Carolinas, which, he said, would "[relieve] Greene from many perplexities." Knox said he wished he could be among the troops joining his friend: "I would fly to you with more rapidity than most fat men." But the war was not over; there still were battles to fight. "[I am] so linked in with the cursed cannon that I know not how to tear myself from them," Knox complained.

Someday, he promised, there would be peace, and they would see each other again. "I sigh for domestic felicity," he wrote, "and I know you do the same."

13 | Forging a Nation

When he heard about the disaster in faraway Yorktown, Lord North, the British prime minister, threw out his arms and exclaimed, "Oh, God! It is all over!"

While there could be little doubt how the war would end, it was not, in fact, over. The British held Savannah and Charleston, along with New York. Bitterness and hatred still ruled the southern backcountry, where no diplomats in powdered wigs and fine clothes could broker peace between Tories and patriots. Rumors of British reinforcements on their way to the South occasionally made their way to Greene's headquarters, and though they proved false, they could not be discounted.

The war was not over.

For some, it would never be over, for they would bear scars, mental as well as physical, for the rest of their days. Greene was particularly concerned about the hundreds of wounded soldiers in his camp, some of them suffering terribly. The autumn of 1781 brought not only the joyous news of Cornwallis's surrender but disease as well. Even in their relative repose in the High Hills of the Santee, Greene's men, wounded and healthy alike, fell ill with dysentry and malaria, while those who had been carried off the field at Eutaw Springs literally rotted away for lack of proper medicine and care. Their plight was all the more heartbreaking with victory so close.

Greene pleaded with Congress to help him relieve the suffering he heard, smelled, and saw every day in his army's rudimentary hospitals: "Numbers of brave fellows, who have bled in the Cause of their country, have been [eaten] up with maggots & perished. . . . Hospital Stores & medicine have been exceeding scarce. . . . To afford the sick & wounded all the relief in my power, I visited the hospitals from Camp to Charlotte."

Neither Congress nor the states had money to buy the supplies Greene needed. Steuben, writing from Virginia, told Greene that "Paper money had no longer a Currency." The self-styled baron was forced to sell some personal possessions—a collection of silver forks—to help pay for the care of a wounded aide.

After pleading in vain for help from Congress and individual governors, Greene was forced to rely on barter for goods and services. Militiamen were offered discharges if they agreed to make two canteens a day and five hundred horseshoes during the remainder of their tour of duty. The system worked, but it was not without flaws; one of Greene's aides noted that "[men] of property are above undertaking such work." On other occasions, goods like tobacco and indigo were exchanged for army necessities like clothing. These measures won the attention of the government's new superintendent of finance, Robert Morris, who praised Greene for his "Genius" in making due despite "the want of Men, Money, Cloaths, Arms and Supplies."

Morris's praise, however, could not be traded for a pair of shoes or a gill of rum or a barrel of gunpowder. Suffering and deprivation remained a southern soldier's lot, and Greene continued to remind political leaders that the army was in dire straits despite the great victory at Yorktown. "We are in the greatest distress . . . for want of shoes," he told the Board of War in November, a month after Cornwallis surrendered. "We cannot march without Shoes nor can we fight without Ammunition." Local officials, too, were on the receiving end of Greene's lobbying. Greene asked North Carolina to provide the army with a "quantity of good hams and bacon."

This tireless dedication to the men who marched and fought with him was one factor among several that led Greene to turn down a new honor that Congress seemed prepared to offer. As part of a reorganization of the government's executive functions, Congress had called for the appointment of a secretary of war to oversee the army on its behalf. Months had passed without an appointment while Congress tried to find a candidate acceptable to all. Among those advocating for Greene was Gouverneur Morris, who told Greene on the sly, "Some Persons . . . think of you for that Office." Greene's reputation truly had been transformed. When he resigned as quartermaster general in the summer of 1780, members of Congress sputtered their denunciations of him, condemned him for his impudence, and made it clear that they would like nothing better than to be rid of a general who failed to show due deference to civilian leaders. Now, however, Congress was considering the very same Nathanael Greene to join the government.

If Greene sought cheap vindication, the opportunity was there for the asking. But the Nathanael Greene of late 1781 was wiser, more mature, and more accomplished than the Greene of even a year earlier. He had vindicated himself on the battlefield, with soldiers who had marched and suffered through the steamy heat of a southern summer. He was not about to leave them. Besides, he had dealt with politicians before and rarely was happy with the exchange. "The more I am in the Army and the more I am acquainted with human Nature the less fond I am of political life," Greene told Morris on November 21. Besides, he had every intention of making money once the war ended—or even before it did—and he did not want jealous critics watching his every move.

> You say that the appointment of a Minister or Secretary of war
> is in contemplation and that among the many I have been
> thought of and proposed by your self and others. . . . To tell

you the truth, my dear Sir, I am poor and I wish not to climb to stations where I have neither fortune or friends to support me. Eminence always begets envy and it is much more difficult to support our selves in high places than to arrive at them.

A congressional salary, he wrote, would hardly support "a growing family." And, of course, there still was fighting ahead. This was no time to relax, and no time to leave an important command: "[If] we fold our Arms and set our selves down at ease, [Britain] will rally her force, and come on to a fresh attack. God grant we not spend the winter in idle amusements."

Congress took the hint and eventually appointed Benjamin Lincoln, who had been at Washington's side when the British surrendered at Yorktown.

Greene had no intention of allowing his army, or himself, to indulge in "idle amusements." The still-volatile political situation in the South required his constant attention. Brazen Tories had captured Greene's friend and ally Thomas Burke, the patriot governor of North Carolina, and a number of state officials and turned them over to the British. It was a desperate gambit to inspire terror and bring about the collapse of civil government in North Carolina, but it failed. An acting governor, Alexander Martin, quickly filled Burke's spot, stabilizing American control over the state. Nevertheless, the incident inspired an upsurge in Tory activity, reminding Greene that the South remained home to thousands of Americans who remained his enemies.

Dealing with the Tories would test Greene's abilities as a politician, regardless of how much he said he loathed politics. If he were to guide the South from war to peace and from conflict to nation-building, he must first bring to an end the brutality of the South's war between fellow Americans. To do that, he decided, he would have to treat his antagonists with moderation. When reports reached Greene of outrages committed against Tories by troops under the command of General Griffith Rutherford—his men reportedly burned houses and mistreated civilians—Greene sent a letter that made his views clear. While patriots had "good reason to be offended" by the Tories, revenge was not the answer: "[In] national concerns as well as in private life passion is a bad [counselor] and resentment an unsafe guide. . . . If we [pursue] the Tories indiscimininately and drive them to a state [of] desperation we shall make them from a weak and feeble force [to] a sure and determined enemy."

It turned out that Rutherford's men probably were innocent of some of the more serious charges. Still, Greene was determined to live by his advice to Rutherford. He understood, too, that while the South's split between Tory and patriot was particularly bitter and complicated, the problem was not limited to the backwoods of the Carolinas and Georgia. There were Tories in New York, in Pennsylvania, and in New Jersey. It was a national problem, and it required a national solution. Greene recommended that "the Governors of every state . . . adopt nearly a similar policy with respect to the proper mode of treating the disaffected." Otherwise, he wrote, "punishment has more the appearance of resentment and persecution than a common measure of justice."

This shrewd observation demonstrated not only Greene's nationalism but his political skills as well. Although he held little regard for the Tories, he would oppose "cruelty" because it was "dishonorable," and "persecution" because it would increase "the number and force of our enemies." There was, as he indicated, a cold calculation to this spirit of reconciliation. While it would be dishonorable to attack the Tories, it would also be a tactical mistake. He told the militia commander Thomas Sumter that it was better "to forgive than to persecute" the Tories because, in part, persecution might lead to even more bloodshed.

So Greene approved of conciliatory gestures, such as a pardon offered to some Tories by South Carolina governor John Rutledge. Greene hoped North Carolina would do the same, but when the state's acting governor, Alexander Martin, refused to issue such a pardon, Greene did not force the issue. "We Military men can only advise and not dictate in these matters," he wrote. While Greene disagreed with Martin's decision, he knew that his men had died for republican ideals, among them the notion that the military was beholden to the people's representatives. He would grumble, but he would not overturn civilian decisions, even though he certainly had the power to do so.

Caty Greene left Rhode Island in early November, soon after hearing the news of the American victory at Yorktown. Winter was approaching, an end to the war was in sight, and the Greenes had not seen each other since Morristown in early 1780. Unlike the winter of 1780–81, when Nathanael was trying to save the Revolution in the South, there was no good reason for the ever restless Caty to remain in Rhode Island. She longed to be at the side of her husband, the war's new hero.

After a four-day ride from Rhode Island, Caty and young George Washington Greene arrived in a joyous, celebratory Philadelphia. Politicians and civilians alike considered the war all but over and were acting accordingly, much to the chagrin of a visitor, General George Washington, who told Greene: "I am apprehensive that the States, elated by the late success, and taking it for granted that Great Britain will no longer support so losing a contest, will relax in their preparations for the next Campaign." Washington was in Philadelphia, in fact, to persuade political leaders that "the most vigorous exertions" still were necessary before America celebrated final victory. Washington had read reports that the British might send thousands of reinforcements to South Carolina, which, if true, promised a bloody reengagment in the South. Washington prudently ordered about a thousand Continentals to march south to join Greene.

None of Washington's cautions, however, would deny Philadelphia its chance to celebrate. Caty was invited to a series of the social engagements she loved, and though she had planned to stay in the city only briefly, her visit stretched into weeks. Poor weather had something to do with her change in plans, but so did the parties and balls. Caty's vivacious presence and her incorrigible flirting worked its charms on Washington, as usual. When Caty finally left Philadelphia to make her way to

South Carolina, Washington told Greene that he would make certain to "strew the way over with flowers."

As the celebrations went on, and even as Washington planned for the following year's campaign, Nathanael Greene was on the march. Determined to complete his reconquest of the South, Greene ordered his men to move out of the High Hills of the Santee toward British positions outside Charleston.

Greene had no intention of forcing a pitched battle, like that at Eutaw Springs. Instead, through the judicious use of his cavalry and of local militia, he planned to bleed the British to death in small, hit-and-run engagements until the units outside Charleston had no choice but to withdraw to the garrison inside the city. There, cut off by land, demoralized by recent events, they might simply sail away, leaving another outpost in American hands.

After a series of marches and maneuvers in late November, Greene saw a chance to strike a lightning blow on a British garrison in Dorchester, South Carolina, just to the north of Charleston. With about four hundred mounted troops, he personally led a march on the garrison. British officers recognized Greene during a skirmish, assumed that they were under attack by the entire southern army, and quickly ordered a retreat toward Charleston.

There was little doubt now that Greene was in command of events in the South. His presence in a small engagement was enough to inspire panic in the enemy's ranks, and Greene knew it. Of the enemy's flight from Dorchester, Greene wrote, "They . . . disgraced themselves not a little by their precipitate retreat." The British were getting pushed back toward the sea.

After a difficult march through coastal swamps in early December, Greene positioned his army between Britain's two remaining strongholds in the South, Charleston, South Carolina, and Savannah, Georgia, in a place called Round O. Though he complained that the army still lacked basic necessities, he was delighted to be on the offensive, to be master of events, to have the British on the run. He wrote to Richard

Henry Lee, a former member of Congress from Virginia: "I have the pleasure to inform you that by a bold Manoeuvre we have obliged the enemy to retire to [Charleston]. . . . Thus the conquerors of the Southern World are pent up with little more than ground enough to encamp upon."

Greene's confidence, however, proved to be a shallow trench when rumors began exploding in the American camp. There were reports—highly exaggerated, but Greene didn't know it—that thousands of British reinforcements were on their way to South Carolina from New York and Ireland. Greene, suddenly frantic, demanded reinforcements from Rochambeau's troops in Virginia, but the French were happy to remain in Yorktown. Desperate and convinced that the British in Charleston would soon outnumber him, Greene put forward a radical idea, one that reminded local civil leaders that the commander of the Southern Department was very much a nonsoutherner. He proposed the enlistment of blacks.

In a letter to South Carolina governor John Rutledge, Greene wrote:

> The natural strength of this country in point of numbers,
> appears to me to consist much more in the blacks, than the
> whites. Could they be incorporated, and employed in [its]
> defence, it would afford you double security. That they
> would make good Soldiers I have not the least doubt. . . .
> Should this measure be adopted, It may prove a great means
> of preventing the Enemy from further attempts upon this
> country, when they find they have not only the whites, but
> the blacks also to contend with.

Blacks already had proved themselves in the Continental service, as Greene saw firsthand during the Battle of Rhode Island. Black troops also had played a prominent role at the Battle of Monmouth.

Political leaders in the South, ever fearful of putting a weapon in the hands of a black man, adamantly opposed Greene's proposal, even though, as he pointed out, blacks constituted a vast pool of potential soldiers. Previous efforts to put more southern blacks in uniform had failed. In 1779, for example, Congress had authorized the recruitment of three thousand southern black slaves, with owners to be compensated a thousand dollars per slave for their loss. But Georgia and South Carolina vetoed the plan. To add to the injustice, state legislators voted to offer slaves as bounties to attract more white recruits.

Greene's observation about the strength in numbers of blacks in South Carolina was undeniable. Of a population of one hundred and eighty thousand in 1789, South Carolina was home to ninety-seven thousand blacks. In Georgia, nearly twenty-one thousand of the state's fifty-six thousand people were black. Blacks were a huge, untapped resource for an army of just a couple of thousand troops.

Greene proposed that slaves willing to serve in the army should be granted their freedom, "and be cloathed, and treated in all respects as other soldiers." As with his views on the treatment of Tories, his plan for black recruitment was based on more than altruism and a sense of justice. There were practical considerations as well. In a letter to Lighthorse Harry Lee, Greene observed that blacks had provided the British with "all their best intelligence." If they were welcomed into the American army, they might be less inclined to do the king's bidding. Blacks, Greene wrote, "will be either more or less useful to [the British] as they are treated well or ill by us."

A Continental officer and member of the South Carolina House of Representatives, John Laurens, put Greene's recommendation to the test. He introduced a bill that would have authorized the state to recruit twenty-five hundred slaves for South Carolina's regiments. As the debate got under way, Greene reiterated his strong support in another letter to Rutledge. The British, Greene told the governor, were still a threat to South Carolina's independence. If enemy reinforcements arrived and reasserted control in South Carolina, Greene said, it was still possible that Britain might claim the state in any peace negotiations. The northern states, he warned, would be justified "in giving you up" if South Carolina continued to bar its immense black population from military service. He conceded that his "remedy may be disagreeable," but he insisted it was the best means to ensure continued American control over the state.

Although Rutledge was a friend and an ally of Greene's, he was "alarmed" by the proposal, and, for a moment, he feared that the arguments of Greene and Laurens might prevail. In the middle of what Rutledge called a "hard Battle on the Subject of arming the Blacks," the governor heard that support for the measure was building. He was greatly relieved, however, to see that "people in general returned to their Senses" and the plan was defeated. One of the measure's opponents, a legislator named Andrew Burke, spoke for many when he saw a larger agenda behind Greene's proposal. "The northern people, I have observed, regard the condition in which we hold our slaves in a different light from us," he wrote. "I am much deceived indeed, if they do not secretly wish for a general Emancipation, if the present struggle was over." He believed that Rhode Island's Greene was one of those secret northern abolitionists. In due course, regrettably, Greene would demonstrate that he clearly was not.

Before the slave-enlistment bill was voted down, South Carolina's legislators and Governor Rutledge passed a motion awarding Greene a plantation—one of the many confiscated from Tory landowners—as a sign of the state's eternal gratitude. This was precisely the kind of premature exhibition Washington warned against, because, after all, the British still were in Charleston and there was no end to hostilities. What's more, Greene was wary about mass confiscations of Tory lands, believing such seizures could only harm efforts to rebuild trust between Tory and patriot once the war was over. He soon supported plans to return confiscated property to Tories who agreed to provide information about British troop movements, arguing that this sort of gesture could help bring together the South's bitterly divided factions. Politicians and militia leaders, however, were not in a particularly forgiving mood, and they opposed Greene's conciliatory gestures.

Despite his personal misgivings, Greene eagerly accepted the confiscated estate that South Carolina offered him. Until now, there was little indication that Greene seriously contemplated remaining in the South after the war was over. His family and his business interests were based in the North, and, as he learned during his argument about slave enlistment, he remained very much a northerner in the eyes of his southern brethren.

Still, the offer of a free plantation came at an opportune time. Greene was taking stock of his financial future and was rapidly coming to the conclusion that his business prospects in the North were dim. He wrote to his cousin, Griffin, about his new interest in the region he had liberated: "This Country affords a fine field for making a fortune." After serving his country so well for so long, Nathanael Greene was determined to make sure that the coming of peace would not diminish his hard-won stature as one of the Revolution's heroes. And that, he knew, would require not medals but money.

On March 22, 1782, the marquis of Rockingham succeeded Lord North as British prime minister, with the understanding that his new government would recognize American independence and so bring the long, bitter war to an end. Three days later, Caty Greene arrived in South Carolina, at last reunited with her husband after their longest separation of the war. She had intended to bring their oldest child, George Washington Greene, with her to camp, but her friends in Philadelphia persuauded her to leave the boy in the capital.

The mild southern winter was over when she arrived, and the roads through the Carolinas were filled with the promise of a welcome springtime. The southern war settled into a comfortable stalemate, with the British safe behind their defenses in Charleston and Savannah and Greene in control of just about everything else. Those thousands of British reinforcements never materialized, save for a few hundred. Yet another new British commander, Alexander Leslie, was reluctant to move out of Charleston to challenge Greene, and Greene was not strong enough to assail the city. So the two sides chose to wait upon events.

Without a campaign to plan, Greene was immersed in administrative and political affairs, tedious work that no doubt reminded him of all the reasons he hated being quartermaster general. But with Caty's arrival, Greene's mood lightened, although only slightly. To Henry Knox, he wrote: "After almost two years absence you may well suppose I was made very happy on the arrival of Mrs. Greene. She is in better health and spirits than I could have expected after such a disagreeable journey. She is kinder to me than I am just to her." Greene was still worried about the British threat in Charleston. His troops, bored with inactivity, were vanishing into the Carolina wilderness. He believed the British, with their superior numbers, were planning a new offensive in South Carolina. And, to further spoil his mood, those unappreciative meddlers in Congress were at it again, refusing to promote his friend Knox to major general. Greene blamed this injustice on "cursed intrigue."

He had good reason to dwell on his fears and anxieties, even with Caty at his side, and even with peace and independence ever so near. Troops from Pennsylvania nearly staged a mutiny in late April over their lack of food and clothing. When he discovered the plot, Greene ordered the ringleader to the gallows. "I act with decision," he told another officer. Although he understood that the soldiers were miserable, Greene would not tolerate rebellion in the ranks. "They had better be quiet," he said of the troops. They were, but Greene admitted that their complaints were entirely justified.

With peace in sight, there were more laurels for General Nathanael Greene, savior of the American South. Following South Carolina's precedent, both Georgia and North Carolina presented Greene with gifts of land, which Greene eagerly accepted. The North Carolina estate was huge—twenty-five thousand acres. But it was the more modest tract in Georgia, a two-thousand-acre plantation near Savannah called Mulberry Grove, that would become Greene's new home when the war ended. These gifts helped persuade the Rhode Islander that his future lay in the South, where he was regarded as a hero and a liberator. It is a tribute to Greene that these gifts did not muffle his voice when he disagreed with the states' politicians on issues like black enlistment and, later, taxation.

And it is equally notable that Greene's criticisms did not lead politicians to withdraw their gifts in a fit of pique.

The summer of 1782, the last summer of the war, was oppressive and deadly. Malaria killed hundreds of soldiers and sickened hundreds more. On August 26, Greene issued a general order that told of the new miseries and deprivations in camp, even on the eve of victory: "The general has observed that the custom of beating the *dead march* at Soldiers funerals has a tendency to depress the Spirits of the Sick in camp & he is therefore pleased to order that in future this practice be discontinued."

With several of his friends and top aides dreadfully ill, Greene asked the British commander, Leslie, to allow a group of sick Americans to take refuge on British-controlled Kiawah Island, off Charleston. Leslie, who had earlier asked Greene for a formal truce and was refused—Greene said only Congress had the power to authorize a truce—agreed. While it was a humane decision, it also simply acknowledged the obvious: the war was nearing its conclusion. The British had abruptly evacuated Savannah in July, leaving only Charleston in their control. There was no point in denying Greene's men a chance to rest and recuperate.

And so the convalescents, including Greene's aide Lewis Morris and Colonel William Washington, spent the last few weeks of summer on the sea-swept island and its beaches, joined by Caty Greene. Although she was not as desperately sick as many others in camp, her husband was concerned about "some disagreeable elements hovering over her" and so ordered her away from the fetid atmosphere of the Carolina lowlands.

She brought along a backgammon table, cards, and other diversions that helped re-create the atmosphere of a winter camp—without the cold and snow. Lewis Morris reported from the island: "We are very much indebted to Mrs. Greene for her vivacity and good humor. She keeps us all in good spirits. . . . We laugh, sing and play backgammon. . . . Your lady has got back her Block Island complexion and looks as she used to."

The patients were not, however, without complaint. One, an aide to Greene named Captain Nathaniel Pendleton, noted with approval that Colonel Washington's new bride, Jane Reily Elliott, often rolled fine cigars for her husband, who smoked them as fast as she could make them. But, he wrote, "I wish they would employ themselves more in this way, and less in kissing."

When Caty returned to camp on the mainland, the army's health crisis had passed, and so, too, had her husband's anxieties. In late September, Greene wrote that his "troubles in this quarter appear to be drawing to a close." Indeed they were.

On December 14, General Leslie's troops in Charleston boarded transport ships and sailed out of the last British stronghold in the South. Several hours later, at about three o'clock in the afternoon, Major General Nathanael Greene marched into town to claim the city on behalf of the people of the United States.

The southern campaign of Nathanael Greene was over, and he and his ill-clad, poorly supplied troops were victorious. Greene had been sent to the South at an hour of extreme peril, with orders to stop the enemy's finest general. He lost or tied every major battle he fought, but in doing so he fulfilled his mission and so preserved the Revolution during one of its darkest hours. He did so with scant resources, no personal knowledge of the terrain, and no small amount of local hostility.

But he was not without his own devices. He was relentless, he was organized, and he was disciplined. He understood that the war was not about territory but about ideas and perception. As long as he could field an army, he could and would not be beaten. He yearned for a famous victory, one that might be forever linked to his name, like Caesar and Gaul, or even Gates and Saratoga. When, to his frustration, the fortunes of war denied him the laurels he sought, he claimed them anyway, at Eutaw Springs.

If victory mattered to him, and it clearly did, it has not mattered to history. Nathanael Greene's name became linked not to a battle but, fittingly, to an idea, to a new method of warfare. "We fight, get beat, rise and fight again," he wrote. In doing so, time and again, he won, and he won at a time when all might have been lost.

General and Mrs. Greene were the toasts of Charleston and the nation in the winter of 1782–83. Congress voted him another resolution of thanks and appreciation. Parties and balls were held in their honor and in honor of imminent victory. On February 6, 1783, as peace negotiators in Europe finished their deliberations, Greene's hero, mentor, and commander in chief, George Washington, dispatched a letter to the commander of the Southern Department: "It is with pleasure [that] I congratulate you on the glorious end you have put to hostilities in the Southern States. The honor and advantages of it, I hope & trust, you will live long to enjoy."

On April 11, eight years after shots were fired at Lexington and Concord, Congress declared an end to the war. It was time for Nathanael Greene and his troops to go home and rebuild their lives. As he prepared for his return to Rhode Island, he replied to Washington's message with a heartfelt tribute to the man who had seen in the young and inexperienced fallen Quaker a military leader of promise and talent. Washington had not cared about Greene's limp, which had so mortified his fellow Rhode Island militiamen. He did not judge him unfit for command because he lacked a formal education in military science, or anything else for that matter. He had turned to Greene in moments of desperation, when the army's supply system collapsed during Valley Forge, and when the southern army collapsed in late 1780. Though not given to sentiment and emotion, Washington revealed through his actions his affection and respect for the energetic amateur from Rhode Island. Greene embraced the man who had been not just his commander in chief but also a father figure to him after he rejected the religion and aspirations of Nathanael Greene Sr. "Every ear feels and every tongue confesses the merit and importance of your services," he told Washington. "The polite Attention which I have experienced since I have had

the honor to serve under your Command claims my particular acknowledgments, and I feel a singular satisfaction, in having preserved your
Confidence and esteem [through] the whole progress of the War,
notwithstanding many jarring interests."

General Greene dismissed his men on June 21, in a moving and elo-
quent salute that suited the occasion.

> We have trod the paths of adversity together, and have felt
> the sunshine of better fortune. We found a people
> overwhelmed with distress, and a country groaning under
> oppression. It has been our happiness to relieve them. . . .
> Your generous confidence, amidst surrounding difficulties;
> your persevering tempers, against the tide of misfortune,
> paved the way to success. . . .
>
>   It is unnecessary, and might be deemed improper on this
> occasion, to enumerate the many trying scenes we have
> passed, of the suffering you have sustained. It is sufficient for
> the General that they have now subsided. It is his happiness
> that he has had the honor to command an army no less
> distinguished for its patience than bravery. . . .
>
>   United by principle and cemented by affection, you have
> exhibited to the world a proof that elevated souls and
> persevering tempers will triumph over every difficulty. The
> orders of government now separate us, perhaps forever. Our
> great object is answered; our first wish obtained. The same
> considerations which led us to the field, will now call upon us
> to retire. In whatever situation the General may be placed, it
> will afford him the highest pleasure to promote your
> interests; and it is among the first of his wishes to see you as
> happy as you have rendered millions of others.

He left Charleston on August 11, accompanied not by Caty—who
was pregnant again and already well on her way home—but by several
aides. Although he was eager to see his children in Rhode Island, he took

his time, looking up friends along the way and soaking up tributes to himself in Wilmington, North Carolina; Richmond, Virginia; Baltimore, Maryland; and Philadelphia, Pennsylvania. He crossed the Delaware into Trenton, the site of that desperate, glorious gamble so many years ago, and was briefly reunited with Washington, in the home of a mutual friend. They had first met on the hills overlooking Boston in the summer of 1775, when neither man, nor anybody else, could imagine what the future might hold. They had suffered together, despaired together, and now they were triumphant together.

And together, in victory, they glimpsed the problems that awaited their infant nation. From Trenton, Washington and Greene traveled to Princeton, where Congress was meeting in exile after fleeing the capital once again. This time the threatening army was not British but American: hundreds of soldiers, most from the perpetually disgruntled Pennsylvania regiments, had marched on Philadelphia to demand back pay. When Pennsylvania's state government declined to protect Congress, delegates chose discretion over valor and crossed the Delaware to be closer to Washington and the troops he had brought with him from Newburgh, New York.

Although both Washington and Greene understood the plight of men who had suffered in service to the Revolution, neither sympathized with troops who wished to use or threaten force against civil leaders. Washington had quashed a near mutiny of officers in Newburgh in March, and Greene himself had negotiated his way out of several near or small mutinies in the spring of 1783. The Princeton exile reminded both men that even though the war was over, peace would bring little respite from conflict, particularly in matters of money.

More uplifting were the expressions of gratitude that the embattled Congress offered to the South's liberator. The lawmakers voted to present Greene with two brass cannon to commemorate his southern campaign, although it was left to Washington to ask Greene where, exactly, Congress might find two brass cannon.

Greene formally requested that Congress accept his resignation as major general, and asked that he be allowed to go home to Rhode Island.

His military career was over. Congress allowed him to proceed to Rhode Island as a civilian.

Nathanael Greene was not at Fraunces Tavern on that night in December 1783 when George Washington said farewell to some of the men who served him for so long. Greene, eager to see Caty and the children, already was home.

He had left Rhode Island in 1775 to fight for a new nation. After a brief reunion with his family, he would soon leave home again, this time to build a new life.

14 | Unfinished Business

Through the long years of conflict and hardship, Nathanael Greene yearned for his return to civilian life and the pleasures of what he invariably called "domestic felicity." Now, at last, he was a civilian again; what's more, he had the fame he had been seeking ever since joining the Kentish Guards in 1774.

He had every right to be satisfied and joyous. The cause he had served so well for so long had ended in a spectacular triumph, one he had helped mightily to achieve. Through talent and determination—not family and heredity—he had made himself a part of history. He had helped defeat a great empire and now would play his part in building a new nation.

Just as important, he was free to introduce himself to the four children born during his absence, to enjoy the constant company of Caty, and to await the birth of their new baby. Years later, their daughter Cornelia recalled these memorable days when the Greene children got to know this stranger who was their father. Although used to command and discipline, Nathanael Greene easily made the transition to doting and forgiving parent. "He was our boon companion and playfellow," Cornelia wrote, "who winked at every atrocity we perpetrated." The Greene family happily established itself in Newport, with the old house in Coventry handed over to Nathanael's brother Jacob.

Still, Nathanael Greene was not at peace. Disillusion, the inevitable residue of revolution, already had left its mark, even before he left the South. He had urged the South's politicians to approve a 5 percent tax on trade to help pay off the new nation's enormous debt. Congress, which did not have the power to tax, could only urge each state to implement the levy. Ever the nationalist in a region that would champion the notion of states' rights, Greene saw the tax as an obligation to be shared equally by all in the name of the new nation. He told the governor of Georgia, Lyman Hall, that the "united efforts of a free people may accomplish great things; but the endeavors of a few will be weak and [ineffective]."

His arguments, however, failed miserably. Georgia did not approve the tax, and South Carolina withdrew its initial support for the plan. Even more embarrassing for Greene, Rhode Island followed suit after he returned, rejecting the measure to the despair of its most famous native son. Greene was appalled as individual states acted as if they were sovereign countries and not part of a united enterprise. He told Washington of his fears for the future: "Many people secretly wish that every State should be completely independent, and that, as soon as our public debts are liquidated, Congress should be no more—a plan that would be as fatal to our happiness at home as it would be ruinous to our interest abroad."

His own financial affairs were in shambles. The family business was in the hands of his brothers, and his secret wartime investment with Barnabas Deane was about to reach an unhappy end, with the company disbanding and Greene collecting nine hundred and sixty pounds sterling for his investment of ten thousand pounds in 1779. Worse yet, he was entangled in yet another complex arrangement that carried an odor of private dealing at public expense. Several months before he rode in triumph from Charleston to Newport, Greene had cosigned a loan to a company that provided his army with one of its final consignments of desperately needed supplies. John Banks, one of the company's principals, was friendly with two of Greene's aides, both of whom secretly became partners with Banks. When the firm, Hunter, Banks & Company, defaulted on the loan Greene had guaranteed, there were whispered accusations that Greene himself was a silent partner with Banks. The evidence suggests that he was not, and Banks offered a testimonial to Greene's innocence, but the suspicions prompted Congress to delay paying Banks's creditors. The creditors, in turn, dunned Greene for the thirty thousand pounds due them from Hunter, Banks.

"I tremble at my own situation when I think of the enormous sums I owe," Greene told his wife. "I seem to be doomed to a life of slavery."

And so, in a desperate attempt to pay off his debts and avoid the life to which he thought he was doomed, he turned to slavery itself.

In principle, Nathanael Greene, like many raised in Quaker traditions, opposed slavery. He told an audience in Philadelphia in 1783, "Nothing can be said in [slavery's] defense." But even as he spoke those words, Greene already was in the business of buying human beings and had found a way to justify it. Slaves, he told that same audience in Philadelphia, were "as much attached to a plantation as a man is to his family."

He put that terrible justification into practice on the plantation he received from South Carolina. The land and its slaves were once owned by the state's royal governor, Thomas Boone, but the new patriot government had confiscated Boone's property. Greene wanted to buy the slaves who had worked the plantation under Boone, and he convinced himself that somehow this was a humane thing to do. He told his Philadelphia audience that the slaves would "not be worse but better" under his ownership.

He also believed he had no choice. If he were to become the rich and influential person he wished to be in postwar America, he first had to clear himself of debt. Turning his gifts of southern land into profitable plantations would help him achieve that goal. He decided he could not do that, however, without using slave labor.

But slaves were expensive, and Greene didn't have a great deal of cash. He told the Speaker of South Carolina's House of Representatives, "[It will be] entirely out of my power" to buy the slaves who had worked the Boone property "unless the State will make the conditions for pay favorable to my wishes." He apologized for making such a request, explaining that he had "a dependant family and children to educate." The state and Greene eventually came to terms.

He had similar plans for the estate he received from Georgia, Mulberry Grove outside Savannah, which was to become his new home. Not long after his return to Rhode Island, Greene told Robert Morris, the new nation's superintendent of finance, "I find I can get my Georgia plantation stocked with good Gangs of Negroes at about £70 a head and the payments made mostly by installment." Greene borrowed money from Morris and from his friend and former commissary general Jeremiah Wadsworth to buy slaves and equipment for the estate. He betrayed no sense that his conscience was troubled as he made the transition from Yankee businessman to slave-owning southern plantation owner, although he later wrote of his wish for the "demolishing" of slavery and an end to the slave trade.

The months following Greene's return to civilian life offered a hint of the role he seemed destined to play in the new nation's government. In March 1784, Congress appointed him to a commission formed to negotiate "Treaties with the different Nations and Tribes of Indians." Ironically, Greene learned of his appointment through a letter from his old antagonist and fellow fallen Quaker Thomas Mifflin, now the president of Congress. He turned down the appointment, not out of any personal resentment but because Caty was recovering slowly after giving birth to their fifth child, Louisa.

The urgency of family and business concerns, however, was no match for personal appeals from Greene's former commander in chief. When Washington asked him, in late March 1784, to travel to Philadelphia for the first meeting of the Society of the Cincinnati, Greene put aside everything else for the sake of his friend and hero. The society was made up of former officers of the Continental army and was designed to "perpetuate" the friendships forged during the war and to celebrate the Revolution's ideals. Washington served as its president, but his presence did not shield the organization from complaints that it reeked of Old World, antirepublican privilege: critics, including Benjamin Franklin and the Adams cousins, were appalled that membership in the exclusive club could be passed down to the eldest sons of members. Washington fairly begged Greene to play an active role in the society, telling him that he wanted "the best abilities of the Society" at its initial meeting. "I cannot avoid expressing an earnest wish that yours may be among them," he added. Greene did not let down Washington but was shocked to discover, as he told Washington, that "the current of public prejudice is directed against the Cincinnati."

The Indian commission appointment, though declined, and his membership in the Cincinnati indicated that Greene could have a place among the new nation's leaders. But his personal finances remained his first concern. Creditors continued to bombard him with bills run up by Hunter, Banks, and he received little help from Congress. In the fall of 1784, after a bitter summer that saw half his crops ruined in a hurricane, Greene rode from Rhode Island to Virginia to confront John Banks in person. He was too late. He informed his lawyer in Charleston, "I arrived and found John Banks dead and buried." He asked his lawyer to file a claim against Banks's estate.

It wasn't just money woes that dogged the hero of the southern campaign. Victory and freedom apparently were not enough to convince some soldiers to forget or forgive old resentments. While visiting Mulberry Grove in the spring of 1785, Greene was confronted by a former officer named James Gunn, who challenged Greene to a duel over a disagreement the two men had had in 1782 regarding a horse. (Gunn believed he was entitled to a new horse courtesy of the Continental army and so helped himself to one. An enraged Greene demanded that Congress intervene, and, to Gunn's chagrin, it sided with Greene.)

Proud men did not easily ignore or decline such challenges at the time, but Greene did. Washington congratulated him for defying convention. He told him that his "honor and reputation" were enhanced by "the non-acceptance of [Gunn's] challenge." Undeterred, Gunn promised to kill Greene without the careful rituals of the duel Greene would not fight. Greene began carrying a pistol with him at all times.

Peace, for Nathanael Greene, was more elusive than he had ever imagined.

Mulberry Grove, Greene's plantation in Georgia, finally was ready for the family. "The prospect is delightful and the house magnificent," Greene wrote of the estate. "We have a coach house and stables, a large . . . kitchen, and a poultry house. Besides these are several other buildings convenient for a family." The main house was a fine two-story Georgian building with a library. In the late summer of 1785, Greene left behind the South's heat and humidity and sailed to Rhode Island to collect his wife and children. Together, they would sail back to their new home and their new lives.

Heartbreak waited on him. While he was gone, Caty had given birth to their sixth child, conceived during a short visit to Rhode Island in late 1784. Named for her mother, baby Catherine developed a terrible cough during the summer. She died despite Caty's loving but futile care.

Still in mourning, the family left Rhode Island for the last time in October. After a short stay in Savannah, they rode out to their new home in November. Though his financial troubles persisted and he still feared for his reputation because of the Banks affair, Nathanael Greene at last allowed himself a sense of contentment. His wife and children were with him, and they seemed happy. In April 1786, Greene offered an idyllic word portrait of his new life.

> It is a busy time with us. We are planting. We have upwards
> [of] sixty acres of corn planted, and expect to plant one
> hundred and thirty of rice. The garden is delightful. The
> fruit trees and flowering shrubs form a pleasing variety.

We have green peas almost fit to eat, and as fine lettuce as you ever saw. The mocking-birds surround us evening and morning. The weather is mild, and the vegetable kingdom progressing to perfection.

Wartime friends were frequent visitors. Anthony Wayne lived nearby, following Greene's example by moving from the North—in his case, Pennsylvania—to the South. Several onetime aides and fellow officers also lived in the vicinity. But Greene's pleasant portrayal of life as a gentleman farmer in the pleasant southern spring was not complete. Privately, he continued to fear for the future. "I am overwhelmed with difficulties and God knows when or where they will end," he admitted to Henry Knox. Greene petitioned Congress to relieve him of the debts owed to John Banks's creditors, and friends like Knox were agitating on his behalf.

All the while, tragedy and setback continued to stalk his doorstep. He lost fifty barrels of rice in a fire, and another forty-five sank in an accident on the Savannah River. Worse yet, in April, Caty—returned to her familiar state of pregnancy—fell, and she went into labor. The baby was premature and died soon after birth.

About two months later, the Greenes paid a social call on the general's former aide Nathaniel Pendleton in Savannah. They stayed the night and then set out for Muberry Grove the following day, June 12. It was a brutally hot day, more like August than late spring, but when they stopped at a friend's house for lunch, Greene insisted on inspecting his friend's plantation.

Hours later, he complained of a headache. He went to bed, but his condition only worsened. His doctors decided that Greene was suffering from sunstroke, and they bled him. Of course, their efforts were in vain. As Greene slipped in and out of consciousness, friends like Wayne and Pendleton rushed to see him, joining Caty at his bedside.

As the southern sun rose on June 19, Major General Nathanael Greene died in the company of his wife and friends. He was forty-four years old, still deeply in debt, still worried about the future prospects of his children. Anthony Wayne, his wife's future lover, was distraught. "My dear General Greene is no more," he told a friend. "Pardon my scrawl; my feelings are but too much affected, because I have seen a great and good man die."

Word quickly made its way northward. Richard Henry Lee, who resumed his political career in Congress, immediately sent word to Washington. "Your friend and second, the patriot Greene, is no more," he wrote from Philadelphia. "Universal grief reigns here. How hard is the fate of the United States to lose such a man in the middle of life! Irreparable loss!"

Washington grieved, not only for the man who had served so capably by his side but also for Caty, for his friend's children—including his namesake—and for his country. He told Jeremiah Wadsworth, Greene's friend and business partner, that he mourned "the death of this valuable character, especially at this crisis, when the political machine seems pregnant with the most awful events."

Lost was a voice for unity and purpose at a time when sectional and state differences threatened the young Republic. Lost was a war hero who, despite his proclaimed distaste for politics, certainly figured to play a prominent role in guiding the nation through its infancy. "The sudden termination of his life," Alexander Hamilton said, deprived the country of a "universal and pervading genius which qualified him not less for the Senate than for the field."

Had he lived, Greene very likely would have joined Hamilton in arguing for a strong, centralized government, for he had seen firsthand the weaknesses of the American confederation during the war: the inability of Congress to raise money for nothing less than national independence; the chaotic supply system that varied from state to state; the petty jealousies that poisoned relations between North and South. Washington would probably have chosen him as secretary of war, an honor that went instead to Henry Knox. His name surely would be better known today had he lived to help his peers in the shaping of the great American experiment.

Instead, on June 20, 1786, the body of this self-made, self-taught soldier and leader was brought to Savannah for a state funeral and burial.

Flags were ordered to half-mast, and the city shut down as the funeral procession moved slowly through the streets.

Nathanael Greene died deeply in debt, and years would pass before Congress finally forgave the money owed to John Banks's creditor. Caty personally lobbied Washington, Knox, and other friends to intervene with Congress, but even that action wasn't enough. Caty eventually lost the South Carolina plantation, Boone Barony, to settle other debts left over from the war years.

In his will, Nathanael Greene spoke of the education he so sorely missed and wished to provide his children. They were the words of an eighteenth-century man who believed in the American idea of merit and hard work, not hereditary privilege.

> As I am convinced that the happiness of my children will de-
> pend . . . [on] their education, it is my last will and earnest re-
> quest . . . that they will attend in a particular manner to the
> improvement of their understanding. As I hope my sons will
> come forward and take an active part in the affairs of their coun-
> try, their education should be liberal. My daughters should not
> be left [behind] . . . but above all things let their morals be at-
> tended to.

A few weeks after Greene's death, Congress, the body that Greene so often criticized for its inaction, formally proclaimed its grief at the passing of a hero, and in fine, moving words, it authorized construction of a suitable monument to him. The statue of Nathanael Greene was unveiled in Washington, D.C., in 1877, nearly a hundred years after his death.

NOTES

A Note on Sources

Nearly thirty years ago, scholars at the Rhode Island Historical Society and the University of North Carolina began publishing the vast and widely scattered correspondence of Major General Nathanael Greene. Twelve volumes have resulted, with one more to come. The bulk of the following citations are from this source—*The Papers of Nathanael Greene,* abbreviated *PNG*—and give the relevant volume and page numbers.

Other abbreviations used here are:

N-YHS	New-York Historical Society
NYPL	New York Public Library
PGW	Papers of George Washington, Library of Congress
PLC	Papers of Lord Cornwallis, University of Virginia
RIHS	Rhode Island Historical Society
WCL	William Clements Library, University of Michigan

Chapter One:

The Quaker General

6   "for God's sake": Hamilton, *The Papers of Alexander Hamilton*, 2:420–21.

Back home with the Greene family: *PNG*, 6:323–25.

"Poor Girl": Ibid., 6:391–92.

If, he told John Mathews: Ibid., 6:335–36.

7   "I commit this important Post": Ibid., 6:347–49.

"I shall be happy": Ibid., 6:350–51.

"Our felicity is not perfect": Ibid., 6:304–6.

"I declare": Ibid.

"O, sweet angel": Stegeman and Stegeman, *Caty*, 49.

8   "Who will that person be?": *PNG*, 6:380.

"Perhaps I should have gone": Ibid., 6:385.

9   "It is my wish": Ibid.

He wanted to return home: Ibid., 6:396.

10   He composed a "my dear Angel" letter: Ibid., 6:397–98.

"Though I do not write much": Ibid., 6:404–6.

11   "Could I leave you happy": Ibid., 6:415–16.

Chapter Two:

A Downright Democracy

14   "My Father": *PNG*, 1:46–50.

Nathanael Greene's descriptions of his father and his childhood are all from this letter to his friend Samuel Ward Jr.

16   He wrote to the earl of Dartmouth: Bartlett, *Records of the Colony of Rhode Island*, 7:182–84.

In fact, in a survey of five Rhode Island Towns: Lovejoy, *Rhode Island Politics and the American Revolution*, 16–17.

17   The colony's charter . . . gave Rhode Island residents: James, *The Colonial Metamorphoses in Rhode Island*, 50.

In reality, England interfered: Lovejoy, *Rhode Island Politics and the American Revolution*, 75.

The colony's charter promised: James, *The Colonial Metamorphoses in Rhode Island*, 50.

19   "You dance stiffly": George Washington Greene, *The Life of Major General Nathanael Greene*, 1:28. Hereinafter cited as Greene, *Life*.

20   "I lament": *PNG*, 1:46–50.

21   Often, according to George Washington Greene: Greene, *Life*, 1:14.

22   "Which one?": Ibid., 1:20.

23 "All government without the consent of the governed": van Doren, *The Portable Swift*, 193.

24 Parliament ordered: Knollenberg, *Origins of the American Revolution*, 142.

A Rhode Island merchant soon reported: Ibid., 181.

The document emphasized the importance of molasses: Simister, *The Fire's Center*, 14–15.

25 When the *Squirrel's* commander: Lovejoy, *Rhode Island Politics and the American Revolution*, 36.

26 Furthermore, he wrote: Bartlett, *Records of the Colony of Rhode Island*, 6:422–23.

A special supplement: *Newport Mercury*, Oct. 28, 1765.

27 Ward played the role: Ibid., Nov. 18, 1765.

Governor Ward informed London: Lovejoy, *Rhode Island Politics and the American Revolution*, 120.

28 Greene very likely wrote the petition: *PNG*, 1:9–10.

29 In his letters: Nathanael Greene's reading habits are discussed at length in Greene, *Life*, 1:22–39.

30 "To pursue Virtue": *PNG*, 1:23–25.

31 "Study to be wise": Ibid., 1:26–28.

Chapter Three:
The Making of a Rebel

33 Rhode Island authorities: Bancroft Collection, documents relative to Rhode Island, NYPL.

He complained: Simister, *The Fire's Center*, 44.

The merchant vessel *Fortune*: *PNG*, 1:33.

"If you do not go into the cabin": Greene, *Life*, 1:29–30.

34 In a letter to his friend Sammy Ward: Ibid., 26–27.

35 One prominent Rhode Islander: Lovejoy, *Rhode Island Politics and the American Revolution*, 158.

"I am . . . informed": Simister, *The Fire's Center*, 43.

"I do not receive instructions": Ibid., 44.

36 "I am the sheriff": Langguth, *Patriots*, 167.

One of the raiders: Greene, *Life*, 1:34.

"I have long feared": Langguth, *Patriots*, 169.

In the meantime: Bancroft Collection, documents relative to Rhode Island, NYPL.

37 "I was surrounded": *PNG,* 1:38–43.

"If Coventry ever was tolerable": Ibid., 1:44–46.

38 The royal commission: Eyewitness accounts of the burning of the *Gaspee* are compiled in Bartlett, *Records of the Colony of Rhode Island,* 7:68–77 and 182–85.

"I should be tempted": *PNG,* 1:51–53.

He told Sammy Ward: Ibid.

39 The minister's talk: *PNG,* 1:61.

"Priests and Levites": Ibid., 1:57–58.

The official record: Friends' minutes, 1751–1806, RIHS.

40 In two letters: *PNG,* 1:26–28; 51–53.

41 John Sherwood: Kimball, *The Correspondence of the Colonial Governors of Rhode Island,* 2:438.

In keeping with custom: Bancroft Collection, documents relative to Rhode Island, NYPL.

A correspondent: *Newport Mercury,* Mar. 21, 1774.

42 Britain's political leaders: *PNG,* 1:64–65.

One observer described her: Stegeman and Stegeman, *Caty,* 10.

43 The ceremony was small: *PNG,* 1:64.

44 Greene's was among eighty signatures: Ibid., 1:67–68.

Tradition has it: This story is told in nineteenth-century biographies by William Johnson and George Washington Greene, with no firsthand evidence.

With their red coats: Kentish Guard Papers, RIHS.

45 He immediately wrote: *PNG,* 1:75–76.

46 The bloodshed: Ibid., 1:79fn.

Greene's commission: Ibid., 1:78–79.

Chapter Four:
An Uncommon Degree of Zeal

48 They heard: Commager and Morris, *The Spirit of Seventy-six,* 92.

After news of the skirmishes: Ketchum, *The Winter Soldiers,* 49.

49 "The rebels": Harvey, *A Few Bloody Noses,* 160.

50 Greene told Thomas: *PNG,* 1:80.

51 Murray was accused: Ibid., 2:96.

In his orders: Ibid., 1:84.

A soldier from Connecticut: Ibid., 1:85.

52 His superiors testified: Greene, *Life,* 1:92.

52   "Let us in": Chidsey, *The Siege of Boston,* 64.
Appropriating money: *PNG,* 1:82.
He would have been happy: Ibid., 1:82–83.

53   He found that many captains: Ibid., 1:85.

54   "My task is hard": Ibid., 1:93.
Despite the discipline: Ibid.
While the Rhode Islanders remained: Ibid., 1:94.
While most of the troops: Commager and Morris, *The Spirit of Seventy-six,* 153.
Other American generals: *PNG,* 1:93.
In a letter to Jacob: Ibid.

55   A shocked Howe wrote: Wright Jr., *The Continental Army,* 20.
He dispatched an urgent message: *PNG,* 1:86.

56   To his brother Jacob: Ibid., 1:92.

58   "I hope we shall be taught": Ibid., 1:99.

59   "Familiarity between the officers and men": Washington to Congress, Sept. 22, 1775, PGW.
A disgusted Greene: *PNG,* 1:95.

60   In a far too candid letter: Commager and Morris, *The Spirit of Seventy-six,* 161.

60   The southerners were themselves puzzled: Thayer, *Nathanael Greene,* 71.
Washington "had not had time": *PNG,* 1:163–65.

61   "His Excellency": Ibid., 1:135.

62   True, Adams wrote: Langguth, *Patriots,* 309.
"Our troops are now very sickly": *PNG,* 1:105–6.
"Void [their] Exerment": Ibid., 1:108.

63   "Provisions bad": Ibid., 1:105–6.
"The fears and apprehensions": Ibid., 1:111–12.

64   "The Author is found": Ibid., 1:127.

65   "So far as regards the Preservation of the Army from cold": Washington to Congress, Sept. 21, 1775, PGW.

66   Then, Greene would contend: *PNG,* 1:194.

67   Henry Knox: Thayer, *Nathanael Greene,* 67.
In October 1775: *PNG,* 1:140.

68   "I would make it Treason": Ibid., 1:140–41.
"This is no time": Ibid., 1:171.

68   He urged Ward and
      Congress: Ibid., 1:177.

69   Of Franklin, Greene wrote:
      Ibid., 1:135–36.

70   "I fear the Colony": Ibid.,
      1:160.

      He told his brother Jacob:
      Ibid., 1:158.

71   If they did: Moses Brown's
      diary, RIHS; also
      published in *Rhode Island
      History*, vol. 15, no. 4,
      October 1956.

      "Our suffering": *PNG*, 1:173.

      Only now were the Americans
      learning: Commager and
      Morris, *The Spirit of
      Seventy-six*, 253–54.

72   "We never have been so
      weak": *PNG*, 1:174.

      His general orders: General
      orders, Jan. 1, 1776,
      PGW.

73   "We have just experienced":
      PNG, 1:178.

      "It is no time": Ibid.

74   "[Playing cards] brings on a
      Habit of Drinking": Ibid.,
      1:180.

      "I am as yellow as saffron":
      Ibid., 1:193.

76   "draw Beer for the Troops":
      Ibid., 1:208.

Chapter Five:
The Dark Part of Night

77   New York, he wrote: *PNG*,
      1:177.

78   "If any should be base
      enough": Ibid., 1:205.

      He forbade his soldiers: Ibid.

79   Greene dutifully dispatched
      word to his troops: Ibid.,
      1:206.

      Greene's troops: Ibid., 1:208.

80   Even if the British: Lee to
      Washington, Feb. 19,
      1776, Lee, *Papers of
      Charles Lee*, 1:308–10.

      After all, he noted: Lee to
      Washington, Mar. 3, 1776,
      ibid., 1:343–44.

81   They should do so "softly":
      PNG, 1:220.

      Local residents complained:
      Ibid., 1:212.

      "Complaints Having Been
      made": Ibid., 1:215.

      Greene was not one: Ibid.,
      1:212.

82   Knox condemned: Scheer and
      Rankin, *Rebels and
      Redcoats*, 143.

      "Tis nobly done": *PNG*,
      1:213.

84   Henry Knox told Lucy:
      Stegeman and Stegeman,
      Caty, 34.

85   Greene said that Adams's
      policy: *PNG*, 1:225.

      Adams replied: Ibid., 1:239.

      "As I have no desire": Ibid.,
      1:216.

      At one point, Greene accused
      Adams, and Congress:
      Ibid., 1:256.

86 "I spied": Flexner, *George Washington in the American Revolution,* 95.

87 "Vegetables . . . would be much more wholesome": *PNG,* 1:252.
"all Filth": Ibid., 1:267–68.
Washington said he hoped: Freeman, *George Washington,* 4:133.

88 He told Adams: *PNG,* 1:255–56.
"[It] is impossible": Ibid., 1:263.

89 Greene's complaints: Ibid., 1:264.
Still, the British waited: Langguth, *Patriots,* 377.
"The fair nymphs": Commager and Morris, *The Spirit of Seventy-six,* 413–14.

90 "Great humanity should be exercised": *PNG,* 1:283.
They would soon "feel my Resentment": Ibid., 1:287–88.
Soon after writing to Washington: Ibid., 1:288.
Within two days: Livingston to Washington, Aug. 17, 1776, PGW.

91 Greene sought to reassure his commander: Blodget to Washington, Aug. 18, 1776, ibid.

92 "Gracious God!": *PNG,* 1:291–92.

92 "I give it": Ibid., 1:294–96.

93 "This in my judgment": Flexner, *George Washington in the American Revolution,* 119.

94 Their performance so embarrassed Washington: *PNG,* 1:300.

95 As Greene noted: Ibid.

96 Washington's secretary wrote: Thayer, *Nathanael Greene,* 112.
"Providence, or some good honest fellow": Langguth, *Patriots,* 397.
"I apprehend the several retreats": *PNG,* 1:303–4.
"The policy of Congress": Ibid.

97 There was, he wrote, "a great change": Tretler, "The Making of a Revolutionary," 249.
"exhibit a Spectacle": *PNG,* 1:311–12.

98 "Here is a gentleman": Dann, *The Revolution Remembered,* 118–19.

100 Although he had told Greene: *PNG,* 1:339–40.
"If we cannot prevent vessels passing up": Ibid., 1:342–43.
"I cannot conceive": Flexner, *George Washington in the American Revolution,* 147.

100 Still, Washington hesitated:
Scheer and Rankin, *Rebels
and Redcoats*, 200.
Lee boldly asserted: *PNG*,
1:347.
"I cannot help": Lee to Reed,
Nov. 16, 1776, Lee, *Papers
of Charles Lee*, 2:283–84.

101 They found themselves:
PNG, 1:352.

102 In it, he did not spare Greene:
Washington to Congress,
Nov. 16, 1776, PGW.
"Oh, General": Flexner,
*George Washington in the
American Revolution*,
152.

103 He claimed that other officers
accused Greene: Lee to
Washington, Nov. 19,
1776, Lee, *Papers of
Charles Lee*, 2:286–88.
"I feel mad": *PNG*, 1:321–22.
"what is said": Ibid.

104 Washington later estimated:
Washington to Congress,
Nov. 19, 1776, PGW.

105 "We retreated to Hackensack":
PNG, 1:362.
"Our people": Commager
and Morris, *The Spirit of
Seventy-six*, 496–97.
the American army "is
broken": Ibid.
"Entre nous": Langguth,
Patriots, 404

106 "These are the times":
Commager and Morris,
The Spirit of Seventy-six,
505.

106 "Fortune seems to frown":
PNG, 1:368–69.
a painting of a rising sun:
Thayer, *Nathanael Greene*,
137. The anecdote is not
verified by any firsthand
testimony.

Chapter Six:
Victory or Death

108 "I hope to give the Enimy":
PNG, 1:375.

109 he noted with "satisfaction":
Ibid., 1:376.
The general, Greene told
Caty: Ibid., 1:368.
Showing off his self-taught
erudition: Ibid., 1:372.

110 "one of the severest" storms:
Ibid., 2:4.

112 "This is an important
period": Ibid., 1:377.

113 "Should we get possession of
the Jerseys": Ibid.
One soldier recalled:
Commager and Morris,
The Spirit of Seventy-six,
519.
"My brave fellows": Ibid.
"God Almighty": *PNG*, 2:4.

114 "This is the greatest
evidence": Ibid.
"[We] have great reason":
Ibid., 2:3.

115 "Push on, boys": Greene,
Life, 1:298.

115 "It appeared to me": Thayer, *Nathanael Greene,* 148.

116 "This line of conduct": *PNG,* 1:374–75.

"The day . . . is our own": Flexner, *George Washington in the American Revolution,* 185.

117 "Great credit is due": *PNG,* 2:3–4.

"The achievements of Washington and his little band": Leckie, *George Washington's War,* 333.

118 "I am exceeding happy": *PNG,* 2:7.

He was installed in the home: Greene, *Life,* 1:306.

"I am unhappy": *PNG,* 2:6–7.

119 Furious civilians: Ibid., 2:4–5.

There, he told Washington: Ibid., 2:24–25.

120 In mid-February: Ibid., 2:26–27.

A loyalist judge: Scheer and Rankin, *Rebels and Redcoats,* 222.

"This . . . is the State of the War": *PNG,* 2:56–57.

According to a letter: Craig to Wayne, Feb. 16, 1777, Bancroft Collection, Wayne Papers, NYPL.

121 "not so much for the annoyance of the Enemy": *PNG,* 2:56–57.

121 Congress passed a resolution: Greene, *Life,* 1:336.

"Could I accomplish": Ibid., 1:337.

"There is not a state": *PNG,* 2:10.

122 "I am sensible": Ibid., 2:29.

In his reply: Ibid., 2:37.

Greene told Adams: Ibid., 2:31.

123 Adams countered: Ibid., 2:40.

Washington explained to Congress: Greene, *Life,* 1:338–39.

Washington told him: *PNG,* 2:44–45.

"There is so much deliberation": Ibid., 2:46–48.

124 Several weeks later: Ibid., 2:87–88.

He was alarmed to find them "insufficient": Ibid.

When he returned: Ibid., 2:50.

He felt duty-bound: Ibid., 2:54–55.

125 "It is to be regretted": Ibid., 2:59–60.

126 "What has kept them": Ibid., 2:60.

"I was almost thunderstruck": Ibid., 2:66–67.

He tried a little tenderness: Ibid.

127 "O, how my heart": Ibid., 2:83.

127 "But remember when you
write to Mrs. Knox": Ibid.,
2:84.

128 "No free people": Ibid.,
2:98–99.

129 He, too, thought: Ibid.,
2:103.
In the same letter: Ibid.,
2:98–99.
Once again, Adams was
on Greene's side: Ibid.,
2:103.
He told his brother: Ibid.,
2:104.

130 "A report is circulating":
Ibid., 2:109.
On July 7, Congress passed:
Journals of the Continental
Congress, July 7, 1777,
Library of Congress.

131 What's more: McCullough,
John Adams, 195.
"I never before took hold of a
pen": *PNG*, 2:111–14.

132 "Phylistines are upon thee":
Ibid., 2:101.
"I can plainly see": Ibid.,
2:121.
Philadelphia, he wrote: Ibid.,
2:140–41.

133 "I am in hopes": Ibid., 2:149.

Chapter Seven:
The Cries of the People

134 "good health": *PNG*,
2:149.

136 Summoning the frustrations:
Ibid., 2:162–63.

136 "Here are some of the most
distressing scenes": Ibid.,
2:155–56.
"dreaded the appearance":
Ibid., 2:156fn.

137 "I am exceedingly fatigued":
Ibid., 2:155–56.

139 "When I came upon the
ground": Ibid., 2:470–72.
"I expect the next action":
Ibid., 2:162–63.

140 "You, sir": Thayer,
Nathanael Greene,
196–97.
He denounced Greene:
Flexner, *George
Washington in the
American Revoluntion*,
226.

141 "My sweet Angel": *PNG*,
2:162–63.
"Let us move": Thayer,
Nathanael Greene, 198.

142 "entertained an exalted
opinion": Ibid.
"The General does want":
Ibid.
he told his generals:
Proceedings of a Council
of General Officers, Sept.
23, 1777, PGW.

143 "it was prudent": Proceedings
of a Council of General
Officers, Sept. 28, 1777,
PGW.

144 "be in readiness": Ibid.

147 "the enemy kept": Thayer,
Nathanael Greene, 203.

147 General Wayne described the
     battle: Ibid., 204.

148 Gates, Rush said: Flexner,
     *George Washington in the
     American Revolution,* 238.
     "Oh, Heaven!": McCullough,
     John Adams, 173.
     Greene snarled: *PNG,*
     2:259–61.
     "[The] foundation": Ibid.,
     2:194–96.

149 "If the Southern Militia":
     Ibid.
     "I have been . . . told": Ibid.,
     2:259–61.

150 "Honor and laurels": Ibid.,
     2:181.
     "[Close] in the
     Neighbourhood": Ibid.,
     2:189–90.

151 "One foot farther": Ibid.,
     2:194–96.
     "If it is possible": Ibid.,
     2:202–3.
     In his reply: Ibid., 2:208.

152 "I cannot promise": Ibid.,
     2:208–10.
     "I shall not be disappointed":
     Ibid., 2:224.
     "If we retire": Ibid.,
     2:225–28.

153 "However desirable": Ibid.,
     2:231–36.

Chapter Eight:
Low Intrigue

155 "General Mifflin": *PNG,*
     2:259–61.

155 Mifflin had complained:
     Flexner, *George
     Washington in the
     American Revolution,*
     225.
     And the Adams cousins:
     Greene, *Life,* 2:33.
     He referred to Greene: Thayer,
     Nathanael Greene, 213.

156 When Conway complained:
     Conway to Gates, Jan. 4,
     1777, Horatio Gates
     Papers, N-YHS.
     "My feelings": Freeman,
     George Washington,
     4:591–92.

157 A certain faction: *PNG,* 2:
     259–71.
     He told other officers: *PNG,*
     2:259–61.
     "the greatest novice": Ibid.,
     2:242–245.
     "men of honor": Ibid.,
     2:252–53.
     "if he fell": Ibid.,
     2:249–51.

158 Clark told Greene: Ibid.
     Lucy Knox . . . observed:
     Thayer, *Nathanael Greene,*
     223.
     The shuttling of his children:
     PNG, 2:349–51.

159 "In the middle": Stegeman
     and Stegeman, *Caty,* 54.
     Greene told Washington:
     PNG, 2:241–42.

160 "The Quarter Master
     General": Ibid., 2:259–61.

160   "No meat!": Scheer and
      Rankin, *Rebels and
      Redcoats*, 291.

161   "the situation of the Camp":
      PNG, 2:280.
      "Cattle and Sheep": Ibid.,
      2:281.

162   "[The] Inhabitants cry out":
      Ibid., 2:285.
      "by way of Example": Ibid.
      "the least neglect": Ibid.,
      2:283.
      His instructions: Ibid.

163   Confronted with evidence:
      Ibid., 2:286–87.
      "I sent on to Camp": Ibid.,
      2:288–89.

164   "The troops are getting
      naked": Ibid., 2:293–94.

165   As he later told Washington:
      Thayer, *Nathanael Greene*,
      227.
      He told Knox: *PNG*, 2:307.
      "All of you": Ibid., 2:376.
      Besides, the job: Ibid.,
      2:293–94.

166   He confessed: Ibid., 2:326.

167   "Money becomes more":
      Ibid., 2:227.
      "I have spent": Ibid.,
      2:300–4.

168   "General Conway is": Ibid.,
      2:422–23.

170   Greene and his two capable
      deputies: Ibid.,
      2:324–25.

171   "In forming your magazines":
      Ibid., 2:327–38.

171   A "large Sum of Money":
      Ibid., 2:330–31.

172   Nathanael promised: Ibid.,
      2:404–5.
      "To git our goods": Ibid.,
      2:401–2.
      "family secrets": Ibid.,
      2:349–50.
      "I am At A Loos": Ibid.,
      2:338–42.

173   "I Fear Billy": Ibid.

174   "Mrs. Knox": Ibid.,
      2:443–44.
      "It has been": Ibid.,
      2:470–73.

175   "I must confess": Ibid.,
      2:446–47.

176   "Delightful": Boatner,
      *Encyclopedia of the
      American Revolution*, 722.

177   "We have suffered": *PNG*,
      2:449–52.

Chapter Nine:
"It Wounds My Feelings"

178   "It would be agreeable":
      PNG, 2:317.

180   "You express": Ibid.,
      2:459–60.
      When several days had passed:
      Ibid., 2:461–63.

181   "Your Excellency has made
      me": Ibid.

182   "I can, and do assure you":
      Ibid., 2:464.

183   "[In] justice": Washington to
      Congress, Aug. 3, 1778,
      PGW.

184 "You are the most happy
man": *PNG*, 2:466–67.
"I am . . . as busy": Ibid.,
2:478.

185 The Frenchman was eager:
Ibid., 2:477fn.
A victory in Rhode Island:
Flexner, *George
Washington in the
American Revolution*, 325.

187 "I am sorry": Greene, *Life*,
2:114–15.

188 "This movement":
Commager and Morris,
The Spirit of Seventy-six,
718–19.
Greene, too, was furious:
PNG, 2:491–92.
"The Garrison is important":
Ibid., 2:480–82.

189 The fleet's retreat: Ibid.,
2:487–89.
American arms . . . would
prevail: Ibid., 2:490fn.

190 Greene was "sensible": Ibid.,
2:491fn.
Washington, who readily
agreed: Ibid., 2:505–6.
"I beg you": Ibid.
Choose three hundred
experienced troops: Ibid.,
2:493–96.

191 "We . . . put the enemy":
Ibid., 2:499–502.

192 "To behold our fellows":
Ibid., 2:506.
He wrote another discreet
letter: Ibid., 2:526.

192 The Americans were relieved:
Ibid., 2:530.
It was exhausting: Ibid.,
2:523.
"My appointment is
flattering": Ibid.,
2:529–30.

193 "all the tender feelings":
Ibid., 1:303–4.
"I am [persuaded]": Ibid.,
2:529–30.
When he heard complaints:
Ibid., 2:546–47.

194 "This is a [malevolent] age":
Ibid., 2:539–40.
A transfer: Ibid., 2:529–30.

195 He desperately wanted her to
come: Ibid., 3:66.
"this pleasure": Ibid.
"I [dined] yesterday":
Ibid.

196 "He is a fine, hardy fellow":
Ibid., 3:122–23.
"His Excellency": Ibid.,
3:353–54.
It hurt him: Ibid., 4:321–24.

197 He told John Hancock: Ibid.,
3:121–22.
"They are [always]
beginning": Ibid., 3:235.
"We had the most splendid
entertainments": Ibid.
"dined at one table": Ibid.,
3:233.

198 "To scourge the Indians":
Ibid., 3:144–45.
He had predicted: Ibid.,
2:546–54.

199 "I have desired Congress":
Ibid., 3:425–28.
"I am sorry": Ibid., 3:428–29.
200 "[It] would be for your
advantage": Ibid.,
4:130–31.
"Mrs. Greene is on her way
Home": Ibid., 4:165–67.
The march to a new camp:
Ibid., 4:125.

Chapter Ten:
"O, This War!"
203 "[It] is my wish": *PNG*,
3:403.
204 The patriot-merchant Robert
Morris: Morris to Deane,
June 9, 1777, Barnabas
Deane Papers, N-YHS.
205 did he not have "the same
right": *PNG*, 4:265.
206 "The military reason": Ibid.,
4:358–60.
"Many times I was almost
ready": Ibid., 4:321–24.
207 "How tenderly would I nurse
you": Ibid.
"I therefore laid down my
pen": Ibid., 4:342–45.
"Methinks you can": Ibid.
"I strongly recommend":
Ibid.
"I wish to hear": Ibid.
208 "I am exceeding unhappy":
Ibid., 4:464–65.
210 "Some people in this
neighbourhood": Ibid.,
5:179.

211 In a petition: Nathanael
Greene Papers, series 3,
American Philosophical
Society, Philadelphia.
Greene sensed that yet
another crisis: *PNG*,
5:187–88.
"We are at this time": Ibid.,
5:181–83.
212 He concluded that the law
was against him: Ibid.,
5:192–93.
"I regret that the Inhabitants":
Ibid., 5:197–98.
On December 19: Ibid.,
5:187–88.
213 "They receive us with
coldness": Ibid.,
5:209–10.
"Our Army is without Meat
or Bread": Ibid., 5:230–31.
"The Army is upon the eve
of disbanding": Ibid.,
5:243–44.
214 If the roads were not clogged:
Ibid., 5:236.
"Such weather as we have
had": Ibid., 5:252–53.
215 He proposed *Clinton:* Ibid.,
5:257–59.
216 Not surprisingly, Greene's
friend and aide Charles
Pettit: Ibid., 5:339–41.
He sent a teasing letter: Ibid.,
5:367.
"The business of my
Department": Ibid.,
5:429–30.

216   "Their conduct": Ibid.
      He told Washington: Ibid.,
         5:471.
      He mentioned to Greene:
         Ibid., 5:479–80.

217   With a nod to his friend
         Thomas Paine: Ibid.,
         5:491–92.
      His presence in the capital:
         Ibid., 5:503–4.
      During a private debate: Ibid.,
         5:594fn.
      "I feel my self . . . soured":
         Ibid., 5:532–33.

218   "I have been among the great
         at Philadelphia": Ibid.,
         5:520–21.
      "Truth and righteousness":
         Ibid., 5:517–18.

219   "Our distress": Ibid.,
         5:582–83.
      "Let go of my hand":
         Stegeman and Stegeman,
         Caty, 76.

220   Greene confided to the
         governor of Rhode Island:
         PNG, 5:582–83.

221   "Society," he explained to
         Caty: Ibid., 6:14.

223   The spy, Greene observed:
         Ibid., 6:31.
      "Their object:" Ibid.
      "The Enemy are out": Ibid.,
         6:32.

224   "The Militia to our aid":
         Ibid., 6:33.
      "Being thus advantageously
         posted": Ibid., 6:37.

224   In his general orders: Ibid.,
         6:41.

225   He warned Congress:
         Washington to Joseph
         Jones, May 31, 1780,
         PGW.
      In a letter dated July 26:
         PNG, 6:155–57.

226   Joseph Jones, a member of
         Congress: Ibid.,
         6:154fn.
      Henry Laurens asked: Ibid.
      Wearily, the commander in
         chief: Thayer, *Nathannel
         Greene*, 276.

227   "The . . . plunder": *PNG*,
         6:233–34.
      "There is so much
         wickedness and villiany":
         Ibid., 6:212–13.
      "We are starving": Ibid.,
         6:268.

228   "In my absence": Ibid.,
         6:289–90.
      "I will venture": Ibid.,
         6:304–5.
      At nine o'clock: Greene's
         orderly book, July 30–Oct.
         8, 1780, NYPL.

229   "Arnold has fled to the
         Enemy": *PNG*, 6:312.
      The discovery of Arnold's
         treason: Ibid.,
         6:319–20.
      He broke the news: Ibid.,
         6:314.

230   On October 1, the tribunal
         found: Greene's orderly

book, July 30–Oct. 8,
1780, NYPL.

230 André, he said: Bobrick,
Angel in the Whirlwind,
419.

"I think I am giving you a
general": Washington to
Mathews, Oct. 23, 1780,
PGW.

Chapter Eleven:
"The Prospect Is Dismal"

232 "I see but little prospect":
PNG, 6:447–49.

"I [entirely] approve": Ibid.,
6:469–71.

233 If the British defeated
Greene: Lee, *The
Revolutionary War
Memoirs of General Henry
Lee,* 247.

234 "I believe the views": *PNG,*
6:488–89.

"Congress can furnish no
money": Ibid., 6:447–48.

235 "[If] there is not public spirit
enough": Ibid.

Cornwallis told his superiors:
Morrill, *Southern
Campaigns of the American
Revolution,* 112.

"They promise me": *PNG,*
6:478–79.

236 "Our prospects with respect
to supplies": Ibid.,
6:485–87.

237 "I cannot contemplate": Ibid.,
6:488–89.

237 "My only consolation":
Ibid.

238 Greene dispatched men:
Ibid., 6:512–14.

239 "Your Services in the lower
Part of South Carolina":
Ibid., 6:519–22.

In describing the "condition
of this army": Ibid.,
6:542–45.

He sent the governor a
blistering letter: Ibid.,
6:530–31.

240 "[While the] subject you write
upon": Ibid., 6:596–97.

Within a few months: Ibid.,
7:5–6.

Greene told Samuel
Huntington: Ibid., 7:7–10.

"The Gentleman": Ibid.,
6:516.

242 They were too weak: Ibid.,
7:18–19.

"There is not a single fruit-
tree": Stegeman and
Stegeman, *Caty,* 85.

"If you will entrust your
letters": Ibid.

"I will not be so impolite":
Ibid., 87–88.

243 "I am posted": *PNG,*
7:16.

Falling back on his youthful
study: Ibid., 7:22.

"When I left": Ibid., 7:17–18.

244 "attempt any thing":
Cornwallis to Rawdon,
Dec. 28, 1780, PLC.

244 He would later write: Bobrick, *Angel in the Whirlwind*, 428.

He assured Cornwallis: Rawdon to Cornwallis, Jan. 11, 1781, PLC.

245 "Amidst the complicated dangers": Freeman, *George Washington*, 5:261.

In fact, Cornwallis encouraged his subordinate: Cornwallis to Tarleton, Jan. 2, 1781, PLC.

"Col. Tarlton is said to be on his way": *PNG*, 7:106.

246 "Just hold up your heads": Morrill, *Southern Campaigns of the American Revolution*, 127–28.

247 "The Troops I had the Honor to command": *PNG*, 7:152–55.

Greene told his friend James Varnum: Ibid., 7:187–88.

248 "Then he is ours!": Leckie, *George Washington's War*, 606.

He was alarmed: *PNG*, 7:192.

"The people have been so harrassed": Ibid., 7:225–26.

249 "Neither will you": Leckie, *George Washington's War*, 606.

"What! Alone, general?": Ibid., 608. Thayer's comments on this anecdote

are in his biography of Nathanael Greene, 313.

250 "His pen never rested": Thayer, *Nathanael Greene*, 314.

"badly armed": *PNG*, 7:261–62.

251 "[It] was determined": Ibid.

"We have no provisions": Ibid., 7:267–69.

252 "All our troops are over": Leckie, *George Washington's War*, 611.

"To have effected a retreat": Commager and Morris, *The Spirit of Seventy-six*, 1160.

Tarleton would later write: Scheer and Rankin, *Rebels and Redcoats*, 440.

"ill-suited to enter": Conrad, "Nathanael Greene and the Southern Campaigns," 140.

253 Cornwallis explained to London: *PNG*, 7:416.

In Late February: Ibid., 369–70.

But, Henry Lee later recalled: Lee, *The Revolutionary War Memoirs of General Henry Lee*, 264.

254 "I have been obliged": *PNG*, 7:419–20.

He kept Washington informed: Ibid., 7:422–23.

254 "Good heavens, Colonel":
Greene, *Life*, 3:186–87.
"violent inflamation:" *PNG*,
7:395.

255 Not surprisingly, he told Lee:
Ibid.
As Greene told Jefferson:
Ibid., 7:419–20.
"I expect Lord Cornwallis":
Ibid., 7:324–25.

257 "Three rounds": Scheer and
Rankin, *Rebels and
Redcoats*, 445–46.

260 "Our Men": *PNG*,
7:433–35.
"Like Peter the Great": Lewis
Jr. to Lewis Sr., Dec. 29,
1780, Morris, *Letters of
Lewis Morris*.
"Another such victory":
Commager and Morris,
The Spirit of Seventy-six,
1160.
"some consolation": *PNG*,
7:446.
"I had not the honor": Ibid.,
7:446–47.
"I was born": Ibid.,
7:469–70.

261 "It is my intention": Ibid.,
7:461.
"In this critical and
distressing situation":
Ibid., 7:481.

262 "I am quite tired": Commager
and Morris, *The Spirit
of Seventy-six*, 1168.

Chapter Twelve:
Victory

264 "Don't be surprised": *PNG*,
8:xi.
Greene told Baron von
Steuben: Ibid., 8:22–23.
"If I can get supplies": Ibid.
"I have been anxiously
waiting": Ibid., 8:129–32.
"[On] this our whole
operation will depend":
Ibid., 8:12.
Although Sumter assured
Greene: Ibid., 8:66.

265 "I . . . regard your affairs":
Washington to Greene,
Apr. 19, 1781, PGW.
"We are at the end": Flexner,
*George Washington in the
American Revolution*, 409.
Greene told a sympathetic
Jefferson: *PNG*, 8:165–67.

266 The Crown's men: Thayer,
Nathanael Greene, 335.
"My greatest dependence":
PNG, 8:118.
Greene inspected Rawdon's
defenses: Ibid., 8:135.

268 One of Greene's aides: Ibid.,
8:159fn.

269 Bitterly, Greene lashed out:
Ibid., 9:134–36.
He confessed to Reed: Ibid.
"You write as if you thought":
Ibid., 8:173–74.
To Washington, Greene
confessed: Ibid.,
8:185–86.

269   "It is true": Ibid., 8:230–31.

270   "Congress [seems] to have lost sight": Ibid., 8:225–27.

Feeling very sorry for himself: Ibid., 8:227–29.

271   The general greeted Dudley: Dann, *The Revolution Remembered*, 224.

"We fight": *PNG*, 8:167–68.

272   "I depend upon your pushing matters": Ibid., 8:249.

"The brilliant repeated successes": Thayer, *Nathanael Greene*, 353.

He told John Rutledge: *PNG*, 8:256.

273   "The Idea of exterminating the Tories": Ibid., 8:349–50.

In an open letter: Ibid., 8:349.

274   "[The] fortifications are so strong": Ibid., 8:299–300.

275   "It is mortifying": Ibid., 8:419–22.

"Had we not moved this way": Ibid.

276   "The difficulties which you daily encounter": Washington to Greene, June 1, 1781, PGW.

"Our army has been frequently beaten": *PNG*, 9:41–42.

277   "I hope I have convinced the world": Ibid.

277   "Your popularity": Ibid., 8:494–98.

"would require a guard": Ibid., 9:35–37.

278   Lafayette made it clear: Ibid., 9:172–74.

279   And he stayed in constant touch: Ibid., 8:446.

280   Stewart later noted: Ibid., 9:334.

281   A "most tremendous fire": Ibid., 9:328–34.

As Greene monitored: Ibid.

284   He stated that . . . he had "left on the field of action": Ibid.

It was . . . "a most bloody battle": Ibid., 9:358.

A British officer: Conrad, "Nathanael Greene and the Southern Campaigns," 256.

285   Even before Eutaw Springs: *PNG*, 9:323.

"How happy I am": Ibid., 9:429.

Congress . . . awarded him a gold medal": Ibid., 9:520–21.

286   A congressional resolution: Lee, *The Revolutionary War Memoirs of General Henry Lee*, 474.

"How you have contrived": *PNG*, 9:317–18.

"[Without] an army": Thayer, *Nathanael Greene*, 381.

287 "This failure": *PNG*,
9:408–10.
His friend James Varnum:
Ibid., 9:501.
"I beg leave": Ibid., 9:519.

288 "It was a happy fight":Ibid.,
9:507–9.

Chapter Thirteen:
Forging a Nation

289 "Oh, God!": Commager and
Morris, *The Spirit of
Seventy-six,* 1244.

290 "Numbers of brave fellows":
PNG, 9:482–83.
Steuben, writing from
Virginia: Ibid., 9:532–34.
The system worked: Ibid.,
9:316.
These measures won the
attention: Ibid.
"We are in the greatest
distress":Ibid., 9:606–7.

291 Greene asked North Carolina:
Ibid., 9:559–61.
Among those advocating for
Greene: Ibid., 9:313–15.
"The more I am in the
Army": Ibid., 9:559–601.

293 While patriots had "good
reason to be offended":
Ibid., 9:452–54.
Greene recommended: Ibid.,
9:456–58.
Although he held little regard:
Ibid.
"We Military men:"
Ibid.

294 "I am apprehensive": Ibid.,
10:61–62.
Washington was in
Philadelphia: Ibid.
When Caty finally left
Philadelphia: Ibid., 10:63.

295 "They . . . disgraced
themselves": Ibid., 9:649.

296 "I have the pleasure": Ibid.,
10:17.
"The natural strength of this
country": Ibid., 10:21–22.

297 Of a population: Boatner,
*Encyclopedia of the
American Revolution,* 883.
Greene proposed that slaves:
PNG, 10:21–23.
In a letter to Lighthorse Harry
Lee: Ibid., 10:12–13.
The northern states: Ibid.,
10:228–29.

298 Although Rutledge was a
friend and ally: Conrad,
"Nathanael Greene and the
Southern Campaigns,"
308.
In the middle: *PNG,*
10:230fn.
"The northern people":
Ibid.

299 "This Country affords":
Ibid., 11:58.

300 "After almost two years
absence": Ibid., 11:60–61.
Greene blamed this injustice:
Ibid.
"I act with decision": Ibid.,
11:100–1.

301 "The general has observed": Ibid., 11:576.

Although she was not as desperately sick: Ibid., 11:577.

"We are very much indebted": Ibid., 11:627–28.

302 But, he wrote: Ibid., 11:682–84.

In late September: Ibid., 11:709.

303 "It is with pleasure": Ibid., 12:419–20.

"Every ear feels": Ibid., 12:626–27.

304 "We have trod": I am grateful to Elizabeth Stevens of the RIHS, an assistant editor of the Nathanael Greene Papers, who found this letter and shared it with me.

Chapter Fourteen:
Unfinished Business

308 "He was our boon companion": Stegeman and Stegeman, *Caty,* 10.

He told the governor: *PNG,* 12:379–82.

He told Washington: Greene to Washington, Aug. 29, 1784, PGW.

309 "I tremble at my own situation": Stegeman and Stegeman, *Caty,* 115.

309 He told an audience: Thayer, *Nathanael Greene,* 422.

310 He told the Speaker: *PNG,* 12:478–79.

Greene told Robert Morris: Greene to Morris, Jan. 9, 1784, Nathanael Greene Papers, WCL.

He betrayed no sense: Greene, *Life,* 3:520.

In March 1784: Mifflin to Indian Commissioners, Mar. 6, 1784, Journals of the Continental Congress, Library of Congress.

311 The society was made up of former officers: Boatner, *Encyclopedia of the American Revolution,* 229.

Washington fairly begged Greene: Washington to Greene, Mar. 20, 1784, PGW.

Greene did not let down: Thayer, *Nathanael Greene,* 433.

He informed his lawyer: Greene to Robert Forsyth, Oct. 2, 1784, Nathanael Greene Papers, WCL.

312 his "honor and reputation": Washington to Greene, May 20, 1785, PGW.

"The prospect is delightful": Francis Vinton Greene, *General Greene,* 311.

312   "It is a busy time": Thayer, *Nathanael Greene*, 441–42.

313   "I am overwhelmed": Greene to Knox, Mar. 12, 1786, Henry Knox Papers, Massachusetts Historical Society.

314   "My dear General Greene": Thayer, *Nathanael Greene*, 445.

314   "Your friend and second": Francis Vinton Greene, *General Greene*, 313.

He told Jeremiah Wadsworth: Washington to Wadsworth, Oct. 22, 1786, PGW.

"The sudden termination": Francis Vinton Greene, *General Greene*, 315–16.

315   "As I am convinced": Nathanael Greene papers, RIHS, ms. 985.

BIBLIOGRAPHY

Manuscript Collections

Abeel, James. Papers. New Jersey Historical Society, Newark, N.J.

Bancroft Collection. Includes the papers of Francis Marion, Anthony Wayne, and documents relative to Rhode Island. New York Public Library, New York.

Continental Congress. Journals. Library of Congress, Washington, D.C.

Cornwallis, Lord Charles. Papers. University of Virginia, Charlottesville.

Friends minutes, 1751–1806. Rhode Island Historical Society, Providence.

Gates, Horatio. Papers. New-York Historical Society, New York.

Greene, Nathanael. Papers. American Philosophical Society, Philadelphia; Rhode Island Historical Society, Providence; New York Public Library, New York; and William Clements Library, Ann Arbor, Mich.

Jefferson, Thomas. Papers. Library of Congress, Washington, D.C.

Kentish Guard Papers. Rhode Island Historical Society, Providence.

Knox, Henry. Papers. Massachusetts Historical Society, Boston, Mass.

Quartermaster Papers. David Library of the American Revolution, Washington's Crossing, Pa.

Washington, George. Papers. Library of Congress, Washington, D.C.

Published Primary Sources

Bartlett, John R. *Records of the Colony of Rhode Island and Providence Plantations in New England.* 10 vols. Providence, 1856–65.

Greene, Nathanael. *The Papers of Nathanael Greene.* Edited by Richard K. Showman and Dennis M. Conrad. 12 vols. Chapel Hill: University of North Carolina Press, 1976–2002.

Hamilton, Alexander. *The Papers of Alexander Hamilton.* Edited by Harold Syrett. 26 vols. New York: Columbia University Press, 1961–79.

Kimball, Gertrude Selwyn. *The Correspondence of the Colonial Governors of Rhode Island, 1732–1775.* 2 vols. Freeport, N.Y.: Books for Libraries Press (reprint), 1969.

Lee, Charles. *Papers of Charles Lee.* 4 vols. New York: New-York Historical Society, 1872–75.

Morris, Lewis. *Letters of Lewis Morris.* New York: New-York Historical Society, 1875.

Thompson, Theodora J., ed. *The State Records of South Carolina: Journals of the House of Representatives.* Columbia,: University of South Carolina Press, 1977.

Secondary Sources

Babits, Lawrence E. *A Devil of a Whipping: The Battle of Cowpens.* Chapel Hill: University of North Carolina Press, 1998.

Boatner, Mark M. *Encyclopedia of the American Revolution.* Mechanicsburg, Pa.: Stackpole Books, 1994.

Bobrick, Benson. *Angel in the Whirlwind.* New York: Simon & Schuster, 1997.

Brookhiser, Richard: *Founding Father.* New York: Free Press, 1997.

Buchanan, John. *The Road to Guilford Courthouse.* New York: John Wiley, 1997.

Chidsey, Donald Barr. *The Siege of Boston.* New York: Crown, 1966.

Commager, Henry Steele, and Richard B. Morris. eds. *The Spirit of Seventy-six.* Edison, N.J.: Castle Books, 2002 (reprint).

Dann, John C., ed. *The Revolution Remembered.* Chicago: University of Chicago Press, 1980.

Edgar, Walter. *Partisans and Redcoats.* New York: William Morrow, 2001.

Fleming, Thomas: *The Forgotten Victory: The Battle for New Jersey, 1780.* Pleasantville, N.Y.: Reader's Digest Press, 1973.

Flexner, James Thomas. *George Washington in the American Revolution.* Boston: Little, Brown, 1967.

Fischer, David Hackett. *Washington's Crossing*. New York: Oxford University
    Press, 2004.

Freeman, Douglas Southall. *George Washington: A Biography*. 7 vols. New York:
    Scribner, 1948–57.

Gaustad, Edwin S. *Liberty of Conscience: Roger Williams in America*. Valley
    Forge, Pa.: Judson Press, 1999.

Greene, Francis Vinton. *General Greene*. Port Washington, N.Y.: Kennikat Press,
    1970 (reprint).

Greene, George Washington. *The Life of Major General Nathanael Greene*. 3 vols.
    Boston: Houghton Mifflin, 1890.

Greenman, Jeremiah. *Diary of a Common Soldier in the American Revolution*.
    DeKalb: Northern Illinois University Press, 1978.

Gutstein, Morris A. *To Bigotry No Sanction*. New York: Bloch, 1958.

Harvey, Robert. *A Few Bloody Noses*. Woodstock, N.Y.: Overlook Press, 2002.

James, Sydney V. *The Colonial Metamorphoses in Rhode Island*. Hanover, N.H.:
    University Press of New England, 2000.

Ketchum, Richard M. *Decisive Day: The Battle for Bunker Hill*. Garden City,
    N.Y.: Doubleday, 1974.

———. *The Winter Soldiers*. New York: Henry Holt, 1973.

Knollenberg, Bernhard. *Origin of the American Revolution*. New York: Macmillan,
    1960.

Langguth, A. J. *Patriots*. New York: Simon & Schuster, 1988.

Leckie, Robert. *George Washington's War: The Saga of the American Revolution*.
    New York: Harper Perennial, 1992.

Lee, Henry. *The Revolutionary War Memoirs of General Henry Lee*. New York: Da
    Capo Press, 1998 (reprint).

Lovejoy, David S. *Rhode Island Politics and the American Revolution*. Providence,
    R.I.: Brown University Press, 1958.

McCullough, David. *John Adams*. New York: Simon & Schuster, 2001.

Middlekauff, Robert. *The Glorious Cause*. New York: Oxford University Press, 1982.

Morrill, Dan L. *Southern Campaigns of the American Revolution*. Mount Pleasant,
    S.C.: Nautical and Aviation Publishing Company of America, 1993.

Schecter, Barnet. *The Battle for New York*. New York: Walker, 2002.

Scheer, George F., and Hugh F. Rankin. *Rebels and Redcoats*. Cleveland: World,
    1967.

Simister, Florence Parker. *The Fire's Center: Rhode Island in the Revolutionary
    Era, 1763–1790*. Providence: Rhode Island Bicentennial Foundation,
    1979.

Stegeman, John F., and Janet A. Stegeman. *Caty: A Biography of Catherine Littlefield Greene.* Athens: University of Georgia Press, 1977.

Symonds, Craig L. *A Battlefield Atlas of the American Revolution.* Baltimore, Md.: Nautical and Aviation Publishing Company of America, 1986.

Thane, Elswyth. *The Fighting Quaker: Nathanael Greene.* Mattituck, N.Y.: Aeonian Press, 1972.

Thayer, Theodore. *Nathanael Greene: Strategist of the American Revolution.* New York: Twayne, 1960.

Van Doren, Carl, ed. *The Portable Swift.* New York: Penguin, 1948.

Wood, W. J. *Battles of the Revolutionary War.* New York: Da Capo Press, 1995.

Wright, Robert K., Jr. *The Continental Army.* Washington, D.C.: Center of Military History, United States Army, 2000.

Unpublished Dissertations

Conrad, Dennis M. "Nathanael Greene and the Southern Campaigns, 1780–1783." Duke University, 1979.

Tretler, David A. "The Making of a Revolutionary: General Nathanael Greene, 1742–1779." Rice University, 1986.

ACKNOWLEDGMENTS

The Rhode Island Historical Society and the University of North Carolina Press began publishing the papers of Nathanael Greene in 1976. The project is ongoing. When the thirteenth and final volume is published, scholars of the Revolutionary period will have at their fingertips one of the era's finest collections of primary documents. Without the work of the scholars and historians who collected Greene's manuscripts from dozens of libraries, this biography could not have been written.

Thanks, too, to the staffs at the following institutions: the American Philosophical Society, the David Library of the American Revolution, Guilford Courthouse Military Park, Independence National Historical Park, Monmouth Battlefield State Park, Morristown National Historical Park, the New-York Historical Society, the New York Public Library, the New Jersey Historical Society, the Massachusetts Historical Society, the University of Michigan, the University of Virginia, and Washington's Crossing State Park.

Members of the Greene family, especially Thomas Casey Greene, welcomed me to the annual celebration of the general's birthday in Rhode Island in 2003. It was heartwarming to see their reverence for their distinguished ancestor. On that occasion, Elizabeth Stevens of the Rhode Island Historical Society shared with me her discovery of the general's final orders to his army before leaving the South in 1783.

Thanks, too, to Mike McLaughlin, Tom Fleming, and Richard Brookhiser for their help and encouragement.

As always, Arthur Carter, publisher of the *New York Observer,* and Peter Kaplan, the *Observer*'s editor, merit my gratitude and admiration.

Jack Macrae, my editor, is a wonderful storyteller and a serious scholar—his contribution to this book cannot be measured. His assistant, Supurna Banerjee, managed to create order out of chaos. Kenn Russell and copy editor Vicki Haire were a pleasure to work with.

My debt to John Wright can never be repaid. Likewise, my wife, Eileen Duggan, and our children, Kate and Conor.

INDEX

345

ABOUT THE AUTHOR

TERRY GOLWAY, columnist and city editor of the *New York Observer,* is a frequent contributor to *American Heritage,* the *Irish Echo, America Magazine,* and the *New York Times.* His previous books include *So Others Might Live, The Irish in America, For the Cause of Liberty,* and *Irish Rebel.* He lives in Maplewood, New Jersey.